# Philosophy for Children
# Through the Secondary
# Curriculum

**Also available from Continuum**

*The If Machine,* Peter Worley
*Teaching Thinking,* Robert Fisher
*Think Again,* John L. Taylor
*Why Think?,* Sara Stanley

# Philosophy for Children Through the Secondary Curriculum

Edited by

**Lizzy Lewis and
Nick Chandley**

continuum

P-T
P5494
2012

**Continuum International Publishing Group**

The Tower Building          80 Maiden Lane
11 York Road               Suite 704
London SE1 7NX             New York NY 10038

www.continuumbooks.com

**British Library Cataloguing-in-Publication Data**
A catalogue record for this book is available from the British Library.

ISBN:  978-1-4411-9661-3 (paperback)
       978-1-4411-7651-6 (ePub)
       978-1-4411-6957-0 (PDF)

**Library of Congress Cataloging-in-Publication Data**
Philosophy for children through the secondary curriculum /
edited by Lizzy Lewis and Nick Chandley.
     p. cm.
Includes bibliographical references and index.
ISBN 978-1-4411-9661-3 (pbk.) – ISBN 1-4411-9661-7 –
ISBN 978-1-4411-7651-6 (ePub) – ISBN 978-1-4411-6957-0 (PDF)
1. Philosophy–Study and teaching (Elementary)  2. Children and philosophy.
3. Philosophy–Study and teaching (Elementary)–Great Britain.
I. Lewis, Lizzy.  II. Chandley, Nick.
B52.P497 2012
108.3–dc23
                                                    2012003515

Typeset by Newgen Imaging Systems Pvt Ltd, Chennai, India
Printed and bound in Great Britain

# Contents

**Contributors**                                                    vii

**Preface**                                                          xi
*Nick Chandley and Lizzy Lewis*


**Introduction to Philosophy for Children**                          1
*Steve Williams*

**1  Working with Concepts**                                        14
*Steve Williams*

**2  P4C in Critical Thinking**                                     26
*James Nottingham*

**3  P4C in English**                                               38
*Steve Williams*

**4  P4C in English Literature**                                    53
*Steve Williams*

**5  P4C in Mathematics**                                           68
*Rod Cunningham and John Smith*

**6  P4C in Science**                                               92
*Lynda Dunlop*

**7  P4C in Religious Education**                                   127
*Patricia Hannam*

**8  P4C in Personal, Social and Health Education (PSHE)**          146
*Roger Sutcliffe*

**9  P4C in History**                                               167
*Doug Paterson*

**10  P4C in Geography**                                            179
*Dick Palfrey*

**11** **P4C in Art** 199
*Sara Liptai*

**12** **P4C in Music** 215
*Sara Liptai*

**13** **P4C in Drama** 235
*Neil Phillipson and Gordon Poad*

**14** **P4C in Physical Education and School Sport (PESS)** 252
*Paul Dearlove*

**15** **P4C in Information and Communication Technology (ICT)** 266
*Nick Chandley*

**Appendix: A Brief History of P4C and SAPERE** 284
*Steve Williams*

**Index** 295

# Contributors

**Nick Chandley** is a teacher and freelance trainer in Philosophy for Children, running courses in schools across the country and having been involved in many creative projects using P4C. He has consulted at local authority level in drama and was responsible for editing the most recent *SAPERE Level 1 Handbook*. He also currently coordinates the Open Futures online learning community for their *askit* strand.

**Rod Cunningham** has worked as a mathematics educator for over 30 years (first as a secondary teacher and then as an adviser). His present post involves working across 40 Welsh secondary schools on addressing disaffection among 11- to 13-year-old students. He has been facilitating P4C for 5 years and in that time has completed training with SAPERE to Level 3. At present he is working with a Year 6 group in a local primary school and is aiming to promote a transition model whereby Year 7 form teachers train with teachers from Years 5 and 6 in their feeder primaries. The proposed outcome is that P4C will become an integral part of the education of 5- to 18-year-olds in the cluster of schools.

**Paul Dearlove** is the owner of Step Up 2 Ltd, a small training company based in the Northeast, that supports the development of thinking, questioning and self-belief in teams and individuals. Paul has been a Merchant Navy Officer, Industrial Training Officer, Teacher, Principal of an Outdoor School in Denmark and latterly a Teaching and Learning Consultant. His 'Out-SMART' programme marries thinking, appreciation and dialogue with an active approach to cooperative learning.

**Lynda Dunlop** is an experienced teacher of science and theory of knowledge. She is currently working as a researcher and completing a Ph.D. in science education at the University of Ulster, United Kingdom.

**Patricia Hannam** is Hampshire County Inspector/Adviser for RE/History as well as a SAPERE Levels 1, 2 and 3 trainer. She has extensive international experience with philosophical enquiry; in particular developing strong links with the Mexican Federation for Philosophy for Children over the past 10 years. She has facilitated a programme of Advanced P4C Seminars, first in Cumbria and now in Winchester, United Kingdom. Her doctoral research is in the field of enquiry in religious education and she has published various chapters and articles on this theme. *Philosophy with Teenagers: Nurturing a Moral Imagination for the 21st Century* was published by Continuum in 2009.

**Lizzy Lewis** began working for SAPERE in 2003 and now works part-time as Development Manager. In this role she has oversight of the running of the charity which includes SAPERE courses, membership, events, website, data, newsletter, communication and staffing. After completing a philosophy degree Lizzy was inspired by 'Socrates for Six-Year-Olds', a BBC programme that featured Matthew Lipman, and joined SAPERE in the early 1990s. Lizzy was a primary school teacher for 12 years, during which time she practised Philosophy for Children (P4C) mostly with infants. Lizzy was awarded a Best Practice Research Scholarship to evaluate her work in P4C in 2001, and co-authored a teachers' resource, 'Thinking on the Edge' (Thinking Activities to Develop Citizenship and Environmental Awareness) in 2003. For her Masters Degree in Education she focused on P4C and children's emotional development. Lizzy was an Associate Tutor of Oxford Brookes University and trained teachers there in P4C between 2005 and 2009.

**Sara Liptai** BA PGCE Ph.D. had worked as a secondary school teacher, translator, linguist and musician in her native Hungary before emigrating to the United Kingdom in 1980. She was a BBC journalist and parent of young children when the lightning struck her in the form of 'Socrates for Six-Year-Olds', causing her to go back into education and to join SAPERE. She completed her Ph.D. on music as stimulus in P4C and has been arguing ever since for a special place for the arts in philosophical enquiry with anyone who is prepared to listen.

**James Nottingham** studied P4C as part of his university degree in the early 1990s before working in primary, middle and secondary schools across the United Kingdom. In 1999, he co-founded a multi-million pound, award-winning regeneration project (RAIS), using P4C as the catalyst for change. Today, James is a freelance trainer working with schools around the world. He is also co-founder of p4c.com, an online cooperative providing resources, advice and collaboration for creating dynamic P4C materials. www.jamesnottingham.co.uk

**Dick Palfrey** works part-time as an Independent Education Consultant in West Yorkshire, United Kingdom. He was School Improvement Officer for history, geography & environmental education, for Kirklees Learning Service, United Kingdom, from 2000–11. Previously, he had been a teacher of geography, geology, environmental studies, a secondary Head of Geography and Advanced Skills Teacher. Dick's interests include philosophy of place and time through local studies, plus wider questions of environmental sustainability and global identity.

**Doug Paterson** is an Advanced Skills Teacher and Head of History at a high school in the North East of England and winner of BT Teacher of the Year for the North East. Doug is particularly interested in enquiry-based learning and making history as interesting as possible. He is a SAPERE trainer and has delivered speeches and workshops at many conferences on wider aspects of teaching and learning.

**Neil Phillipson** is a Teaching and Learning Consultant with Stoke-on-Trent Local Authority, United Kingdom. He is interested in working with teachers to support the progressive development of learners' independence through enquiry.

**Gordon Poad** is a creative learning practitioner, trainer and consultant. He is the director of Cap-a-Pie Associates, United Kingdom, who aim to design creative programmes that bring about positive changes in teaching, learning and curriculum design.

**John Smith** has taught for more than 30 years and he is a SAPERE registered P4C trainer. He has worked as a primary mathematics specialist for more than 15 years, first as a primary teacher and numeracy coordinator and then in his current role as a senior lecturer in the Manchester Metropolitan University Institute of Education, United Kingdom. John has been interested in children's thinking as it is expressed in talk throughout his career and he is the author of *Talk, Thinking and Philosophy in the Primary Classroom*. Recently, he has brought together his work with children and adults in P4C and mathematics, as he believes that, in combination, these two disciplines provide many valuable learning opportunities.

**Roger Sutcliffe** has been President of both SAPERE and ICPIC, the international network, and is a director of www.p4c.com. Having read philosophy at the University of Oxford, United Kingdom, he taught various subjects at both primary and secondary level for 20 years before he saw the BBC documentary, 'Socrates for Six-Year-Olds' in 1990. He has spent most of the 20 years since then developing and promoting P4C in the United Kingdom and beyond.

**Steve Williams** taught English and media studies for 14 years and served for 5 years as Head of English department. He helped to found SAPERE, the Philosophy for Children network in the United Kingdom, and was the first person in Britain to introduce P4C as curriculum subject in a secondary school. He is a member and director of p4c.com, a cooperative producing online resources for teachers.

# Preface

This book has been in our minds for many years. How Philosophy for Children (P4C) can be used through the curriculum – in subjects – has been an issue since it was introduced in the United Kingdom in the early 1990s. The challenge lay in trying to use P4C in the context of teaching particular subject matter because it is primarily a democratic process that so importantly gives participants ownership over their philosophical enquiry and the natural direction that it takes.

Over the years, P4C practitioners have experimented with introducing stimuli and activities that might steer or influence the students' creation and choice of philosophical questions. There is a conflict for the teacher, in the role of facilitator, between ensuring that the path the participants can take is genuinely open while also attempting to guide them in a particular way. This guidance is usually in the form of a stimulus or activity presented to the participants in order to focus their thinking on a particular philosophical concept.

From our work with teachers and young people we have discovered a phenomenally rich layer of philosophical concepts that underlie the curriculum. Our experience is that when students are helped and encouraged to explore philosophical concepts then the subject matter they are working with takes on a whole new meaning. Equally, the use of P4C in curriculum subjects reveals questions and concepts to students that they do not usually reach. Finding meaning and subject matter that is meaningful to young people is crucial to their engagement with, and enjoyment of, learning and the model P4C offers is ideally suited to this.

Our experience at SAPERE, having worked with tens of thousands of teachers in the United Kingdom since the early 1990s, is that the discovery of philosophy not only wakens young people to a new way of thinking but also their teachers, parents and governors. Seeing the curriculum with a fresh perspective, through philosophical concepts and the experience of philosophical enquiry and dialogue, is exciting and motivating. Feedback from many teachers and schools that have adopted P4C shows that it has transformed how they teach and how they approach the curriculum.

Over the years, issues and questions about how to use P4C through the curriculum have been raised on our training courses. With the tremendous work of hundreds of secondary classroom teachers and the support and collaboration of SAPERE trainers, we are now in a position to present what we hope is a useful resource. Each chapter is written by an experienced P4C practitioner and aims to present the case for using P4C within specific subjects. In addition to this, practical activities are included to give you, the teacher, the opportunity to use it in your classroom. In these activities are sample stimuli for philosophical enquiry, but there will be countless others already within your schemes of work. Likewise, the concepts and questions attached to each activity will doubtless be supplemented by ones that both you and your students begin to ask.

This is, therefore, only the start of a journey. To acquire the philosophical understanding and skills to capably and confidently facilitate philosophical enquiries requires commitment, time and training. This book is intended to support those who have already undergone P4C training, to offer those who have not a rationale for P4C and to show what is possible in the context of the secondary curriculum. The field of philosophical enquiry is an incredibly rich one but one that ultimately reaps a significant harvest as your classroom becomes a true community of enquiry, with you as co-enquirer. This book is designed to be the catalyst for that journey, but further advice and training can be found at www.sapere.org.uk

We are profoundly grateful for the support of the SAPERE trustees, staff team, trainers and members, and we would like to give particular thanks to all our authors and especially to Steve Williams, Roger Sutcliffe and Chris Rowley.

Nick Chandley and Lizzy Lewis

SAPERE
communities of enquiry

*A wide range of resources and stimuli have been suggested throughout the book and we advise that teachers use their discretion in selecting suitable and age appropriate materials for their students.*

# Introduction to Philosophy for Children

Steve Williams

## Chapter Outline

| | |
|---|---|
| P4C as a practice | 2 |
| Methods: What does P4C look like? | 2 |
| Philosophizing: Where is the philosophy in P4C? | 6 |
| Standards and expectations: What does progress in P4C look like? | 7 |
| The importance of relationships | 10 |
| P4C in secondary schools as a scale of involvement | 11 |

Philosophy for Children (P4C) aims towards the appropriation of the practice of philosophizing by young people of all ages. That involves students being willing and able to think for themselves, and to think *well* in the sense of having their thoughts under rational control. They actively seek out alternative perspectives to their own because they prefer to make judgements in the face of all relevant considerations. Doing P4C in schools demonstrates confidence that young people are capable of being curious and making judgements about matters of significance – with assistance from their peers and teachers.

That confidence, when supported by sound teaching methods, has borne fruit with many groups in over 60 countries where P4C has been introduced during the past 30 years. It has been researched extensively and the following results seem consistent (Trickey and Topping, 2004):

- Students make significant gains in cognitive ability, intellectual confidence and self-esteem.
- Students show improvements in critical reasoning skills in dialogue.

- There is evidence of improvements in students' communication skills and concentration, and in their ability to self-manage their impulsivity more appropriately.

So what is P4C, what might it have to offer in secondary schools for students from 11–16 and what is the significance of the word 'Philosophy' in the title?

# P4C as a practice

The origins of P4C and its development in the United Kingdom are presented in the Appendix. The version of P4C described here has been widely adopted by schools in the United Kingdom and promoted by SAPERE (Society for the Advancement of Philosophical Enquiry and Reflection in Education).

P4C is best thought of as a practice rather than another subject. It could be given a separate timetable slot; for example, some schools find regular time for P4C under the heading of Personal Learning and Thinking Skills (PLTS). However, it can also become a collaborator with established subjects – helping out with conceptual work and enquiry.

In common with other practices, P4C has distinct methods and its own standards of excellent performance – for both teachers and students. The 'philosophy' of P4C refers to the activity of philosophizing – examining reasons and presuppositions, reflecting on concepts, exploring meaning and value, and considering significant questions leading to making judgements about what to think and how to act. Let's look at the main aspects of the practice in more detail.

# Methods: What does P4C look like?

P4C is dialogical and, as Robin Alexander argues, 'teaching is more likely to be effective if it actively engages student's attention and interest, and is reciprocal rather than merely transmissive' (Alexander, 2006a). He draws on a long history of research and theoretical writing to support this case (Alexander, 2006b). Dialogue, however, is demanding. According to Alexander, it requires 'willingness and skill to engage with minds, ideas and ways of thinking other than our own, it involves the ability to question, listen, reflect, reason, explain, speculate, and explore ideas; to analyse problems, frame hypotheses . . . defend, probe and assess arguments' (2006a). Importantly, dialogic teaching aims for an *appropriation* of concepts, principles and attitudes by learners so they can think for themselves. P4C provides a means to facilitate that appropriation.

## A structure for dialogue

Dialogue in P4C starts with a shared stimulus. The teacher and students identify points of interest and significance; then students spend time formulating questions. These are shared and analysed by the whole group. One question is chosen to start the dialogue, which then proceeds according to guidelines negotiated and regularly re-evaluated by all members of the group. The dialogue continues in the spirit of a community of enquiry (see p. 4). At the end, there is time for individual reflections on the content and process of the dialogue. These tried-and-tested routines (expanded in the box below) provide a helpful structure with which to navigate the difficulties of classroom dialogue. Even so, the routines should not be seen as ends in themselves but always as the means to achieving a classroom community of enquiry.

---

### The sequence of enquiry in P4C

*Adapted by Steve Bramall from SAPERE Level 1 course handbook (2010)*

The steps are presented as guidelines for the teacher but they also serve to explain what happens.

1. **Preparation**
   Start by sitting in a circle so everyone can see and hear one another. Give guidelines on conduct, ground rules and aims of enquiry (these are always able to be reviewed by the group). Use warm-ups to aid cooperation, speaking, listening and thinking.
2. **Presentation of stimulus**
   Present the stimulus. It might be a narrative, a news item, a selection of contrasting arguments or explanations, a picture, video, work of art – anything that engages students and prompts them to raise interesting ideas and questions.

⇨

**Cont'd.**

**3. Thinking time**

Give time for individual reflection on the stimulus – maybe a minute of silent thinking or jotting down key words. Ask students to share with a partner their thoughts about issues raised.

**4. Question making**

Split the class into small groups to generate questions. Have each group choose one open-ended question. Have them present their chosen question so all can see it.

**5. Question airing**

Invite authors to explain or clarify their questions. Ask participants to link, appreciate or evaluate any of the questions aired.

**6. Question choosing**

Have all students vote to select a question as a dialogue starter or negotiate an agenda of questions with them.

**7. Dialogue: First thoughts**

Ask authors of the question selected to open the dialogue by sharing their initial thoughts – perhaps their expectations of where the question might lead or the answers they currently have in mind.

**8. Dialogue: Building**

Bring other community members into dialogue by inviting comments, responses, examples, agreements, disagreements, reasons, and so on. Introduce other relevant perspectives or possible arguments if the dialogue is too limited in scope.

**9. Dialogue: Last thoughts**

Invite each individual to share final thoughts with the community. Ask for volunteers or go around the circle – but do allow people to 'pass'.

**10. Review**

Invite reflective and evaluative comments about the enquiry throughout the dialogue or at a particular stage. What went well? What could be improved?

## Community of enquiry

The ideal of a community of enquiry regulates classroom dialogue and guides all the methods and activities of P4C. The phrase itself was taken by Matthew Lipman, the founder of P4C, from American Pragmatist philosopher, Charles Peirce. In P4C, the community of enquiry represents an explicit aspiration towards maintaining respect for other people while also agreeing, disagreeing, questioning and bringing others into the dialogue. The overall aim is for individual participants to achieve better understanding, make better judgements and to be accountable to a community of peers. The community of enquiry is an ideal that provides a direction and towards which teachers and students can advance together by degrees. Whatever the starting point, they work for more trust and intellectual risk taking, more sharing of responsibility, better reasoning and greater philosophical curiosity. The nature of the teacher's input into the dialogue is the subject of the next chapter.

## Skill-building activities

Routines leading students from the questioning of a stimulus to dialogue are not sufficient in themselves to achieve two key objectives of P4C: the sharpening of students' cognitive tools and the in-depth exploration of concepts. Therefore, the practice of P4C involves the use of tasks to focus dialogue around concepts such as 'justice' and 'assumption'. Though the tasks are short, they are no less dependent on the ethos of the community of enquiry than the longer, more open, sessions of dialogue described above. They elicit the making and justification of judgements and they translate into 'moves' that students can make in their own thinking, discussing and writing throughout the curriculum. There are many examples of skill-building activities in this book.

## Ongoing questioning, dialogue and connection-making

The ideal of a community of enquiry is not suspended at the end of a single dialogue. The teacher establishes a learning environment in which ongoing connections can be made to new experiences in life and learning. For example, once students have reflected in some depth on the concepts of justice and injustice, then they are likely to want to overlay their considered perspectives on experience to see if there is a reasonable fit. Teachers of P4C keep the avenues of ongoing dialogue open using devices such as student journals; they create opportunities for students to reconsider their judgements in the light of new facts, arguments or perspectives. Though teachers may fear that this sort of approach will divert time away from the already demanding task of covering the curriculum, they may be reassured to find that students become more interested and engaged with learning the more they feel part of a community of enquiry.

# Philosophizing: Where is the philosophy in P4C?

We have talked so far about routines, shaped by the ideal of the community of enquiry. But why is the practice called 'philosophy for children'? Where is the philosophy in it?

There is always a basic and spontaneous philosophizing that arises when people use words like *is, real, should, fair, know, beauty* and *purpose* – words that suggest the speakers are making judgements about existence, morality, knowledge, aesthetics and the ends of life. There are also traces of philosophical thought contained in the 'common sense' of communities: in established maxims, customary convictions, familiar metaphors and popular political opinions (Gramsci, 1982, p. 323; Jaspers, 1960, pp. 11–12).

There is no escape from this kind of spontaneous philosophy. However, like the proverbs of old, it is often incoherent, contradictory and lacking in critical awareness. Deliberate philosophizing is therefore required in order to 'bring to light' contradictions, and also categories, models and standards in terms of which people interpret, judge and make meaning in the world (Berlin, 1978, p. 11). Deliberate philosophizing is part of the creative and critical attempt by humankind to understand and influence reality. P4C is a practice of deliberate philosophizing with the following features:

- *P4C is dialogical and reflective.* Participants are in dialogue with each other to question presuppositions, seek alternative arguments and perspectives, and decide what to think in the face of those alternatives.
- *P4C is conceptual.* Participants pay particular attention to the way that concepts guide our actions and judgements. Through dialogue they try to make better sense of those concepts so as to make better judgements.
- *P4C is imaginative.* Participants wonder and speculate; they imagine consequences, connections, possible scenarios and 'thought experiments'. They create analogies to 'fit' experience and make it more meaningful. Then they compare and evaluate their analogies. They imagine how changes in thinking and conduct could make societies better or worse.
- *P4C is interrogative and collaborative.* To philosophize is to question others and open oneself to being questioned. In a community such as a school this necessarily involves collaborating to sustain an

ethos of questioning in pursuit of wisdom. For the philosopher Karl Jaspers, this involves a 'loving contest' (1960, p. 13). Similarly, P4C adopts the ideal of the community of enquiry.
- *P4C is concerned with a matrix of enduring themes.* In P4C people ask questions that cannot be answered adequately using scientific or empirical methods: What kind of person should I want to be? What are my obligations to people in other countries? What is 'my community'? Should some values always carry more weight than others? How can I tell a good argument from a bad one and a truth from a falsehood? In response to questions like these, it is helpful to attend to significant connected questions and answers from the past. Therefore, teachers of P4C will be actively interested in some of the enduring themes and arguments of philosophy and in the philosophical dimensions of their own disciplines.

Spontaneous philosophizing is present in all areas of life because it is embedded in language and the 'common sense' of cultures and sub-cultures. Yet, it will not help students make 'good sense' out of all the knowledge, information and advice that flies at them every day. That is, it will not enable them, sufficiently, to understand, join up and prioritize their experiences. Therefore, an effort of deliberate philosophizing with young people is required to help them become more self-reliant and purposeful thinkers. P4C provides a way forward to achieve this end.

# Standards and expectations: What does progress in P4C look like?

If P4C is a practice, there should be standards for success and failure that can be recognized and shared by the people who do it – teachers and students. The overriding success criteria for P4C is that participants make progress towards the ideal of a community of enquiry and they become more capable of deliberate philosophizing. This is a good in itself. However, when P4C becomes a collaborator with other subjects, there are additional expectations.

The following standards would therefore apply, depending on the degree of commitment to P4C in a school (see the section 'P4C in secondary schools as a scale of involvement' on p. 11). A standard in this case is a criterion to indicate whether an action is being carried out or an expectation met.

### Standards for P4C in general

**Students** are developing dispositions such as: curiosity; eagerness to hear alternative viewpoints; patience when alternatives contradict their own views; courage to stick to their own views and also to abandon them on reflection; civility in both agreement and disagreement with others. Students have a sense of care: for others, for ideas that shape conduct in thought and deed, and for precision in the use of language.

**Teachers** display these dispositions and are working to create an environment in which they can flourish.

**Students** are developing tools of reasoning and reflection by giving reasons and examples, identifying differences and similarities, determining relative importance, establishing criteria, identifying assumptions, and so on.

**Teachers** use these tools in dialogue, draw students' attention to their various uses and to the ways they combine to enable further enquiry. This work will be ongoing and take place both within whole-class dialogue and in focused small-group and paired work.

**Students** will become more reflective about their reasoning and more aware of the philosophical dimensions of experience. So, for example, they will not only give reasons but also ask what kind of reasons they are (e.g. based on observation, example, principle or deduction). They will tend to identify conceptual aspects of discourse that require attention and they will become more attuned to some of the enduring themes and arguments that infuse deliberate philosophical thinking.

**Teachers** stimulate and guide this philosophical awareness through their choice of resources and activities, and their own contributions to dialogue. Stimulating students' philosophical thinking goes hand in hand with developing their own because deliberate philosophizing does not end with the completion of a single session; it persists in the minds of teachers and students. For example, questions about 'what is just' in a given situation are bound to return in relation to others. Therefore, one of the standards of P4C is that teachers, as well as students become more philosophical.

## Standards for P4C with other subjects

When P4C is practiced, regularly, anywhere in the curriculum, the standards for P4C in general apply both as goals and as criteria for evaluation. However, the following additional standards are pertinent to the role of P4C as a collaborator with other subjects and with cross-curricular themes.

**Students** are becoming more motivated in their studies for at least three reasons:

1. A concentration on the exploration of values and ethics has given them more motivation to find out facts. For example, when they have discussed the justifications for war, they are often more interested in finding out facts about particular wars. And when they explore justifications for stem cell research, they are interested in finding more precise information.
2. When students argue, they have emotional responses that can motivate them to learn – either to support their own arguments or to establish new, more coherent, positions. When curricula are mostly directed towards the acquisition of knowledge or techniques, there is little room for regular argument with its motivating properties.
3. In a community of enquiry, students' beliefs and arguments are at least acknowledged and sometimes valued by their peers and teachers. This boosts their intellectual self-confidence, which is also a source of motivation.

**Students** are better able to use tools of reasoning and they are more able to combine the conceptual and empirical aspects of knowledge in order to gain a deeper understanding of their subjects.

**Students** are better able to understand the significance of the key concepts of each subject area and to compare the application of concepts such as 'evidence' and 'truth' across subjects.

**Teachers** are enabling dialogue, enquiry and the fusion of conceptual, empirical and practical aspects of learning. This reveals itself in their planning and their organization of time. They are able to recognize and defend the benefits of this approach against the objection that 'there just isn't time for such things'.

How is it possible to discover the extent to which these standards are being achieved? Mostly by observation of what teachers and students say and do in lessons. There will be peer and group evaluation so that students will be prompted to ask themselves, for example: Did we give reasons? Were we patient when people disagreed with us?

There will also be ongoing observation by teachers, both in and out of P4C sessions in order to find out whether:

- more questions are being asked and more reasons given
- students are getting better at handling the conceptual and philosophical dimensions of learning
- there is more constructive dialogue
- students are displaying positive dispositions and reasoning skills in dialogue with each other – both with and without prompting by the teacher
- students are becoming more motivated to learn
- teachers are giving students sufficient guidance with their reasoning (e.g. by showing them how to make arguments and question assumptions)
- students are becoming more precise in their use of language
- students and teachers are taking a greater interest in philosophical questions.

Students and teachers will not be evincing all these things in all lessons but, over time, they will be making progress.

## The importance of relationships

Relationships are central to the practice of P4C in schools. Teachers and students live together during school hours. The introduction of P4C aims to make that life more reasonable, stimulating and philosophical. The quality of the relationships and the quality of P4C will affect each other. P4C is a practice that all teachers can, to some extent, undertake with their students. It is not just for teachers (or other experts) with a background in academic philosophy. One aim of P4C is to improve relationships and learning throughout the school. Input from expert philosophers can supplement the work required to achieve that aim but it cannot replace it. Indeed, a great stimulus to philosophical reading for teachers is to philosophize with students about the problems they identify spontaneously from living together in the pursuit of learning. Some teachers may have previous experience of studying philosophy. However, all teachers can foster more deliberate philosophizing and we believe their efforts will be rewarding for students and for themselves.

# P4C in secondary schools as a scale of involvement

It is useful to present P4C as a scale to avoid the mistaken notion that there are only two levels of involvement – minimum and maximum – with the minimum level being insufficient to realize any significant benefits and the maximum level requiring unfeasible commitments from teachers and schools. Rather, all levels of involvement in the practice of P4C can be beneficial and each level in the scale can build comfortably on previous ones. However, at certain points on the scale, one could expect transformations to occur rather than just incremental changes – transformations in attitude, motivation and intellectual self-reliance on the part of students. The variables in the scale include the following:

- *Levels of training and resources*: Breadth and depth of training will be relevant considerations. At first, a small group of staff may take introductory courses in the practice of P4C. Then, if the pioneers find it to be beneficial, other staff will become involved. Further training and support will be available at a range of levels to improve the practice. The school will invest in resources to assist teachers with their planning.
- *Levels of responsibility*: A school will give responsibilities to teachers for the coordination of P4C across the school.
- *Levels of integration*: P4C may appear in one or two subject areas or be more fully integrated into the whole curriculum and the life of the school. Philosophical events and clubs will be considered. Guest philosophers might be invited to work with teachers and/or students. All staff and governors will work together to create a philosophical ethos.

The practice of P4C is worthwhile at whatever level it is adopted. It can make school life more intellectually and emotionally satisfying for all concerned.

# Further resources

There are many books, articles and resources on P4C. Here are some that may be of special interest to secondary teachers and managers.

*SAPERE Level 1 Handbook,* SAPERE, 2010. SAPERE (Society for the Advancement of Philosophical Enquiry and Reflection in Education) has produced this resource for its introductory courses in P4C. It is available from the Society (see www.sapere.org.uk).

*Socrates for Six-Year-Olds.* This documentary was broadcast by the BBC in 1990. It provides the historical background of P4C and shows it operating in several American schools. There are interviews with Matthew Lipman, the P4C pioneer who died in 2010. The programme inspired many of the 'early adopters' of P4C in the United Kingdom. It is part of a DVD called *The SAPERE DVD Collection,* which includes other short items filmed in the United Kingdom. It is available from SAPERE (see www.sapere.org.uk).

*20 Thinking Tools* by Philip Cam, ACER, 2006. This book provides a wealth of ideas for the sort of concept-building activities that are a necessary feature of P4C.

*Teaching for Better Thinking: The Classroom Community of Enquiry* by Ann M. Sharp and Laurence Splitter, ACER, 2005. This is a very comprehensive book on the principles of the community of enquiry, classroom dialogue and philosophizing with children.

*Philosophy Goes to School* by Matthew Lipman, Temple University Press, 1988. This interesting book presents the thinking of the original team of P4C educators in America about how P4C might support learning and thinking across the school curriculum.

*Philosophy with Teenagers: Nurturing a Moral Imagination for the 21st Century* by Eugenio Echeverria by Patricia Hannam, Continuum, 2009. A book promoting the use of P4C with teenagers.

*Cross-phase books on P4C.* The following three books are written mostly with primary schools in mind but also have interesting passages on P4C in education generally:

- Fisher, R. (2008) Teaching Thinking: Philosophical Enquiry in the Classroom, Continuum.
- Haynes, J. (2011) *Children as Philosophers,* Routledge.
- Stanley, S. (2006) *Creating Enquiring Minds,* Network Continuum Education.

*Research Summaries.* A summary of research into P4C can be found at http://p4c.com/benefits-p4c There are links to research articles. The SAPERE website has a similar page: http://tinyurl.com/p4cresearch2

*Concept activities.* There is a document on the website at www.p4c.com that explains different types of exercises with which to explore concepts. Teachers could use the examples and instructions to make their own activities for students. http://p4c.com/files/p4c/Conceptsnew2.pdf

*p4c.com* (see www.p4c.com). This is the website of a cooperative of writers producing advice and resources for P4C. I am one of the members of the cooperative. Some materials are available for free and there is a subscription for full access to an ever-growing resource. The site is for all age groups. One resource is an e-book titled *The Philosophy Club* by Steve Williams and Roger Sutcliffe. It was written with secondary pupils in mind and contains advice and printable resources.

# References

Alexander, R. J. (2006a) *Education as Dialogue: Moral and Pedagogical Choices for a Runaway World*. Hong Kong Institute of Education in conjunction with Dialogos.

— (2006b) *Towards Dialogic Teaching: Rethinking Classroom Talk* (3rd edn). Dialogos.

Berlin, I. (1978) 'The Purpose of Philosophy', in Henry Hardy (ed.), *Concepts and Categories*. Princeton, NJ: Princeton University Press.

Gramsci, A. (1982) 'The Study of Philosophy', in *Selections from the Prison Notebooks of Antonio Gramsci*. London: Lawrence and Wishart.

Jaspers, K. (1960) *Way to Wisdom*. New Haven and London: Yale University Press.

Trickey, S. and Topping, K. J. (2004) '"Philosophy for Children": A Systematic Review', *Research Papers in Education*, 19 (3), 363–78.

# 1 Working with Concepts

Steve Williams

---

> ## Chapter Outline
>
> The language of reasoning      14
> Philosophical concepts      20

Teachers can help students to philosophize: to reason well, explore concepts philosophically and ask questions that move enquiry forwards. With support from their teachers, students can aspire to be more systematic and imaginative in their thinking.

## The language of reasoning

The first step for students towards deliberate philosophizing is to gain more control over their thinking by becoming more expert in using the language of reasoning.

There are certain words, phrases and concepts that structure thinking, discussion or writing of any complexity. They are necessary in order to make judgements, organize them and defend them in discourse with others. Here is a selection of the most important of these expressions organized under four headings related to the kind of work they do. Some expressions necessarily appear under more than one.

- **Degree:** All/some/none, always/sometimes/never, more/less important, better/worse, impossible/possible/probable/likely/certain, degree
- **Kind:** Quality, attribute, criterion, all/some/none, is/isn't, if . . . then, group, class, is/are, part/whole, example, alternative, addition, kind

- **Relation:** Cause, effect, consequence, if . . . then, same/similar/different, opposite, part/whole, important, significant, best/worst, before/after/at the same time, certain/possible/probable/impossible, means/end/purpose, connection, relation
- **Discourse:** question, answer, statement, proposition, hypothesis, opinion, reason, premise, argument, grounds, principle, maxim, assumption/presupposition, evidence, conclusion, if . . . then, unless

The English educationalist, philosopher and literary critic I. A. Richards suggested that words like these are among the most 'resourceful' in the language because they help people think about everything else: In a striking sentence, he says: 'The senses of these chief words – and their ways of working with and against one another – are the rules of reason' (Richards, 1955, p. 10). Let's relate Richard's thoughts to some common conceptions of 'thinking skills'.

Most of the expressions in 'the language of reasoning' are necessary for the sorts of operations emphasized by thinking skills initiatives: sorting, classifying, analysing, recognizing part/whole relationships, comparing and contrasting, hypothesizing, drawing conclusions, justifying conclusions, distinguishing fact from opinion, relating causes and effects, generating options, and so on (see Schwartz and Parks, 1994).

We can see that all these operations require the enlightened use of the language of reasoning. In fact, comparing *is* the enlightened use of terms like similar and different for a purpose; justifying *is* the enlightened use of terms like reason and conclusion.

If students are to 'think for themselves' then the language of reasoning should be developed deliberately and regularly in conversation and writing. Consider what someone might have to do in a conversation when they disagree with a partner.

**John:** I think stem cell research should not be allowed because we shouldn't mess with human life. It's a *principle*. We shouldn't play at being God.

**Yasmin**: I *disagree*; stem cell research could help people with serious illnesses to live a *better* life. Maybe we shouldn't try to do it just because we can, or for cosmetic uses, but only to cure serious illnesses.

In order to progress further with this argument, John and Yasmin would have to recognize that *principles* and *consequences* are involved. They would need to share background information and relate it to their *reasons*. Yasmin might present more information about various treatments. John would consider whether or not to modify his *principle* into 'You shouldn't mess with human life *unless . . .*'

They might *agree*, at least, that they both valued human life. Yasmin might say 'people mess with human life all the time, like people get operations. Why is stem cell research *different* in *principle* from those things?'

The resourceful words in italics have two uses; to help John and Yasmin make the arguments and to help them reflect on the arguments together. The words are tools as are the moves of agreeing and comparing. However, this 'tool' metaphor only goes so far. We don't use the tools one at a time like a carpenter. We have them in our minds all the time, ready to be used together in whatever combination is required in a particular context of thinking, dialogue or writing in any subject area. They are more than tools; they are constituents of the people we have become. Students become reasonable when they are able to use the language of reasoning to keep control of their thoughts, when they understand how resourceful that language can be and when they are disposed to reason with others. And if students can become more reasonable, they will bring their reasoning selves to lessons in all subjects – willing and able to learn better and understand more.

## Routines to develop reasoning

Here are some ideas for helping students to appropriate the language of reasoning in the course of regular classroom dialogue.

1. Show students how they can enquire systematically into any issue using a succession of questions which incorporate key expressions from the language of reasoning. Show them how *you* go about putting a series of questions together; prompt them by asking 'What questions do you have at this point?' or 'What do you think your next three questions will be about this?' Draw their attention to the usefulness of the expressions in framing questions such as 'What are the alternatives?' 'What is similar and different about them?'

'What would the consequences be if one of those alternatives were chosen?'

2. Include short sessions in your lessons in which you draw the attention of students to the different senses of the reasoning words. For example, things can be the *same* in different senses.
   - Hitler and Stalin were the same. They were both tyrants.
   - Cloning means remaking an organism to be the same as the original with an identical genetic structure.
   - A cloned sheep and the original are not the same sheep. How could there be two of them?
   - These poems are the same; they both express feelings of lost love.

3. Help students to use diagrams and written lists when reasons, examples, similarities or causes need to be gathered and analysed. Diagrams and lists operate to focus joint attention. However, don't be tempted to think that the benefits of using 'graphic organizers' will leak out across the curriculum with no further effort. Regular classroom dialogue is essential.

4. Stress the language of reasoning in all the dialogues you have with pupils. Use the language yourself by overlaying it onto students' contributions; so if one says: 'I've got another idea', ask them if they think it is a *different* idea from those raised so far and, if so, in what ways is it *different*. If someone says: 'X happens because of Y' you might say: 'So that's a *consequence*, what are some of the other *possible consequences*?' and 'which *consequences* do you think are *most important*?' These kinds of moves initiate students into using the language of reasoning to reflect on their own thinking.

5. Talk to students about their writing in terms of the language of reasoning. Where are they comparing? Where are they exploring consequences or categorizing? How are they doing all these things? Share your own writing with them to show them you do it.

6. Use 'Question and Ideas Books' for students to record and develop their thoughts. One idea for the books is to provide prompts such as: 'Write at least four *examples* of . . .?' or 'What are some of the *criteria* for . . .?' Then let the students write freely about what follows from their lists or what further questions they have.

7. Focus from time to time on one resourceful expression and create an activity to help students become more familiar with the part it plays in reasoning. The activity 'It's just a matter of opinion!' (see box pp. 18–20) explores the concept of *opinion* and relates it to other expressions.

### 'It's just a matter of opinion!'

*The following resource was written by Steve Williams and Jason Buckley for the website: www.p4c.com. It is reproduced here with permission.*

The phrase 'it's just a matter of opinion' is often heard but it is not clear, without further dialogue, what users of the phrase mean. There is a range of possibilities. For example:

- This is an opinion as opposed to a fact. Only facts can be true so this can't be true.
- This is an opinion and, although some opinions can be true, this isn't one of them.
- This is no more than an opinion because there are no good reasons to support it.
- There is no such thing as objective truth.

In this activity, you provide a list of opinions and ask students if the phrase 'it's just a matter of opinion' should be applied to each one. You also provide a list of concepts to stimulate the students' thinking and prompt their replies.

### Suggestions for doing the activity

Have the opinions (listed below) available for your students. Also have the 'concept list' available. For each of the statements, ask students to decide whether or not they think 'it's just a matter of opinion'. When they have made their decision, ask them to explain it using the concepts on the concept list as prompts. Which of those are relevant to their answers and why? If the students don't know the meanings of the concept words, take some time to explain. Question the students and encourage them to question each other about their decisions, justifications and choices of related concepts. Discussion is likely to focus on whether each opinion can be supported by reasons, what kinds of reasons can be identified and what the power of each kind of reason can be in each case. There is plenty of scope for making distinctions between concepts such as opinion, belief, truth and knowledge, and for asking whether some opinions are more justifiable than others.

Discussion about some opinions may focus on what particular terms mean. For example, what does 'harder' mean in the statement

**Cont'd.**

'maths is harder than English'? If both parties could come to an agreement about the criteria for 'hard' and the appropriate contexts for its application, could the statement be more than 'just a matter of opinion'? If they can't agree criteria, must it only be a matter of opinion'? The activity is as complicated as you want to make it and could give you scope for plenty of discussion in lessons that follow.

## Variations and practicalities

There is plenty of scope for doing the activity in different ways. For example, you might make a selection of the statements and present them to students one opinion at a time or let students see all the opinions from the start. You could get students moving to designated positions or standing on a line to indicate their choice, or you could sit them at tables sorting their items into groups and labelling them. You could have them making decisions individually or by trying for a group consensus.

## List of situations

- David Beckham is better looking than Brad Pitt.
- Manchester United is a better football team than Tranmere Rovers.
- Manchester United is a better football team than Chelsea.
- Brussels sprouts taste disgusting.
- You get what you deserve.
- It's wrong to kill humans for sport.
- It's wrong to kill animals for sport.
- Brussels sprouts contain lots of vitamin C.
- Beethoven is a better composer than Justin Bieber.
- Maths is harder than English.
- The world is warming up because of human activities.
- If you want to get a good job, you need to do well at school.
- It's wrong to tease people because they are fat.
- Whole-class detentions are unfair.
- When someone dies, their eldest son should inherit everything.
- All people are selfish.
- Smoking is bad for your health.
- Smoking makes you look grown-up.

> **Cont'd.**
>
> List of concepts
>
> - Opinion
> - Criteria
> - Belief
> - Truth
> - Knowledge
> - Attitude
> - Justify
> - Certainty
> - Evidence
> - Probability
> - Reasons
> - Taste
> - Likes/dislikes
> - Fact
> - Supportable
> - Insupportable

# Philosophical concepts

Another step towards deliberate philosophizing is for students to recognize the kinds of concepts that are often present in philosophical questions and discussions.

Concepts unite a number of different things into a class. The members of the class are said to share common characteristics that can be defined or described. Thus, 'square' and 'bee' are concepts and, although the instances of each may differ in certain ways, they should nevertheless be distinguishable from shapes that are octagons and insects that are damselflies. In the field of natural science there is some room for conceptual contestability and change under pressure from new discoveries. The change of Pluto from 'planet' to 'dwarf planet' is an example.

However, in philosophical areas of investigation, conceptual contestability is often persistent. For example, 'being treated equally' and 'getting what you deserve' are two competing definitions of justice but perhaps it is also possible to be treated equally *and also* get what you deserve. Then again, there are overlaps between the concepts of justice, fairness, equality, reward and freedom. The relations between them are not cut-and-dried but open to argument. An important part of the practice of philosophy is to reflect systematically on contestable concepts in the light of their applications in life and their implications for action.

The English philosopher R. G. Collingwood (2005, pp. 26–53) suggested another difference between philosophical concepts and those arising from the exact and empirical sciences. He claimed that all people have some awareness, through normal conversation starting in childhood, of philosophical concepts such as 'fairness', 'beauty' and 'knowledge'. In philosophizing, there is no 'absolute zero' of knowledge. Rather we come to understand philosophical concepts better and apply them more wisely through a process of systematic reflection on the ways they work with and against each other in a field of enquiry.

In a thorough and influential book on P4C, Laurance Splitter and Ann Sharp (1995, p. 130) suggested that philosophical concepts are: *common, central* and *contestable*. We can use those related headings to sum up the discussion about concepts so far but apply slightly different definitions for the terms than did the original authors.

- *Common*. Philosophical concepts such as 'fairness', desert', 'beauty', 'knowledge', 'truth', 'time', 'history' and 'evidence' are common in that most people are at least aware of them or concepts closely related to them. Therefore, philosophizing about these concepts involves coming to know them in a clearer more complete way and understanding how they can be applied to experience.
- *Central*. Philosophical concepts are central to the human condition, to fields of human endeavour or to persistent controversies.
- *Contestable*. Philosophical concepts work with and against each other in relations that are contestable and have histories. Differences of judgement and interpretation cannot be resolved by reference to a single authoritative definition or foundational principle. Philosophical discussion will therefore work towards wiser judgements by recognizing complexity, and appreciating that consensus may not be possible.

Simply to discuss concepts like 'justice' is not necessarily to discuss them philosophically. So someone might say 'fairness is about equal treatment' while another might respond, 'no it's about getting what you deserve'. They may fall back, impatiently, to the position that: 'it's all subjective anyway' and that it is pointless even to put one's case to others. How, then, could teachers help students to reflect philosophically on contestable concepts and what would be the benefits of doing so?

## Asking the right questions

In order to move forward in thinking one must ask questions. In a philosophical enquiry, the right questions to ask are ones that move it forward.

A starting question will contain, or at least imply, a philosophical concept (i.e. one that is common, central and contestable). It will also be an open question in the sense that it will not be asked from a position of authority with a preconceived answer in mind. A starting question may have a 'yes' or 'no' answer and still be regarded as an open question because the answer begins a process of discussion rather than ending it. Hence, the following questions are open and each has a philosophical dimension.

- Is graffiti art or vandalism?
- Could 'fair trade' ever be possible?
- Can it ever be right to invade another country?
- Are great extremes of wealth unjust? If so, should there be rules about maximum and minimum levels of wealth?
- Who should I respect and why?
- Do I have more than one culture?
- If one person in a class misbehaves, is it always wrong to keep the whole class behind?
- Should scientists decide what societies should do about global warming because they are more knowledgeable about global warming than non-scientists?
- Is democracy always the best form of government?
- Is toleration a virtue?

Teachers will help students to recognize open questions with philosophical dimensions and to create their own. Let's look at how an enquiry into one of these questions might proceed, what other questions could be asked to move the discussion forward and how the language of reasoning presented earlier in the chapter could help.

## A worked example: Is toleration a virtue?

Participants in a discussion need to consider not only the concepts contained in the question but also those implied by it. Let's assume that a virtue is a good habit of conduct that is influenced by intelligence and by other virtues. Let's also assume the students and teacher have discussed this concept before and, in that sense, have something to build on. So, is toleration a good habit to cultivate in oneself and others?

Underlying the concept of toleration is a historically established web of related concepts working with and against each other, for example, restraint, opposition, abhorrence, prejudice, violence, force, reasonableness, sincerity, respect, consequence and power. Hence, the concept of toleration and its applications are highly contestable and unstable. In discussion, participants will soon become aware of this clash of concepts, particularly when they begin to consider examples. Below are some suggested strategies for the teacher, not only for enquiring into this question but any other questions that include contestable concepts:

- help students establish a field of related concepts
- help them see how concepts can work with and against each other
- help them raise appropriate examples for consideration and comparison

Let's say that some students agree that toleration is to do with showing restraint towards something you oppose or even abhor. But there is a question that needs to be asked: Is it possible to show restraint *and* still oppose? Perhaps students will find it *is* possible when they start thinking of examples. But then other questions need to be asked: Would all forms of opposition be justified, including those that involved violence? And if one stopped short of violence but nevertheless opposed through persuasion, could one still claim to be tolerant? Teachers should be prepared to ask the questions that need to be asked but also to encourage students to ask of those kinds of questions too.

On another track, if a person is prejudiced about many things but stops short of allowing his prejudice to turn violent, he might claim proudly that he is a tolerant person. Perhaps it would be better, therefore, to think of lack of prejudice as being more virtuous than toleration. But is prejudice *always* wrong? Shouldn't people be prejudiced against cruelty, for example?

Having identified a web of philosophical concepts and considered their complex interrelations, the teacher can ask for questions arising from examples of their application. We might hear: 'Should a school have "zero tolerance" of bad behaviour and expel children if they disrupt lessons?', or 'Should states invade other states to prevent acts of mass slaughter?' In order to explore these questions further, participants can use the language of reasoning.

- Ask what the *consequences* would be of taking the proposed action or refraining from it.
- Ask what *alternative* courses of action there might be. What reasons could be given for supporting each of the alternatives?
- Ask what *degree* of 'badness' should, in their opinion, trigger action and what attributes make the 'badness' bad.
- Ask what *questions* students have at each stage of the discussion.
- Ask what *connections* there are between concepts such as toleration and prejudice. If students don't suggest concepts you think are relevant and important, then you should introduce them.
- Ask students to make *arguments* and offer *examples.* Encourage them to think of possible counter-arguments and examples. If there are arguments you think they should face but haven't raised, then offer them yourself by asking: 'What would you say to someone who put this *alternative argument . . .?*'

## What is progress in philosophical enquiry?

Progress does not necessarily depend on students coming to a consensus of opinion. There may be reasonable disagreement. Progress would still be in evidence if:

- Participants are developing a shared language of value. Understanding that their responses 'are shaped by some of the same vocabulary can make it easier to agree to disagree' (Appiah, 2007, p. 30).
- There is realization that rival uses and applications of a concept are 'not only possible' but can be 'of potential critical value to one's own use or interpretation of the concept in question' (Gallie, 1955, p. 193).
- Participants have come to understand the concept better *and* they grasp fresh aspects of it.
- Participants have come away with a more complex position than they held at the beginning and, as a result, subsequent dialogues are

more thoughtful – not only because people are more familiar with concepts in this field but also because they are more willing to learn from others, even though they come to the question with their own preconceptions.

- Participants have built up an understanding of a concept such as toleration and a view of its application that is satisfactory to them and that they can defend systematically against challenges.
- Teachers and students become interested in the histories of the webs of related concepts that stimulate their philosophizing. Participants want to find out more, keep enquiring and apply their enquiries to their own lives.

## Summary

Teachers can help students appropriate the language of enquiry through the practice of philosophizing, which is not limited to discussing words and their meanings but relates to real life. In the process of thinking about both, students can become more confident thinkers and more reasonable people.

# Further reading

Teachers can also help students explore concepts by devising or obtaining exercises and discussion plans that focus on a single concept or collection of related concepts. There are some excellent examples written by Matthew Lipman, the originator of P4C published in the journal: *Analytic Teaching*, volume 16, number 2. They are available at www.viterbo.edu/analytic/table5.htm

# References

Appiah, K. A. (2007) *Cosmopolitanism: Ethics in a World of Strangers*. London: Penguin.

Collingwood. R. G. (2005) *An Essay on Philosophical Method*. Oxford: Clarendon Press.

Gallie, W. B. (1955) 'Essentially Contested Concepts', *Proceedings of the Aristotelian Society*, New Series, 56 (1955–6), 167–98.

Richards, I. A. (1955) *Speculative Instruments*. Chicago: University of Chicago Press.

Splitter, L. J. and Sharp, A. M. (1995) *Teaching for Better Thinking: The Classroom Community of Inquiry*. Victoria: ACER.

Swartz, R. J. and Parks, S. (1994) *Infusing the Teaching of Critical and Creative Thinking into Content Instruction*. Pacific Grove, Canada: Critical Thinking Books & Software.

# 2 P4C in Critical Thinking

James Nottingham

## Chapter Outline

What is critical thinking?                                     27
Wobblers                                                       32

Critical thinking is the study of claims. When a person tries to persuade another of something then he or she is making a claim.

For example:

- I think it is wrong to steal because it is against the school rules
- I reckon you should tell the teacher then she can sort it out
- An apple a day keeps the doctor away

These are all claims. A student of critical thinking will be expected to test these claims, give reasons for what they say in return, look for assumptions and evaluate analogies. They will need to be aware of circular, slippery slope and straw man arguments. Ultimately, they will be expected to create their own persuasive arguments.

This chapter provides an overview of how P4C can help develop these and other critical thinking skills, and provides a supplement to the introduction by exploring in detail some of the possibilities of thinking and reasoning in enquiry.

Before that though, a word of warning from Matthew Lipman, the creator of P4C:

For the vast majority of school students, critical thinking has not fulfilled its promise; there were a number of deficiencies that doomed it from the start:

1. The critical thinking approach was, by itself, narrow and skimpy. It needed to be based much more solidly on informal logic, formal logic, educational psychology, developmental psychology, and philosophy, but this was seldom done.
2. Little effort was made to devise, as part of the approach, a creative thinking component that would engage students in imaginative thinking, and in thinking about the imagination.
3. Likewise, no serious effort was mounted to construct a valuational component, in which students would be able to talk together freely about the different sorts of values, and how they were to be appreciated. (Lipman, 2003, p. 5)

There are more in Lipman's list but these three make the point – critical thinking is not, in itself, a recipe for success. If, however, it is taught within a community of enquiry that seeks also to build caring and creative thinking, as well as sound judgement and reflection, then it has a chance.

# What is critical thinking?

'Critical' comes from the Greek *kriticos* meaning: 'able to make judgements'.

This is a useful reminder when running P4C sessions: Are students expressing received ideas or are they weighing up pros and cons and making a reasoned judgement? If it is the latter then they are probably engaging in critical thinking. If it is the former then, no matter how articulate they might be, they may still only be engaging in opinionated debate.

Very often early P4C sessions (and other class dialogues) result in an exchange of opinions only. Student A offers an opinion to which his or her peers respond with their own opinions until such times as an impasse or agreement is reached. We ought to be pressing for a higher quality of thinking, beginning with the use of reasons.

Here are some steps for developing critical thinking. Each idea is explored in more depth and there could be many more, including a look at logic (formal and informal) and judgement making, but this is an introductory chapter.

1. Invite students to respond to the question they have chosen. This will normally result in a series of opinions being offered.

2. Ask for reasons to support the opinions already expressed. These reasons could come from the students who offered the opinions or from any other student.
3. Develop argumentation – a claim that is intended to be persuasive, has a conclusion and is supported by at least one reason.
4. Use cognitive conflict to create more reflection within students' own minds, rather than only when in dispute with other people.
5. Examine the quality of each claim in terms of credibility, assumptions they might be based upon, response to counter-claims, and so on.

## Stage 1: Listening to opinions

Generally speaking, students will respond to questions and prompts with their opinions. Rarely in the early stages of the development of a community will they offer reasons for their points of view; this tends to come later.

Though opinions are only really the starting point for critical thinking, it is important that these opinions are listened to and understood. Some ways to achieve this include:

**Repeat** – invite a student to give their opinion about the subject matter then ask the other students to repeat that opinion to each other in pairs

**Paraphrase** – invite a couple of other students to give their opinions then ask the other students to repeat these ideas using different words or phrases

**Build** – once again, invite some more views, then ask the other students to repeat or paraphrase, and then add something in support of this view opinion (whether they agree with it or not – at this stage, it is about listening and understanding, rather than agreeing or disagreeing)

**Check for understanding** – a facilitation move where you ask if anyone knows what Student A is saying. Typically, a number of students will nod their heads. Invite one of the 'head-nodders' to explain what they think Student A meant. Then go back to Student A to ask whether this was indeed what they meant. More often than not, Student A will respond with a 'Yes, but . . .' and then go on to clarify further.

## Stage 2: Asking for reasons

The aim of a thinking skills program such as P4C is not to turn children into philosophers but to help them become more thoughtful, more reflective, more considerate and more reason-able individuals. (Lipman et al., 1980, p. 15)

The hyphen to *reasonable* has been added to draw attention to the breakdown of the word. Experience shows that the more students are 'able to reason', the more 'reasonable' they become. In fact, it was this aspect of P4C that helped me to justify its inclusion in the programmes of study in a number of schools. After all, who doesn't want more reasonable students? And the best place to begin developing reasonableness is by improving one's ability to reason.

Thus, critical thinking begins when students give reasons for their opinions, or views about the world. For example:

- I think we should protect trees (*this is an opinion*) because they improve the look of the countryside (*this is the reason they give*).
- I support euthanasia (*opinion*) because I would like to choose when I die (*reason*).
- He believes we should keep British Summer Time throughout the year (*opinion*) so that we don't have to walk home from school in the dark (*reason*).

Once your students are ready to move beyond giving opinions, ask them to justify their ideas by offering supporting reasons. This could be achieved using a similar progression to those suggested for listening to opinions:

**Reason** – ask Student A to support their opinion with a reason
**Repeat** – ask students in pairs to repeat the reason given by Student A
**Check** – ask students in pairs to check whether they think the reason given by Student A supports their opinion (whether or not they agree with Student A should be put to one side for now)

**Build** – ask students in pairs to think of other reasons that might also support Student A's opinion

I agree or I disagree, because . . .

Asking students to begin with 'I agree with X because . . .' or 'I disagree with Y because . . .' is a popular convention in P4C. However, it doesn't necessarily lead to reasoning.

For example, let's say Susan is waiting to give her opinion that red cars are the best. She then hears Tom saying he thinks white cars are the best, so she responds with 'I disagree with you Tom because I think red cars are better.' Though this gives the impression of Susan's reasoning, she is actually giving her opinion with the preface 'I disagree with'. That is not to say that the convention is weak – it can be a very useful tool for enhancing thinking but beware of the problems!

## Stage 3: Developing argumentation

Putting reasons together with opinions leads to argumentation. Not in the layman's terms of 'arguing' a point, but in terms of an argument that:

1. is intended to be persuasive
2. has a conclusion (opinion)
3. is supported by at least one reason

Without all three aspects, a statement is not considered to be an argument – instead it is thought of as opinion, debate, a question or a difference of opinion.

For example, which of these would be considered to be a sufficient argument?

1. I believe England will win a World Cup within 10 years.
2. Student A states: Students shouldn't have to wear school uniforms and Student B responds – But it's better to wear a uniform than worry about having the right labels.
3. Schools should insist upon uniforms because it generates a sense of identity and belonging.
4. The shop closes at 5 p.m. because that's what it says on the door.

Only number 3 is a critical thinking argument. The first one is an opinion; the second one is an exchange of opinions; the third one is an argument because it fits all three characteristics (opinion, supported by reason and is intended to persuade). Number 4 has the appearance of an argument but isn't because it does not intend to persuade – it only informs.

To begin developing argumentation, we need to teach our students the differences above and then encourage the presentation of arguments.

For example, if Student A offered the opinion: 'stealing is wrong', instead of agreeing with him, we should ask him to justify his opinion with a reason. For example: 'because it is against the law'.

Once students have started to get into the habit of giving reasons, we can then ask them to consider whether the reasons they have given support their conclusions (opinions), as well as how strong the reasons are. For example:

Argument: Cars should be banned because they emit dangerous greenhouse gases.
Challenge: Should everything that emits $CO_2$ be banned? For example, pets, farm animals, people?

Note that the challenger is not agreeing or disagreeing; instead they are questioning the validity of the reason.

## Stage 4: Creating more reflection

Once your students are getting the hang of argumentation, I would suggest intervening a bit more so as to develop some cognitive conflict in their minds. This then leads to more ideas and eventually to habitual reflection and more sophisticated critical thinking. Cognitive conflict is about setting up a conflict of opinions within a person's mind (as opposed to a conflict between two or more people). This conflict, or dissonance, then unsettles the thinker and causes them to reflect more deeply on what it is they actually think.

For example, ask your students if they think Robin Hood was a 'good man' – they will probably say 'yes'. This is thought number one: 'Robin

**Figure 2.1** Cognitive conflict: A disagreement in one's own mind

Hood was a good man.' However, if they are then asked whether it would be good if someone in the class stole from a supermarket and gave the proceeds to the poor, their usual answer is 'no'. This then prompts the second thought in their minds, 'it is wrong to steal.'

This conflict of opinions between thinking that Robin Hood was a good man, while also believing that stealing is wrong (see Figure 2.1), is the tension that causes the children to think or reflect more. This can be shown thus:

The prime reason for setting up cognitive conflict is that it encourages students to think more. When students know the solution to a problem, they have less reason to think about it; they tend to simply solve it and move on. However, if they experience cognitive conflict in their minds then the tension between the two ideas should cause them to think more. It also gives rise to more claims with which to enhance critical thinking.

# Wobblers

*Wobblers* are a great way to create cognitive conflict (Nottingham, 2010).

## *Wobbler* One: If A = B

This is a process of asking what a concept is, taking whatever the student says and then testing it by turning it around and adding an example. For example:

**Teacher**:   What is food?
**Student A**: What we put in our mouths.
**Teacher**:   Does that mean whatever we put in our mouths is food?
              For example, if I were to chew this pen lid.

This structure can be represented as:

If A = B then does B = A?
A is the concept that you are considering, in this case 'food'
B is the students' response, in this case 'What we put in our mouths'

### Some examples of *Wobbler* One

If bullying (a) means hurting someone (b) then does that mean if I hurt
   someone (b) that I'm bullying them (a)?

For example, what if I foul someone in a football match? Or give someone some bad news?

If a holiday (a) is taking a break (b) then if I take a break (b), am I on
   holiday (a)?

For example, taking a tea break or going outside to play a game for half
an hour?

If a hero (a) is someone who is brave (b), does that mean a brave person (b) is a hero (a)?

For example, someone who runs across a motorway might be brave but
are they are hero?

## *Wobbler* Two: NOT A

An alternative to the first *wobbler* is to add a negative. The structure
then becomes:

If A = B then if it's NOT B, is it NOT = A?
A is the concept that you are considering, for example, 'food'
B is the students' response, in this case 'what we put in our mouths'

So this time, to challenge the students' answer, we ask:

'Does that mean if we do not put it in our mouths (not b) then is it not
   food (not a)?

### Some examples of *Wobbler* Two

If bullying (a) means hurting someone (b) then if I don't hurt someone (not b) am I not bullying them (not a)?

For example, if I don't hit them but instead encourage everyone to ignore them, am I not bullying?

If a holiday (a) is going away somewhere (b) then if I don't go away (not b), am I not on holiday (not a)?

For example, if I stay at home during the school holidays, am I not on holiday?

If a hero (a) is someone who I respect (b), does that mean if I don't respect them (not b) then they are not a hero (a)?

For example, the apartheid government in South Africa didn't respect Nelson Mandela for years but to millions around the world he was (and still is) a hero.

## Wobbler Notes

Sticking to the advice of the following suggestions will improve the success rate of all the wobblers:

### *Wobbling, not point scoring*

Wobblers are not designed to prove students wrong. Rather, it is about encouraging students to go beyond the 'easy answer' or first response; to help them identify contradictions and misconceptions; and ultimately to develop the habit of questioning their own ideas.

### *Humour and humility*

Putting students on the spot in an attempt to discredit or disprove their hypotheses is rather disingenuous. Instead, it seems to be far more productive if we laugh with the students (rather than at them) and admit we don't know what the concept means any more than the students do. This helps to develop a sense of co-inquirers rather than the 'usual' teacher–student relationship. This adds a new dimension to curriculum approaches, as shown in the following chapters.

## A little bit of trickery

Still keeping in mind humour and humility, this type of challenge could be said to be a form of trickery. Of course, trickery has negative connotations (the trickery of a conman) as well as positive ones (the trickery of a children's magician). This is partly why it's worth mentioning: these wobblers seek to provide trickery that is positive, fun and engaging.

# Stage 5: Pushing for quality

Once your students have mastered the basics covered above, it is time to begin pushing for depth and quality. Here are some of the aspects of quality that are most useful, together with a few of the problems often encountered with dialogue in schools:

## Values

Very often an argument in critical thinking is considered in terms of its merit or credibility. However, not to be ignored should be considerations in terms of relative worth or importance – socially, ethically, historically, and so on. Questions for your students to consider might include:

1. Is this argument ethically sound?
2. If this argument might cause offence, then should it be withheld?
3. Is this an appropriate context in which to express my arguments?
4. Who might this argument affect?
5. What are the implications of this argument socially, emotionally, historically, culturally, and so on?

## Credibility

There are two key questions to ask when considering credibility: Can we trust the sources of information upon which our arguments are based? Why? In many cases students find this difficult because their opinions often cloud their judgements (e.g. if they agree with the argument then they tend to trust the sources; and vice versa – if they don't agree then they don't trust the sources).

### Straw man arguments

A straw man argument misrepresents another's argument. It rears its head very often in school (and the media!). The most common forms of this type of fallacy are:

1. misrepresenting another argument so that it appears much weaker than it was originally (e.g. through oversimplification)
2. quoting an argument out of context, so that it misrepresents the actual intentions of the argument
3. implying that one or more people who have presented the argument poorly are representative of all supporters of the argument

### Argumentum ad hominem

An ad hominem tries to discredit an argument by pointing out a negative aspect of the person (or group) that supports it. For example:

- Of course that policy is wrong – the BNP support it.
- Yes, but that's what Tom says and we all know we can't trust Tom.
- Why should we uphold Christian values when there are so many priests who are convicted paedophiles?
- The problem is, he's a Liverpool supporter so what he says must be biased.
- He would say that, wouldn't he? After all, he's a teacher.

## Summary

This chapter provides an overview of some of the ways to respond to claims. Of course, to start with these are merely the mechanics of critical thinking. Success in curriculum subjects is more likely to occur when these guidelines are applied many times over, within many different topics, through the use of a community of enquiry. That is one of the reasons P4C can be so powerful: it gives the opportunity to develop the skills of philosophical enquiry until they become habitual, almost natural, forms of thinking for students and teachers alike.

## Further resources

McCall, C. (2009) *Transforming Thinking*. London: Routledge.

Nottingham, J. A. (2010) *Challenging Learning*. Cramlington: JN Publishing.

Van den Brink Budgen, R. (2000) *Critical Thinking for Students*. Oxford: How to Books Ltd.

Vansieleghem, N. and Kennedy, D. (2011) 'Philosophy for Children in Transition: Problems and Prospects', *Journal of Philosophy of Education*, 45 (2), 171–82.

# References

Lipman, M. (2003) *Thinking in Education* (2nd edn). New York: Cambridge University Press.

Lipman, M., Sharp, A. M. and Oscanyan, F. S. (1980) *Philosophy in the Classroom*. Philadelphia: Temple University Press.

Nottingham, J. A. (2010) *Challenging Learning*. Cramlington: JN Publishing.

# 3 P4C in English

Steve Williams

## Chapter Outline

Connections between English and P4C          38

Activities using English and P4C             45

# Connections between English and P4C

The teaching of English is central to the notion of a humanistic education. There is an expectation that students will become competent readers, writers, speakers and, by implication, thinkers. They will reflect, critically and creatively, on the human condition – not least in response to literature. They will think for themselves about values and the ends of life in awareness of a range of cultural traditions and perspectives. This is a vision that aims beyond functional literacy towards people being willing and able to make their own contributions to discourse in civil society – at work, in church congregations, in political groups, in clubs and societies, in communities of commitment and in schools and colleges. The vision is proclaimed through the aims and key concepts of the National Curriculum Programme of Study for English.

Yet, in the poetic words of T. S. Eliot (2004): 'Between the idea and the reality . . . falls the shadow.' In English teaching, as in so many subjects, the shadow falls when attainment targets and exam results are seen as ends in themselves rather than means to the greater ends of intellectual, cultural and social empowerment. Teachers who plan a unit of work on 'persuasive writing' may calculate that students are more likely to meet the attainment targets if the set topic is: 'design a holiday brochure for your local area' rather than 'present your ideas on the principles of a just society'. They may avoid the justice topic either because they think students lack sufficient background information or are incapable of thinking and writing well about such abstract principles.

Yet, perhaps, students have most to gain from tackling the most demanding of topics – topics that are fundamental to everyone, require high levels of conceptual discernment, direct students towards significant writing from the past and present, and are open to arguments from a range of perspectives. Philosophical dialogue can help students and teachers of English to achieve high standards while at the same time becoming more intellectually self-reliant. It can help teachers fulfil the humanistic promise of their subject in the following ways:

- Prompting students to reflect, at a general level, on the ideas they give and receive in discourse in order to argue, explain, criticize, clarify and justify.
- Making students aware of those philosophical arguments that are part of a cultural heritage. Many of the ideas and perspectives students take for granted about such themes as equality, liberty, choice, fairness and respect relate to such arguments, as are many of the sentiments and dilemmas conveyed in literature. However, the students' ideas may be contradictory, incoherent or limited in scope. Philosophical dialogue helps to widen and sharpen their responses.
- Ensuring that students take time to consider the moves they are making when they are trying to understand or challenge ideas – moves such as comparing, giving examples, using analogies, and so on.

Experience has shown that this is not a project suitable only for the elite few. All students are capable of thinking more philosophically – and they usually enjoy it. In the past, philosophical writing was not always considered a discrete field of discourse. Raymond Williams (1983, p. 121), writing on the philosopher David Hume states: '[I]n 1762, Boswell called Hume, quite simply, "the greatest Writer in Britain"', and that according to his biographer Ernest Mossner, Hume 'regarded philosophy as part and parcel of literature'. Today, philosophical dialogue would be a valuable addition to the teaching of English, while philosophical writing, for and by students, would be a medium for reflection about what they take for granted and what they come to believe. English teachers who have introduced one or both have reported excellent outcomes.

Perhaps the best way of explaining how philosophical dialogue might contribute to English lessons is to imagine a sequence of activities and provide some commentary on the thinking behind each one. The example I have provided is concerned with what follows when we ask the question 'Why?' In terms of discourse, we seem to be requiring an explanation. Certainly, 'the explanation' is an important type of writing required in English courses and examinations. Explanations often present causes, reasons, motivations and justifications. We should be able to recognize which is which, otherwise we will not be able to give coherent explanations, nor understand the nature of the explanations we read and hear.

## Dialogue and thinking for oneself

The first thing to stress is that the activities in the following imaginary sequence are meant to complement and build on each other. Therefore, the way of working is necessarily dialogical. By that, I mean there is a back and forth movement of responses that is ongoing and cumulative rather than being limited to a single oral discussion. The dialogue would refer to things discussed in previous lessons, texts read and written by the students and questions they have created. A piece of argumentative writing could be a response to a class discussion; a further discussion could be a response to that piece of writing; a work of fiction might be introduced to explore similar conceptual territory, and so on.

The following sequence of activities is meant to illustrate this spirit of ongoing dialogue. The sequence might be spread out; an item may not follow the previous one in the same lesson or week. In each part of the sequence, I have indicated those items I think have a philosophical dimension to them.

## Reading and viewing texts

Students study several newspaper articles, video reports and interviews about 'the UK riots' in the summer of 2011. The material contains accounts and interpretations of the events. There is no particular philosophical dimension here. The students are reading reportage and editorial about current affairs, as one would expect in English lessons. However, the texts are likely to contain and to rouse moral responses and ascriptions of causes. There is evidently some potential for philosophical reflection.

## Questioning and discussion

Students are invited to enquire into what they have read using strategies for philosophical dialogue introduced in Chapter 1. Some of their questions address the interpretations and commentaries that are offered. A question they choose to discuss is: 'What caused the riots?' In the course of the discussion, students put forward different candidates for consideration. Some offer groups of items acting in combination as 'the cause'; some offer them as causal factors with one, the 'cause', being the most important. The discussion reflects many of the ideas put forward in the media at the time including:

- criminal opportunism
- local tensions with police
- the shooting of a black man acting as a 'spark'
- practices like 'stop and search' used in a discriminatory way against black youths
- recreational violence
- gang culture
- the ease of organizing a crowd through social media
- the intoxicating feeling of power that comes with being part of a mob
- unemployment and cuts in public services
- social exclusion; poverty; the growing gap between rich and poor
- the lack of response by the police when confronted by the protest, leading to people thinking they could 'get away with it'
- youth clubs are closing so there are less things for young people to do
- boredom
- not being at school
- parents not controlling their children
- a general selfishness and lack of concern for others throughout society (the metaphor 'moral compass' has been used in the media to signify what it is that certain people lack)
- youthful impetuousness

It becomes clear in the conversation that students are using the word 'cause' in different ways. Some are imagining a cause to be like an irresistible natural force: if an event happens or a situation pertains, then another event is certain to take place. Others want to talk about multiple causes and see a cause as a factor, in combination with other factors that makes certain events more likely to happen – although when people are involved you can never be certain. These differences of meaning can lead to exchanges like this that go around in circles:

**Student 1**: I think the cause is poverty. When people are poor, they are more likely to cause trouble, steal and riot.
**Student 2**: Not everyone who is poor riots and steals. Most don't. I think you are stereotyping poor people.
**Student 3**: Some of the people who looted had jobs and were not poor; so to say poverty was the cause has to be wrong.
**Student 1**: I still think poverty is the cause.
**Student 4**: But that's stereotyping.

Another confusion is that some students talk about the 'cause(s)' of the riots – why the riots started in the first place – while others talk about the 'reasons' for people joining in with acts of looting that were already happening. And this last point requires a further distinction between people making conscious choices and trying to explain or justify their actions and people who are thought to be 'forced' to do something by external or internal influences, their choice-making capacities being diminished in some way by those influences.

We are into philosophical territory here, or at least territory where argument and philosophy overlap. There is a philosophical dimension in trying to introduce and make sense out of terms such as 'cause', 'reason', 'more likely' and 'certain' – and in considering the extent to which people are free agents and/or 'victims of circumstance'.

References in the media to some people's perceived 'lack of moral compass' also invite questions that have philosophical implications such as:

- 'What would it mean to have a moral compass?'
- How would it relate any of the following moral processes: considerations of consequences, internalization of moral 'rules', application of empathy or exercise of conscience?
- Is 'moral compass' a useful metaphor?

Some people might recoil from these suggestions, thinking that there is a danger of leading students into a philosophical quagmire from which they may never emerge. However, I argue that these distinctions and considerations are necessary for any reasonable discussion about the issues in question. The alternative is to have the students talking past each other without questioning any of the things they have previously taken for granted. There are obvious reasons for this: either they fail to grasp the significance of what other people are saying, they have not reflected on the concepts they are using, or they are unaware of the range of arguments that are possible.

How, then, should teachers handle this kind of discussion? There is an explanation of the general principles of enquiry in the Introduction; therefore, it is enough to say here that teachers would be sensitive to the importance of conceptual clarification and distinction making. In the time available for discussion it would be sufficient to prompt reflection by asking questions like:

- Are you saying this is the only cause or do you have other causes in mind?
- Is everything caused by something?
- Is there a difference in talking about the cause of something like water boiling and the cause of a riot?
- Is there a difference between the cause of the riot in the first place and the cause of people taking part when it is already happening?
- Which factors are one-off events and which are ongoing? Can they both be causes?

A teacher might finish off the lesson by inviting students to write their own versions of a causal chain in relation to the riots. One example of a chain would be: Unemployment → youth gangs in the area → police shooting a black man in Tottenham and the protest as the 'spark' → excitement of seeing riots and looting on TV → some people's lack of self-control. Students would then underline any they think are particularly interesting or important and give their reasons.

The teacher would then ask students to write *either* (a) an explanation of the riots based on their causal chains *or* (b) a dialogue between two characters who are talking about the causes and having a reasonable disagreement *or* (c) a personal response in some other form. The forms – explanation, dialogue and personal response – could be compared to see what features were similar and different.

## Time for reflection

The teacher decides that it is worth spending some time getting students to think, in a more systematic way, about the concepts they raised in the discussion. She has read the students' writing, she does some background reading on causation and causal arguments, and she creates an activity for focused discussion – or acquires one from one of the support websites for P4C (see the resource list at the end of this chapter and the example of such an activity given in Part 2). The teacher believes that the exercise will help students to think for themselves in all future discussions involving the concept of 'cause' in that it will introduce them to the sorts of questions they will need to ask, the judgements they will need to make and the kinds of arguments they will need to take into account. She also thinks this will have a bearing on the higher attainment targets for speaking, listening and writing that require sensitivity to a range of viewpoints and the ability to order them in a coherent way. She is aware that when students use causal connectives such as 'because', 'therefore' and 'as a result of' they are often unclear about the work the words are doing in sentences. Their writing seems muddled even though it exhibits an abundance of connectives (see Williams, 2008). The teacher wants to wean them off the writing frames upon which they have come to depend and instead follow a structure based on their own questions and distinctions.

## Archiving and questioning

The teacher makes a class book with a title like 'causes and choices'. She selects some of the students' writing – their causal chains, explanations, dialogues and reports of their discussions – to start the book off. In future, if any poems, novels, plays, essays, philosophical dialogues or reports relate to the themes of the class book, then the teacher will reference the text (e.g. with a selected quote, summary or dustcover design). She will also add new responses from the students that are creative as well as critical – poems and stories juxtaposed with commentary on ideas and uses of language. The students are invited to write new questions and enter them in the book. From time to time the teacher brings some of the students' questions or writing to the attention of the whole class. Here, the philosophical, literary, rhetorical and generic dimensions of the topic combine without diminishing the enjoyment that students gain from their reading, writing and discussing. I believe that these approaches would enhance the study of English.

## Conclusion

This possible sequence of activities is only one example of how teachers of English might integrate philosophical dialogue into lessons. It would not be necessary for them to be experts in philosophy, but they would need sensitivity to conceptual, moral, aesthetic and logical dimensions of discourse so they could lead the students towards more critical, creative and coherent thinking. The aim would be not only to help them speak, read and write competently but also interestingly, independently and reflectively about matters of significance. With regard to examinations and other assessments, we can choose either the high road or the low road. We take the low road when we give students undemanding work and ready-made content to arrange in ready-made structures. We take the high road when we give students challenging work and provide them with the resources to rise to the challenges. Philosophical dialogue helps English teachers take the high road.

# Activities using English and P4C

## Activity 1: Causes and choices

*Stimulus*
Make a selection from among the suggested 'causes' the students raised in their discussion about the riots (see the sequence of activities in the previous section). Write them down in one list and call them 'factors'. A full list appears on the companion website if you'd like to use it.

### Guidance

Have sets of blank index cards to give to students. Split the class into groups of four or five. Each group gets a copy of the list and a set of cards. Below the list, write a set of statements to prompt groups to select combinations of factors. The statements could be as follows:

- We are the most important/interesting factors because . . .
- I am the X (extra) factor because . . .
- Together, we could have caused it because . . .
- Together we were not enough to cause it because . . .

(The 'X (extra) factor' represents something out of the ordinary that, given certain background conditions, could be said to have sparked an event.)

The groups of students would try to match one or more of the factors to the statements. They write their selection of factors on the index cards. Then they present their conclusions to the class and prepare themselves to be questioned by their peers. There is no need for every group to use all the statements. Allow a period of question-and-response after each presentation to fit the time you have available.

### Philosophical questions and concepts

The same activity could be used for any inquiry into 'causes' where students are seeking to *explain* an event or situation. Ask the students what are the most *important* things they would like to be explained.

## Activity 2: 'It just happened?'

*The following resource was written by Steve Williams and Jason Buckley for the website: www.p4c.com. It is reproduced here with permission.*

### Stimulus

This activity requires students to consider some statements and decide whether they could be explained causally or be better categorized as chance happenings. However, other concepts might also be relevant such as *voluntary, predictable, deliberate*, and so on. Often, our understanding of actions depends on our use of related families of concepts rather than one single concept. Our starting point is a commonly used phrase: 'It just happened!'

## Guidance

Have the situation descriptions (listed below) available for your students on cards. We've included this list on the companion website in case you'd like to use it. Also provide them with the 'concept sheet' listed below and available online. For each of the situations, ask students to decide whether or not they think 'It just happened!' would be a reasonable explanation. When they have made their decision, ask them to justify it using the concepts on the concept sheet as prompts. Which of those are relevant to their answers and why? If the students don't know the meanings of the concept words, take some time to explain. Question the students and encourage them to question each other about their decisions, justifications and choices of related concepts. There may be several alternative interpretations of each situation. So you might ask students: 'Could you ever know that this interpretation is the best one? How?

There is plenty of scope for doing the activity in different ways. For example, you might give students one statement at a time or let them see all the statements from the start. You could get students moving to designated positions or standing on a line to indicate their choice, or you could sit them at tables sorting their items by making lists and diagrams. You could have them making decisions individually or by trying for a group consensus. You will probably only need about five of the situations for the activity. We've provided more to give you plenty of options.

## List of situations

- You are eating dinner on the sofa in front of a football match. Your team scores, and you spill spaghetti bolognese on the carpet.
- Two of the fish in your aquarium die on the same day.
- You win a race on sports day.
- You come top of the class in a maths exam.
- A bird messes on your school uniform just before your school photograph.
- You are walking along talking to a friend and step in some dog poo.
- You meet someone who looks exactly like you when you are out shopping.

- It's been sunny all week while you are at school, then at the week-end it rains.
- Your pet rabbit is ill. You pray that she gets better. The next day, she is better.
- One day, you observe a black person being questioned by a police officer. A week later, the same thing happens.
- Most of the children in your class are off sick on the same day.
- You are about to have your school photograph taken when you notice a big spot of ink on your shirt.
- Someone trips over his shoelaces on the way into assembly, and you laugh.
- The weather always seems to be miserable on your birthday.
- You go back to school after the summer holidays and notice that many of the boys have got the same hairstyle.
- You go back to school after the summer holidays and notice that many of the girls have got the same bag.

> **List of concepts**
>
> - Coincidence
> - Cause
> - Random
> - Voluntary
> - Involuntary
> - Deliberate
> - Unintentional
> - Spontaneous
> - Controlled
> - Uncontrolled
> - Predictable
> - Unpredictable
> - Systematic

## Routines: Writing for dialogue in English lessons

I am using dialogue here to refer to the to-and-fro of ideas over time – in writing as well as speech. Philosophical teaching and learning requires consistent dialogue because there is an ongoing and cumulative process of collaborative reflection among students and teachers. One purpose of writing that is often neglected is that it is a tool for generating thoughts, ordering them and preserving them so they can be analysed and discussed. Here are some ideas for using writing in the service of dialogue.

### Questions and Ideas books

Questions and Ideas books (or simply QI books) are journals that students can use both in and out of lessons. They write questions and ideas about classroom discussions and reading. QI books are vehicles for intellectual encouragement. Here are some possible uses:

- To check on levels of interest and understanding and to stimulate dialogue. The teacher reads the books, gathers questions and ideas and uses a selection as a stimulus for small- or large-group discussion
- To enable small groups of students to compare questions and ideas and suggest a topic for enquiry
- To elicit some 'first thoughts' from participants in a discussion. Ask students to pick out significant thoughts from their writing to share. The creation of first thoughts through writing rather than speaking could be helpful to students who rarely speak. They will have time to gather and record their ideas before the most uninhibited of their peers start to dominate the session
- To enable a 'thinking break' or 'cooling-off period' during an oral dialogue to gather and sort ideas
- As a means of reflecting on an oral dialogue or a sequence of dialogues
- As a means of discovering 'what one knows' prior to an oral dialogue, writing or reading
- As a means for students to reflect on their extended writing
- As a means for students, in private, to record their own ideas for future refinement or elaboration

### Freewriting in QI books
#### Explanation

Freewriting is a term invented by the writer and educator Peter Elbow (1973, 1998). It simply means writing continuously for a fixed period of time. The challenge of freewriting for students is to write when they might not feel like writing; it's about 'getting on with it'. Normally freewriting takes the form of continuous prose but it does not have to be grammatically correct, syntactically complete or carefully considered. Form is not stipulated. The writing often looks like a set of notes with sentences, key words and phrases happily mixing together.

The purpose of freewriting is to get ideas out and to overcome the anxiety that can arise when students are worried that their writing will not be correct or clear enough. In freewriting sessions, they are encouraged not to worry but to keep going and have faith that, with pen in hand, they will discover their own thoughts.

### Freewriting and dialogue

Imagine you have just shared a text or a segment of teaching with students. You might ask them to use freewriting to make connections between their own lives – their interests, curiosities, values and experiences – and the text. You might say: 'write non-stop for 10 minutes to see if you can discover something that connects what you think is important with the story (or text) we've just read together or the discussion we've had.'

At the end of the freewriting session, ask students to underline anything they felt was significant, important, surprising or interesting. It's good to use this vocabulary in your conversations with students because you will be helping them to name and understand evaluative concepts that will assist their writing and thinking. Ask them to share, with their peers, points they have underlined, either in a whole-class or small-group setting. They shouldn't necessarily read the actual words they wrote, although they can if they wish. The point is to have used freewriting to discover some ideas. Students may want to re-express those ideas, or elaborate on them, in the course of further discussion.

The advantage of using freewriting in a dialogical context is that students' ideas are not ignored. They contribute to ever widening cycles of response and enquiry. The freewriting itself is disposable or, if students use QI books, it can remain as part of an archive of each student's ideas and interests. Eventually, students may, unprompted, use freewriting as a tool for thinking.

### *Prompts for QI books*

Sometimes set the students a timed writing task and ask for a minimum number of items or lines. The precise numbers in these examples can be changed to suit your class and topic. Timings can be set as appropriate. The items are not writing frames to direct thought, only prompts to stimulate it. They are based on some of the language of reasoning presented in Chapter 1 (p. 14).

- What were the most *significant* points from your reading/discussion about . . . . Fill six lines or more.
- What different or connected *reasons* would you give for agreeing or disagreeing with the claim that . . .? Write five lines to explain.
- Write two *important questions* about . . . .
- For a passage you have just read on . . . write down the *questions* you think the writer is answering. After reading, take five minutes to complete your questions.
- Write two questions about . . . because you would like to hear what other people think.
- Explain at least three *arguments* you found in the unit of work you have just studied. Fill five lines or more.
- Write at least four *examples* of . . . .
- What are some of the *criteria* for . . .? Fill five lines or more.
- What are the most likely *causes* of . . . . Fill five lines or more.
- What is the *evidence* for . . .? Fill five lines or more.
- Explain some *differences* and *similarities* between . . . and . . . . Fill five lines or more.

# Further resources

Many of your favourite resources will have a philosophical dimension. Here are a few that I have come across or written that might provide something extra.

*Philosophy for Teens: Questioning Life's Big Ideas* by Sharon M. Kaye and Paul Thomson, Prufrock Press, 2006. This is a book of dialogues between imaginary American teenagers about philosophical themes such as *beauty, justice* and *truth*. They are supported by information on the philosophical background to the themes and suggestions for further discussion and writing. Though the dialogues could be better, the book not only provides plenty of practical suggestions, it also highlights a neglected genre of argumentative writing – the dialogue – which can stand alone and also serve as preparation for writing in other genres such as *essay* and *speech*. There is also a selection of 'thought experiments' that students may enjoy arguing over.

*The nano-conscience* by Steve Williams. This is a role-play designed to encourage the discussion of moral issues at Key Stage 3 and above. Students are invited to consider two contrasting ways of making moral judgements and then apply them to real-life situations. The role-play uses the idea of a computer, small enough to be placed inside a person's ear, acting as a conscience (see http://p4c.com/articles/nano-conscience).

*p4c.com*. The *nano-conscience* is one of the resources that is available on the cooperative website www.p4c.com. That resource is free but you can get access to others if you subscribe. I am one of the members of the cooperative. The site is not restricted to English teaching or secondary schooling but there are stories and scripts on philosophical themes and activities with which to explore concepts.

*Famous speeches.* There are many websites where famous speeches are freely available (see, for example, www.famousquotes.me.uk/speeches). Many of the entries provide good material for philosophical enquiry because they highlight virtues such as courage and justice, they promote values such as freedom and equality, or they appeal to a common identity or purpose.

# References

Elbow, P. (1973) *Writing without Teachers*. New York: Oxford University Press.

— (1998) *Writing with Power: Techniques for Mastering the Writing Process* (2nd edn). New York: Oxford University Press.

Eliot, T. S. (2004) 'The Hollow Men', in *The Complete Poems and Plays of T. S. Eliot*. London: Faber and Faber.

Williams, R. (1983) *Writing in Society*. London: Verso.

Williams, S. (2008) 'Connectivitis and Its Remedies', *Teaching Thinking and Creativity*, 25, 60–5.

# P4C in English Literature

Steve Williams

**4**

---

## Chapter Outline

Connections between English literature and P4C          53

Activities using English literature and P4C          60

## Connections between English literature and P4C

Thinking philosophically and thinking about literary works are both activities that require high levels of sensitivity to the use of language. But are they compatible? Would deliberate philosophical thinking add anything to students' appreciation of literature or would it be a distraction? The experience of many English teachers who have given over some time in their lessons to dialogue about philosophical questions is that it can complement the study of literary fiction. One example of this is in the exploration and application of concepts. Fiction writers employ concepts in their work; philosophers seek to explore, explicitly, the meanings of concepts, their relative importance and the consequences of their application.

We can illustrate this point with reference to a novel that is popular with Key Stage 3 students. *The Boy in the Striped Pyjamas* by John Boyne (2010) describes the experiences of the 9-year-old son of a concentration-camp commandant. He is unaware of what is really happening to the prisoners and asks his father who 'those people' are. The story continues: "Ah, those people", said Father, nodding his head and smiling slightly. "Those people . . . well, they're not people at all, Bruno'" (ch. 5, p. 53). Later on, in presenting Bruno's thoughts about his own family, the prisoners and the camp guards, the writer uses the word 'people' no less than eight times in the space of a couple of paragraphs.

Bruno does not differentiate between the various groups as either people or non-people as his father does, and wonders innocently why none of them have been 'invited back to the house' (ch. 9, p. 100). Five pages later he sees an approaching shape on the prison side of the fence and notices that 'the thing was neither a dot nor a speck nor a blob nor a figure, but a person' (ch. 10, p. 105). The writer's deliberate use of the terms 'person' and 'people' seems central to the meaning and moral significance of the book. In an encounter with the family's maid, Bruno 'looked across the room at Maria and realized for the first time that he had never fully considered her to be a person with a life and a history all of her own. After all, she had never done anything (as far as he knew) other than be his family's maid' (ch. 6, p. 60).

In English lessons, students might normally be asked to explain, with supporting quotes from the text, the father's attitude towards the people in pyjamas. They might be asked to identify the main themes of any of the chapters. They might be asked to write an imaginative response to the text such as pretending they are Bruno and writing a letter home to a friend. They might be asked for their speculations on the intentions of the author, and the author's uses of language. However, there is a philosophical background to the theme of 'person' that could also be explored. The term generally signifies a human being with capacities to be an agent – to make life-plans and choices with values and standards in mind. So students might choose to discuss questions like:

- Must you be free to be a person?
- If someone is not free, are they no longer a person?
- What might be the consequences of not seeing someone as a person? Any examples?
- If you treat someone only as a means to your own ends and not as an end in herself, are you treating her as a person?
- What might be the consequences of seeing all humans as persons? Any examples?

- Do either of these things always come first: not seeing someone as a person and treating them badly, or treating them badly and not seeing them as a person?
- Should we think of persons having certain 'rights' just because they are persons?
- What is the history of the term 'rights' and how is it applied in arguments about morality and politics?

The above list of questions is available on the companion website. In the process of discussing such questions, students will gain a deeper understanding of 'the intentions of the writer' in using the term 'person' in the way he does. They will also relate literature to life, past to present and future. And they will be doing what experienced readers of novels often do: appreciating a book as an imaginative work made out of language but also as a means of meditating on the human condition with reference to concepts and beliefs that are embedded in cultures. Philosophical dialogue helps students to explore those concepts and beliefs by making them visible and open to question.

## Objections to philosophical dialogue in literature lessons

There are at least two possible objections to this line of argument. First, that English teachers do this sort of thing anyway. The time they spend talking about ideas is already sufficient for the overall aims of literary study in schools to be achieved – including, most importantly, good exam-pass rates. It is neither possible nor advisable to cut into time spent on the traditional areas of literary study. Secondly, philosophy and literature are separate subjects. Literature enables readers to achieve a complex and rich view of life; it is an antidote to some of the cruder generalizations about conduct and belief offered by philosophers. The encroachment of philosophical dialogue into literature lessons is something to be avoided.

The first objection would be difficult to uphold as an accurate generalization. Teachers will vary as to the extent they are willing to delve into the philosophical background of the concepts that arise from reading literary texts. The argument presented here is that they should be willing to do so and that the delving should be thoughtful and coherent. Teachers who have adopted some of the practices of P4C are well equipped to do that. But why delve into these matters?

One answer is that reading and discussing stories is an important humanistic activity. As the philosopher Kwame Anthony Appiah (2007, pp. 29–30) puts it:

'evaluating stories together is one of the central human ways of learning to align our responses to the world'. In exemplifying his point using an Afghan film, *Osama* (2004), Appiah writes: 'Our response to the film, when we discuss it with one another, reinforces our common understanding, and the values we share. *Murderous, waste, courage, dishonesty, oppression*: these are value terms . . . . And if the story is truly representative, our discussion of it will help us not only to decide what we feel about the characters but how we should act in the world. . . . It keeps our vocabulary of evaluation honed, ready to do its work in our lives.'

It would surely be wrong to deny this connection between texts, life and evaluation and to propose any reductionist approach that would dull rather than hone the 'evaluative vocabulary' of students.

Robert B. Louden (1992, p. 157) summarizing an argument by Richard Wolheim writes that:

Challenging works of fiction require commentaries; and in the process of commenting on, and seeking to understand, the moral insights expressed in a work of fiction, we inevitably employ the theories of others or engage in theorising efforts of our own.

Philosophical dialogue of the sort advocated here is a means for teachers and students to make their own theorizing efforts together in a critical spirit. For although people share values in a broad sense, as Appiah maintains, they often disagree about how to apply them to a given situation. We can all agree, for example, that fairness is a good thing but we might put a different emphasis on the notions of 'equality of treatment', 'rights' and 'deserving of reward' when discussing the treatment of individuals and groups in society.

When evaluations differ, some justification is required and that, too, is part of the work of philosophy – sustained reflection on the justifications for particular ways of living and acting. At Key Stage 3, it is possible to incorporate that kind of sustained reflection into the curriculum because literature is integrated into a programme of writing, reading, speaking and listening covering a wide variety of genres and topics.

In later key stages, as the study of literature becomes more special-ized, philosophical dialogue is harder to 'fit in'. However, if the students' 'vocabulary of evaluation' is sufficiently well honed, then their apprecia-tion of literary works and the literary techniques employed by writers are likely to be richer and more critically astute.

## An 'A' level text

We can illustrate this with reference to Shakespeare's *Twelfth Night*. The character Malvolio is a self-important and officious servant who is tricked by a fake letter – seemingly from his grieving mistress – into declaring his love for her. In doing so, he reveals his inflated ambitions in a most ridiculous way. The fake-letter strategy was executed by a disgruntled group of servants and hangers on. They were angry at the threats Malvolio made when putting a stop to their late-night party-ing. After he humiliates himself before his employer and is thought to be mad, he is carted off to a cell where he is brutally treated. Is the way Shakespeare handles Malvolio indicative of comedy, tragedy, both or neither? Students' answers to this question will depend, at least to some extent, on their reflections using evaluative moral concepts like *justice*, *vice* and *virtue*.

Shakespeare is making use of a comic tradition stretching back to Greek times in which life-denying comic villains who judge others over-harshly undergo a well-deserved fall. Malvolio's undoing is certainly very funny. Yet as one 'A' Level student wrote:

If Malvolio were to lose his reputation and influence or be locked up for a brief period, then I think the audience would be satisfied. But what the revellers do next makes Malvolio seem like a victim. They lock him up in a dark room and give him no hope of release while trying to convince him he is mad. This is cruel, inhumane treatment, bordering on sadism. It makes us re-assess our views of Malvolio and his tormentors. . . . We could take a more charitable view of Malvolio's intervention in the party. Lady Olivia is in mourning, having lost both her beloved father and brother. Her uncle Toby responds by inviting his 'friends' to drink and sing until the early hours. He is sponging off a grieving woman. Malvolio could be acting out of honourable loyalty to Olivia.

There is some consideration of proportionality here, and a questioning of the comeuppance seemingly sanctioned by the comic tradition. There is an awareness that it is often not a straightforward matter to assess the virtues and vices implied by writers. It requires a reflectiveness akin to what Aristotle called 'practical wisdom'. This particular student is aware of possible alternative or complementary ways to judge Malvolio's character. In returning to the text to dig deeper she becomes aware of the complexity that makes Shakespeare so interesting and humane as a writer.

The more general point is that students who have, over time, developed an adequate evaluative vocabulary of ethics and had opportunities to apply it in ongoing dialogue will be willing and able to read texts more closely and appreciate the ways that an author's own view (or philosophy) of life manifests itself through patterns of language and generic convention. An author's view of life is, as Arnold Kettle (1972, p. 24) believes, 'there in every word he writes, and it is his view of life which will determine the nature and profundity of the pattern of his book'.

## Invitation to philosophize

In my experience, it is always interesting to give students a text or selected extract and ask them to devise a set of questions that they would find interesting to explore. The questions will tell you something about what the students find significant. You may be delighted or disappointed by their responses. Either way, you have a starting point for dialogue. It would not be appropriate in my view to prescribe the sorts of questions you are looking for at the outset, although you will want to make the students aware of the range of types of questions they could ask in response to a literary text.

So as well as questions about use of language, voice, genre, convention, imagery, and so on, there will be questions about underlying concepts and explicit arguments contained in a text. There will be questions leading to the analysis of character but also to considerations of assumptions about virtue, vice and those visions of 'a good life' that readers bring to the analysis.

After questions have been chosen and ranked by interest and significance, the teacher and students explore one or more together as explained in Chapter 1. At the end of the discussion, ask students to share their current states of mind. It would be most useful to have them record some of their ideas and opinions and to collect them to be part of an ongoing archive of literary and philosophical commentary – subdivided into the most persistent themes. Each different text studied might prompt students to reassess their thoughts and, as the thoughts grew more comprehensive, complex and discriminating, students might become more aware of subtleties in the art and world view of writers.

## Conclusion

Philosophical dialogue and the formal study of literature are complementary activities. There is a philosophical dimension in the creation of literary texts (in the sense of an author realizing a view of life through the pattern of fiction). There should be a philosophical dimension to dialogue *about* literary texts. I have concentrated mostly on ethics in this chapter but there is also scope for dialogue about questions of aesthetics and epistemology, for instance:

- Why do people prefer one work to another?
- In what ways can people's preferences be justified?
- Should some kinds of justifications carry more weight than others and, if 'yes', then why?
- Is it possible to say that some works of fiction are 'truer' than others? If so, in what ways are they 'true' and on what grounds is it possible to argue for their truthfulness?
- In assessing a literary work, how should we view the connections between truthfulness, a vision of a good (and bad life) and aesthetic quality?

This list of questions is available on the companion website.

# Activities using English literature and P4C

Philosophical teaching adopts two complementary approaches: open questioning followed by dialogue in response to a stimulus and dialogue focused around an activity designed to explore a particular concept or to invite arguments. The suggestions in this section represent both approaches. Although only a few texts are offered as examples, these strategies could be adapted and used with any text.

## Activity 1: *The Merchant of Venice*

### Stimulus

Act IV, Scene I of this play is the famous court scene. The foundation of the scene is a series of arguments and justifications that are either implied or stated directly:

- The Venetian merchants' attempts to persuade Shylock not to claim his bond and Shylock's justification of his intention to take it
- The argument about what the Venetian law allows and forbids
- The justification for the punishment of Shylock

### Guidance

The concepts and precepts on which the scene's arguments and justifications are based include: *justice, judgement, mercy, pity, equality of treatment, contract as public promise keeping, inhumanity, killing and murder, law, malice, giving reasons and withholding them in public debate, interpretations* (of the law) and *universality* (in the sense of treating others as one thinks all should be treated).

Provide students with this list (you can find it online) and ask them to identify parts of the scene where any of the items are mentioned or implied. Then ask them to use the concepts or precepts to make their own judgements about the characters in the scene, taking into account what has gone before in the play. Also ask them to think of examples from life where the concepts or precepts might be applied. Finally ask them what questions they have about any of the items and/or about the scene itself.

*Philosophical questions and concepts*

- When and how do people justify the use of the law for malicious intent?
- Who is to decide what is malicious?
- Should laws be always applied irrespective of intent?
- What do people mean when they say someone is acting 'inhumanly'?
- Should people feel obliged to accept someone's claims if they refuse to give reasons? If so, can you think of examples?
- Is justice achieved by the end of the scene? Why and why not?
- Is it possible to have justice when there is racial and religious discrimination?
- Should some values always be given more consideration than others? Why?

## Activity 2: *The Boy in the Striped Pyjamas* – dehumanization

### Stimulus

One of the main themes of the novel is dehumanization. The writer implies the moral imperative of seeing others as being fully human. In this light, parts of the novel stress the concept of 'person'. This activity picks those parts out for scrutiny and enquiry. The activity combines close reading with philosophical questioning.

### Guidance

Give students the following three extracts to read.

1. In chapter 5 (p. 53), Bruno asks his father who the people on the other side of the fence are. The story continues: '"Ah, those people", said Father, nodding his head and smiling slightly. "Those people . . . well, they're not people at all, Bruno."'
2. In chapter 10 (p. 105), Bruno sees an approaching shape on the prison side of the fence and notices that 'the thing was neither a dot nor a speck nor a blob nor a figure, but a person.'
3. In chapter 6 (p. 60), Bruno 'looked across the room at Maria and realized for the first time that he had never fully considered her to be a person with a life and a history all of her own. After all, she had never done anything (as far as he knew) other than be his family's maid.'

Then ask them to read page 100 and underline the word 'people' when it arises. After they have completed the task ask them to spend 10 minutes 'freewriting' in response to all that they have read.

Freewriting is explained in Chapter 3, Part 2. It simply means writing continuously for a fixed period of time. After students have completed their freewriting, ask them to underline, or otherwise highlight, any ideas they think could be worth pursuing; then invite them to share those with their peers.

Take their work away and read it. Don't mark it but, instead, write a letter back to the whole class highlighting some of their thoughts and responding with ideas and questions of your own using a phrase like 'I wonder . . . .' You are not telling them what to think here, you are showing your active interest in their ideas. When you have read your letter, ask them to create questions they think would be interesting to discuss. Negotiate the choice of a starting question and during the dialogue have one or more students summarize the main points orally or in writing.

If questions about concepts with long histories such as 'rights' come up, encourage the students to research and reflect on them after the lesson and do the same yourself. Find a way to allow those reflections to be shared in speech and writing. That is the essence of philosophical learning: teachers and students enquiring together over time into questions and concepts that matter and that tend to return in life and literature. In this case there are possible overlapping concepts of 'person', 'freedom' and 'rights'.

 *Philosophical questions and concepts*

- Must you be free to be a person?
- If someone is not free are they no longer a person?
- Should we think of persons having certain 'rights' just because they are persons?
- Should everyone have the same rights?
- Does everyone have the same rights?

## Activity 3: *The Boy in the Striped Pyjamas* – father

### *Stimulus*

The novel sets the father's actions towards the prisoners against the esteem he requires and receives from his family and Maria, the servant.

Bruno's intuitive good will is the device the writer uses to draw out the contrast and stimulate our thinking.

## Guidance

Ask students to read the following quotes and think about the portrayal of the father in the book as a whole.

'Of course', said Gretel, who always spoke of Father as if he could never do anything wrong and never got angry and always came in to kiss her goodnight before she went to sleep which, if Bruno was to be really fair and not just sad about moving houses, he would have admitted Father did for him too. (p. 25)

My mother knew your father . . . 'said Maria after after a few moments. 'She worked for your grandmother . . . And after your grandmother retired, of course my mother stayed friendly with her and received a small pension but times were hard then and your father offered me a job, the first I ever had. A few months later, my mother became very sick and she needed a lot of hospital care and your father arranged it all even though he was not obliged to. He paid for it out of his own pocket because she had been a friend to his mother. And he took me into his household for the same reason. And when she died he paid all the expenses for her funeral too. So don't you ever call your father stupid Bruno. Not around me. I won't allow it . . . he has a lot of kindness in his soul, truly he does. (pp. 61–2)

And while Bruno realized that Father was generally a very kind and thoughtful man, it hardly seemed fair or right that no one had stopped Lieutenant Kohler getting so angry with Pavel, and if that was the kind of thing that went on in Out-With then he'd better not disagree with anyone any more about anything; in fact, he would do well to keep his mouth shut and cause no chaos at all. Some people might not like it. (p. 149)

Introduce students to the idea of an 'opinion line'. One end of the imaginary line represents 'strongly agree', the other 'strongly disagree'. Ask the students to arrange themselves on the line in response to the statements that follow. These can also be found on the companion website. It is often best to use small numbers of students in turn so they can be questioned by the rest of the group. Ask them to give reasons for their positions, respond to questions and then confirm or change their position with good reasons.

- The Commandant was a good person because he was a good father
- The Commandant was a good father but a bad person
- The Commandant was a bad father and a bad person
- The Commandant was a bad father but a good person
- The Commandant was a good person because Maria said it was true that he had 'kindness in his soul'
- You are a good person if you care for people who are close to you
- The Commandant deserved to lose his own son. It was just

*Philosophical questions and concepts*

- 'Good' and 'bad' are very general terms expressing moral approval or disapproval. The idea of this activity is to get students to support their initial judgement of the father with some reasons incorporating specific examples of acts that could be judged as 'good' or 'bad' and also to weigh those examples against each other and to judge some to be more significant and serious. You might ask them whether or not the terms 'true' or 'fact' are appropriate to any of the statements.

## Activity 4: *The Boy in the Striped Pyjamas* – being reasonable

*Stimulus*

The father and other managers of the camp regime depend on unquestioning obedience to authority. Bruno, is becoming increasingly upset about what he witnesses at the camp. He tells his father with all the assertiveness he can muster that he wants to go back to Berlin. In the following part of the scene, the initial reply comes couched in reasonable language.

*Guidance*

Ask students to read these extracts from chapter 5 and then follow the instructions below:

'I remember when I was a child', said Father, 'there were certain things that I didn't want to do, but when my father said that it would be better for everyone if I did them, I just put my best foot forward and got on with them.' . . . 'I was just a child and didn't know what was for the best. Sometimes, for example, I didn't want to stay at home and finish my schoolwork; I wanted to be out on the streets, playing with my friends just like you do, and I look back now and see how foolish I was.'

'So you know how I feel', said Bruno hopefully.

'Yes, but I also knew that my father, your grandfather, knew what was best for me and that I was always happiest when I just accepted that. Do you think that I would have made such a success of my life if I hadn't learned when to argue and when to keep my mouth shut and follow orders? Well, Bruno? Do you?' (pp. 48–9)

1. Bruno's father wants him to follow orders. Summarize his argument, in single short sentences.
2. In groups, imagine situations where people are trying to persuade others using similar arguments. Think of situations where such arguments would be reasonable and unreasonable for:
   • adults trying to persuade children
   • adults trying to persuade teenagers
   • teenagers trying to persuade teenagers
   • adults trying to persuade adults

Ask students to write some of the arguments and reasonable responses in dialogue form. Share the writing and ask them for their thoughts on the meaning of the concept 'reasonable'.

Students would need to know that the term 'argument' here means an opinion supported by reasons. The extract is an argument from authority and from consequences used to persuade one person to follow the command or advice of another because:

1. the other person is better qualified to give the command
2. following the command will lead to good consequences (in the case above, happiness and success) while not following an order from a powerful person can get you into trouble

Requesting that people follow orders and take advice from others who 'know better' is often very reasonable; sometimes it is not.

The activity for students described above requires that they think about those general principles that would help them discriminate between reasonable and unreasonable arguments for following an authority rather than whether Bruno or anyone else could be expected to resist.

A further and valuable discussion could emerge about power, courage and practical wisdom. After all, one of the most important questions in life is: 'When and why should I refuse to follow where others lead and command?' This could be a question for ongoing dialogue through writing, discussion, reading and viewing.

# Further resources

You will make your own decisions about what texts will be most fruitful for philosophical dialogue, depending on your own favourites and the demands of schemes of work. Here are four recommendations.

1. *Tuck Everlasting* by Natalie Babbitt (Bloomsbury Publishing, 2003). This novel is a great read for students in Year 7. It is gripping and very well written with themes well suited to philosophical treatment such as: friendship, the purpose of life, freedom, responsibility, free will, obedience to authority and evil. Gaye Hubble has produced a teaching resource for 'Tuck' using a P4C approach. Not all the items will be useful but there are some good ideas and the resource is extensive and freely available at www.viterbo.edu/analytic/table4. htm (see Analytic Teaching, vol. 18, no. 1).

2. Stanley Milgram's experiments. Film extracts for these famous experiments on obedience to authority can be found easily on YouTube with an appropriate search, as can the recent reconstruction by British TV presenter Derren Brown. Milgram and his colleagues 'measured the willingness of study participants to obey an authority figure who instructs them to perform acts that conflict with their personal conscience'. See http://en.wikipedia.org/wiki/Milgram_experiment The films provide a complement to any book such as *The Boy in Striped Pyjamas* that touch on themes of authority, conscience, humanity and free will.

3. *Harrison Bergeron.* This is a classic satirical short story by Kurt Vonnegut (see www.tnellen.com/cybereng/harrison.html). It is a good choice with which to see how P4C could open up dialogue beyond interpretation of the given text and towards wider discussion of philosophical themes before coming back to the text again. In this case those themes are the foundations of politics: liberty and equality. There are more complex tensions between those ideals than are represented in the story; students' questions might lead to them being considered. Leszek Kolakowski's article, 'How to Be a Conservative-Liberal-Socialist' from his book *Modernity on Endless Trial* (University of Chicago, 1990) provides an insight into some of the problems. See www.mrbauld.com/conlibsoc.html

4. There are many poems that could provide starting points for complementary literary and philosophical dialogue. Here are three:

- *The Craftsman*, by Marcus B. Christian: www.poetryfoundation.org/poem/242256
- *A History Without Suffering*, by E. A. Markham: www.poetryfoundation.org/poem/242378
- *Theme for English B*, by Langston Hughes: www.eecs.harvard.edu/~keith/poems/English_B.html

# References

Appiah, K. A. (2007) *Cosmopolitanism: Ethics in a World of Strangers.* London: Penguin.

Boyne, J. (2010) *The Boy in Striped Pyjamas.* London: David Flicking Books.

Kettle, A. (1972) *An Introduction to the English Novel, Volume 1.* London: Hutchinson University Library.

Louden, R. B. (1992) *Morality and Moral Theory.* New York and London: Oxford University Press.

# 5

# P4C in Mathematics
Rod Cunningham and John Smith

## Chapter Outline

Connections between mathematics and P4C                    68

Activities using mathematics and P4C                      71

Conclusion                                                89

# Connections between mathematics and P4C

There are many mutually beneficial connections between these two areas of enquiry. Students' mathematical ideas can be developed directly through the P4C community of enquiry, which could legitimately form part of some mathematics lessons, while the kinds of skills developed through P4C outside the mathematics classroom can support the development of mathematical skills.

## Reasoning

One connection lies in the importance attached to careful reasoning and justification and attempts to establish proof in both P4C and mathematics. Just as the mathematical student attempts to justify arguments in the mathematical domain, the philosophical student attempts to justify a wide range of positions that might be taken in philosophical discussions. Both students have the same logical tools available to them and, while formal, symbolic logic is not often appropriate in secondary maths enquiries; the activities in which students are engaged can provide a good foundation for the development of these formal conventions at a later stage. A student who argues that a computer cannot have emotions because it is a machine and a machine cannot have emotions, is using the same kind of deductive reasoning as the student who explores claims that corresponding angles are equal when a straight line intersects two parallel lines. Both students must rely on assumptions. The student making the claim about computers, for example, may assume that machines are incapable of emotion and the student who claims the equivalence of corresponding angles may assume that the angles at a given point on a straight line add up to 180 degrees. Given those assumptions however, both students can demonstrate and extend their use of deductive reasoning in a way that most other subjects do not generally allow.

This highlights an important feature of mathematics. Although it can and should be applied in the world around the student, it can be used for reasoning without reference to the world. Philosophers refer to this as a priori reasoning, as opposed to a posteriori reasoning which requires some kind of knowledge or experience of the world. Most subjects in the school curriculum deal with a posteriori knowledge, for example, scientific, historical or geographical knowledge, whereas a mathematical problem can involve deductions about number, for example, which do not require direct experience of the world. We certainly need to have been introduced to the names of numbers used in our language community but the essence of number – the 'fiveness of five' if you like – is independent of its arbitrary name.

## Dialogue

Another important area of similarity is that the use of dialogue and discussion is (or should be) common to both mathematics and P4C. The place of these in philosophy is readily apparent but effective mathematics lessons should also feature dialogue and discussion prominently. The 'conflict' approach to mathematics teaching, developed by Malcolm Swan and others, is a good example of mathematics teaching which relies on extensive, rich dialogue, while teaching which follows the Dutch approach, known as Realistic Mathematics Education or RME, is another. This approach uses realistic contexts to stimulate and develop mathematical understanding and places great emphasis on children 'making sense' of these situations through their talk and diagrammatic representations. There is a considerable amount of evidence to suggest that children from Holland are particularly able to cope with mathematical problem-solving situations and the implication is that this approach has allowed them to develop this ability. Students used to P4C practice often appear to have a greater capacity to question and to draw from their own experience.

## Mathematical ideas and concepts

Although some mathematical ideas which might give rise to philosophical speculation require a good understanding of mathematics – the notion of limits in calculus, for example, or the study of chaos and complexity – others can be approached by students with levels of understanding more typical of the secondary student. The concept of infinity and notions of multidimensions too could lead to fruitful enquiries among advanced students of mathematics and physics but students in the primary and early secondary age phases are also fascinated by ideas of infinity – 'numbers going on forever' – and of the abstract nature of two-dimensional representations – 'shapes we cannot hold'. Another example will be given later in the chapter. Discussion in a community of enquiry could allow students important opportunities to share and clarify their thinking about such concepts. The methodology of P4C is an excellent vehicle for stimulating and exploring these and many other ideas. Resources such as the artwork of M. C. Escher and the Mobius strip can provoke and sustain enquiries about infinity, for example, while questions, always highly valued within P4C (as discussed in the introduction), could be formed about a particular mathematical situation or starting point as exemplified in the work of Marion Bird (1991).

While advanced study of probability can be challenging, more fundamental concepts of certainty and uncertainty are within the grasp of virtually all learners. This kind of discussion links to the distinction between a priori and a posteriori truth claims mentioned earlier, regardless of whether we introduce these terms in our discussions. The proposition 'The sun will rise tomorrow' may be offered as an example of absolute certainty but it may be challenged on the grounds that, although it is almost unimaginable that it will not happen, we are still reliant on our knowledge of the world in making that claim. In that sense it is something that we can only claim a posteriori rather than a priori. Similar examples are given later in this chapter. The concept of irrational numbers is also intriguing to many students. This is apparent in paradoxes such as the fact that we can draw the hypotenuse of a right angled triangle whose other sides each measure one unit but we cannot say precisely how many units long the hypotenuse is. Similarly, we cannot state precisely how many times greater the circumference of a circle is than its diameter. We can however, comfortably use the symbols $^2\sqrt{}$ and $\pi$ in our mathematical considerations of these cases, the two symbols being precise descriptions of numbers which defy notation as fractions or decimals.

# Activities using mathematics and P4C

What follows are some activities within particular areas of mathematics that we hope will help develop understanding of specific concepts as discussed in the previous section. Use is made of dialogues that could be given to students to read out, asking the students themselves to either continue the dialogue or launch into a more general discussion. Reference is also made to paradoxes that have puzzled philosophers in the past and may still set your students thinking. The aim here is to present some examples of what is possible in different areas of mathematics in order to stimulate teachers of mathematics to explore the use of communities of enquiry within the subject.

## Activity 1: Mathematical knowledge

*Stimulus: Sorting and categorizing statements*
The aim of this first activity is to explore the difference between mathematical and other types of knowledge. Knowledge in mathematics seems to be different from that in science or history, say. This activity helps to explore that difference.

*Resources*

Photocopy the statements 1 to 8 below and cut them into strips, each strip containing a statement. Provide a set of statements for each group of students.

*Guidance*

Form the class into small groups. Give each group a set of statements as shown below. Use the introduction above and explain to the groups what the task is. When they have spent 15 minutes on the task bring them together to share ideas.

Ask the students to look at the statements below and sort them according to whether they (a) must be true or (b) could possibly be false. You can find the list of statements online to print off as cards. In each case they should say either why the statement must be true or, if not, how they would test to see if it is true or false.

1. Triangles have three angles.
2. Swans have yellow beaks.
3. Bipeds have two feet.
4. $2 + 2 = 4$
5. Bachelors are not married.
6. Athens is the capital of Greece.
7. Mount Everest is the highest mountain in the world.
8. If I drop a stone it always falls towards the Earth.

Continuing work on statements:

Let's look again at $2 + 2 = 4$

Could this ever be false? Two people have been doing the exercise above and here is part of their discussion afterwards.

*You could get two students to take the parts in the following dialogue and read it to the class.*

**Jake**: I don't see what the fuss is, I can just see that $2 + 2 = 4$, this is obviously a matter of looking at examples.

**Carol**: But would you ever expect to find $2 + 2 = 5$, for example? What would you do if you did?

**Jake**: I'd count them again, that's for sure.

**Carol**: So it can't be false can it! What about $2,000 + 2,000 = 4,000$? Do you count those?

**Jake**: No, but I know how numbers work.

**Carol**: So what you know about numbers isn't based on observation.

**Jake**: Well it could be, in theory anyway, though it might take a while.

**Carol**: OK, but there are occasions where mathematics can give you a result which seems to contradict observation, and we can see an example of this by looking at Galileo's paradox.

*Ask the students to give their reactions to the dialogue above and to suggest philosophical questions that arise from them. The following questions might also be useful.*

## Philosophical questions and concepts

- What is the status of truth claims in mathematics?
- Do we need observation to back up mathematical statements?
- How are these statements different from those made by scientists?

### Notes

The students will probably find that some of the above statements must be true and that they don't need to do any observations to check this. We might say that these are true by definition or convention. Other statements are not certainly true, although some will seem more certain than others. If we wanted to show these to be false we would have to find a counter-example. This would certainly require some form of observation.

Galileo's paradox is mentioned by Carol in the dialogue above. This paradox acts as a starting point for a discussion about the structure of number.

## Activity 2: Number theory

### Stimulus

Finding the square of a number and Galileo's Paradox.

### Guidance

*Ask the following question in a whole-class setting.*

How do you find the square of a number?

*The following interaction between teacher and students is likely.*

1 squared = 1
2 squared = 4
and so on

**Teacher**: So from 1 to 100 how many whole numbers are there and how many squared numbers?

**Students**: 100 whole numbers and 10 square numbers.

**Teacher**: So there are many more whole numbers than squared numbers up to 100, do you agree?

But Galileo showed that there are as many squared numbers as there are whole numbers. How did he do that?

Get the students to work on this question in pairs and then be prepared to present their ideas to the whole class.

*Hint for the teacher: He paired each whole number up with its square. This is essentially what we do when we count anything, we place it in one-to-one correspondence with the whole numbers and take the last whole number to be the size of the set. Hence any number up to infinity can be matched against its square.*

### Extension work

*Students who enjoyed Galileo's Paradox might like to explore the paradox of Hilbert's Hotel which is a challenge devised by the mathematician David Hilbert.*

Hilbert's Hotel has an infinite number of rooms. All the rooms in the hotel are full. Mr and Mrs Smith want to book a room. The staff say that unfortunately it is full, but Mr and Mrs Smith have a solution to the problem. 'Why not', they suggest, 'ask everyone to move over one room, and then there will be a free room for us?' (see also http://ierg.net/lessonplans/unit_plan.php?id=33)

### Philosophical questions and concepts

- How does our idea of infinity fit with what we can observe in the world? If there were a finite number of rooms, the Hilbert's Hotel problem could not be solved. Does the solution sound like a 'cheat'?
- How can we cope with such an idea?

## Notes

This would be a good place to explore the concept of infinity using a community of philosophical enquiry. You could ask students to bring a picture, a story or just a statement which helps them to think about infinity to the next meeting. You could download some pictures from the Hubble telescope collection on the internet which inspire thinking about the universe and beyond and run an enquiry based on a chosen stimulus from the images of infinity.

## Extension work

*Return to the dialogue between Jake and Carol*

**Jake**: What does Galileo's paradox show us, apart from being a neat trick?

**Carol**: It shows that we can demonstrate things in mathematics without relying on observation. We set up some definitions at the start and everything follows from that.

**Jake**: But we do discover things in mathematics. We don't just decide which numbers are going to be called prime numbers. Mathematicians (or rather computers programmed by mathematicians) are discovering new prime numbers all the time.

**Carol**: That's right and this is what makes mathematics unusual. On the one hand it helps us describe the world but we don't seem to rely on observation like we do in science. We can be led astray. Here is another paradox which was puzzled over by the Greek philosopher Zeno who was born 500 years before Christ.

## Guidance

Read Zeno's Paradox out and ask students to discuss it in groups of four. The aim is for them to explain how the two conclusions can be reconciled. Let them spend about 10 minutes on this before drawing their ideas together in class discussion.

*Achilles and the tortoise have a race. Because Achilles thinks he will win*  *easily he gives the tortoise a head start. The race gets underway, Achilles gets to the point where the tortoise has started from. By this time, the tortoise has moved on to a new position. Again, Achilles makes it to that new position, but the tortoise has moved on again. . . . Following this reasoning it seems as though Achilles can never actually catch up with the tortoise. Surely this is absurd since we know Achilles will win.*

So how can this be explained?

*Hint for the teacher: The mistake is to think that time can be cut up into distinct pieces. The passage of time is independent from the progress that Achilles and the tortoise make. Back to the dialogue.*

**Jake**: So that is just about definitions really, just like the infinity paradox you mentioned before.

**Carol**: We have found out something new just by thinking about it that time must be continuous and can't be carved up. That is more than we find out from a definition where if you know the definition you also know the word and its meaning.

**Jake**: I'm getting a bit confused about all this. Mathematics seems to be about the world but we seem to be able to work things out by thinking about them rather than going out and observing the world.

**Carol**: Galileo said that 'Mathematics is the language in which God has written the universe.' That's what makes it so important and fascinating.

**Jake**: So it's a language that can have very precise terms and concepts?

**Carol**: Yes and what makes it a difficult language to learn is that the concepts can be difficult. We probably don't spend enough time on clarifying concepts.

**Jake**: Can you give me an example?

**Carol**: How about 'randomness'? Are we really clear what this is?

*Philosophical questions and concepts*

In an enquiry you might like to focus on Galileo's comment that the world is written in the language of mathematics.

- What is the significance of this statement?
- Is the structure implied by Galileo's statement out there in the world or is it in our heads?

## Activity 3: Probability – Do you feel lucky?

*Stimulus: Predicting the next toss of a coin*

The concept of 'randomness' is worth exploring. Undertaking an activity and then reflecting the underlying concepts can help students make progress in their understanding. The branch of mathematics known as statistics is based on the idea of randomness so it is important to be clear about what it is.

## Guidance

Toss a coin a few times at the front of the class, asking students to predict whether it will be a head or a tail, then move into the following thought experiment.

Tell the class that you have just tossed a coin four times and that it came up heads on all four occasions. Ask the class to decide which of the following outcomes is most likely if the coin is tossed again.

1. A head will come up
2. A tail will come up
3. There is no way of knowing

Identify three positions in the room and ask students to go to the place that best represents their choice of answer. Ask each group to come up with the best arguments for their case and spend some time sharing.

Explain that if we asked people in the street all three answers would be represented. How might this be reflected in their different views on gambling and taking part in lotteries?

Now ask students in pairs to come up with the best definition of randomness that they can think of.

One common definition is that 'The next action is independent of the last, that is, it is not influenced by it in any way.' Another useful comment is that 'the coin has no memory.'

## Further stimulus ideas

There are a number of starting points for enquiry here.

1. Say that the same coin-tossing experiment was performed ten times and a head came up each time. Tell the class that the coin had previously been tested and shown not to be biased. What questions would the class raise?
2. Use the story book *Two Frogs* by Chris Wormell (2003). The story is about two frogs sitting on a lily pad, one has a stick as insurance against possible happenings. This leads into questions about risk and probability.

3. Use the story, 'The Rocking Horse Winner', in the book *The Pig That Wants to Be Eaten* by Julian Baggini (2005), about a boy who is able to predict the outcome of horse races. Incidentally, this book has a number of interesting starting points for mathematical and other inquiries.
4. Choose a news or gambling story or get students to bring in stories about luck or risk or chance.

 *Philosophical questions and concepts*

- Is there such a thing as true randomness?
- How can we reconcile the idea of randomness with the fact that we expect an event to have a cause?
- If we use the probability scale from 0 to 1, what sort of events would students put at the extremes of 0 and 1, that is, impossible and certain?

This brings up important philosophical issues about certainty and our grounds for claiming it. Many of these issues are what philosophers would call epistemological issues.

### Notes

Some students will be interested to explore tests for randomness and pseudo-random numbers. The decimal places of $\pi$ are sometimes used as a source of randomness because there are no repeating patterns, but how can they form a random sequence when they are generated by a definable process, namely, dividing the circumference of a circle by its diameter?

A note on thought experiments: An important philosophical strategy is to set up a thought experiment and use this to work through possible outcomes in order to clarify a concept. In the case of our coin-tossing activity above the participants' beliefs are revealed by asking them to consider a hypothetical situation and its possible outcomes.

## Activity 4: Functional mathematics

For many people the importance of mathematics lies in its usefulness. An example of this is the 'base ten' number system. This is one of the most significant ideas in the history of human development. Why do we need to spend time ensuring that students really have the concept embedded? Imagine that we tried to teach people to learn to drive before they fully appreciated that the whole point of a car is to provide mobility and open up travel opportunities. 'Place value' in our number system is not an easy concept to grasp and providing a reason to persevere with its understanding is time well spent. Here is an activity to develop understanding.

### Stimulus
Tally system.

### Guidance
Try this activity yourself before using it with students.

Imagine that you have some important reason to keep track of large objects (it could be sheep passing through a gate or bales of hay being stacked up). You don't want to have to keep returning to the sheep to check on numbers so you could make a mark to stand for each one. How do you then remember how many marks you have made? The obvious way to do this is to use a tallying system, grouping marks together so that you have less counting to do since a group contains a constant number. But what if you have lots of groups? Could you create 'supergroups' so that you spend less time counting groups. Try inventing different tallying systems and investigate how effective these might be for keeping track of, say, 1,000 sheep.

### Resources
Counters for students to use when they act out the sheep counting activity above.

Now that you have chosen a tallying system how will you record this? You could just use marks on paper but it would become laborious to draw them out all the time. Could you invent marks to stand for singles, groups and supergroups?

If you have undertaken the above activity you will have some idea of how number systems have developed. Think about this statement as a further stimulus for discussion:

Our number system underpins the organization of modern, industrial society.

*Philosophical questions and concepts*

- Is the learning of difficult concepts facilitated by a narrative like the one above?
- In the base ten system, any number can be represented by just ten different symbols. We say that this number system is 'to the base ten'. Why might base ten be important? What other bases could be used effectively?
- Is our thought affected by our understanding of number – would we 'see the world differently' if we had a different number system?

*Notes*

For further work on this topic see the Innovative Education Research Group (IERG) that contains a wealth of material inspired by the educationalist Kieran Egan. You might like to use his story of the crow and the farmer to introduce/reinforce the difficult notion of place value.

Egan argues that students do not truly understand until they can internalize the concepts involved and this is often facilitated by a story. In mathematics this is notoriously difficult which is why a narrative starting point followed by an enquiry can help. Egan explores the key learning frameworks that fit with students' perceptions of the world as they grow and develop. He capitalizes on these in the development of units of work.

Go to http://ierg.net/lessonplans/unit_plan.php?id=26 for the place-value reference, and www.ierg.net for a more general introduction to the work of the IERG.

## Activity 5: Growth

Growth is a natural phenomenon. It is useful to be able to describe growth mathematically in order to make predictions, on the one hand, and to help understand what is happening on the other.

*Stimulus*
Story graphs.

### Guidance

Use this activity as a whole-class starter for thinking. Use the following introduction:

Look at the following two graphs (Figure 5.1). They both show growth.  Try to describe to a partner what is happening in each case.

### Resources

The story graphs in Figure 5.1 could be projected onto a whiteboard.

### Notes

The important point is that one growth pattern is additive and the other is multiplicative. Ask the students to think of examples of each type of growth.

### Stimulus: Story

Here is another story that will encourage students to think about growth patterns and the power of multiplicative growth.

### Guidance

You could read the following story to the students.

The King of Siam wanted to reward a loyal subject for a job well done. The King asked:
'What can I give you as a reward?'
'I don't want much, your highness, just a little rice', his subject replied.
'A bag, two bags, name your price', said the King

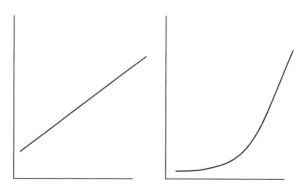

**Figure 5.1** Two representations of growth

The King's subject pointed: 'Do you see that chessboard over there? Just let me have a grain of rice on the first square, then double on the second, double again on the third, and so on, keep doubling until we get to the last square. Then if we can just gather up all the rice calculated for each square, I'll take that.'

'I would've thought you'd be better to have the two bags, my boy.' The King answered, looking slightly puzzled.

What do you think? What would have happened if the subject had asked for just two more grains on each square?

You could model the loyal subject's suggestion by using a calculator in the following way (students might work on this in pairs):

Key in: $2 \times 2 = = =$

Keep keying in = as many times as there are squares on the chess board or you could model this on a spreadsheet which would have the added advantage of adding up the total on all squares more easily.

### Notes

There are a number of other growth models that could be explored.

For example:

1. Model the growth of a forest fire. You could use either square, triangular or hexagonal paper (or have different groups use different types of paper). Assume the fire starts in one shape then moves outwards at equal intervals of time, setting light to any shape with at least one side touching the previous shapes that are alight.
2. Explore the Fibonacci sequence that appears in many natural growth patterns in nature (1, 1, 2, 3, 5, 8, . . .). *The Rabbit Problem* by E. Gravett (2009) is a picture book that explores the Fibonacci sequence.

### Philosophical questions and concepts

The above section talks about 'models', what is the relationship between a model and 'the real world'? For follow-up work collect examples of models and pictures of 'reality'. For example, a model car and picture of the real thing, the graph at the beginning of this section and world population figures, and so on. Use this as a stimulus for an enquiry.

- Can there be models which we can't see or touch?
- How does the idea of a model fit with the discussion in Activity 3 about thought experiments?
- What does the above suggest about the importance of imagination in mathematics?

## Activity 6: Patterns in nature and those we create

### Stimulus: Art and architecture

Pictures of patterns in nature provide a good starting point for discussing pattern. Some examples include, a sunflower, branching patterns of plants, honeycombs. Shapes don't need to be regular. Hubble telescope pictures of the universe are readily available on the internet and can inspire deep questions about our place in the world. You could also use created images; in particular, some of the 'impossible' drawings by M. C. Escher provide the sort of 'cognitive dissonance' that stimulates questioning. Considering art and architecture further, the 'golden mean' represents a rectangle of particular proportions which are observed in classical building facades and in works of art. This proportion of shape appears to be satisfying to the human eye. Is this a function of the structure of our brains, or is it a conditioned response? Philosophers are concerned to identify the basis of aesthetic judgements.

### Stimulus: Musical chords

The auditory field is also a rich mathematical realm. Play a major, minor and seventh chord on a piano or other musical instrument (or ask one of your more musical students to do this!) What images and feelings do each of these inspire in us? What is the basis of these chords and the musical scales from which they are derived? (String length has a bearing on this.) Over the ages our appreciation of harmony and dissonance has changed. The mathematics of musical scales is a rich source of investigation. Added to this is our perception of pitch. For example, piano tuning relies on very fine adjustments by a human expert to make the instrument 'sound right', which is not a simple mechanical measure.

### Guidance

Read out the preamble above and use some of the images described as stimuli for communities of enquiry. It may be useful to use a number of images in quick succession, asking the students which they might be interested in focusing on as a stimulus for question posing.

### Philosophical questions and concepts

- Why do some patterns 'resonate' with us and others do not? (Considering the beauty of music takes us again into the philosophical area of aesthetics.)
- Are the patterns a characteristic of the physical world or do they reside in our heads?

## Activity 7: Space, shape and dimensions

### Stimulus: Book Flatland

Edwin A. Abbott (1838 to 1936) wrote a book called *Flatland: A Romance of Many Dimensions* (present edition published by Penguin, 1987). In this he imagined what it would be like to live in two dimensions. He surmised that such a world would be made up of shapes, such as circles, triangles, hexagons including a range of regular and irregular forms. Inhabitants of Flatland would not be able to take a bird's-eye view of each other, but would have to recognize another shape by moving around it and noting the number of sides a shape has. In this scenario the fewer sides a shape has, the more important a shape it is, hence circles are of the highest status.

### Guidance

After introducing the book to students read out the quotation below. Get the students to visualize each step. They will readily identify the last as making a cube, but what about the next step? By putting 'hypercube' or 'tesseract' in your search engine you will come up with a number of animated versions of a four-dimensional shape. This is our three-dimensional equivalent of the struggle experienced by A Square's grandson in two dimensions. You can use this visualizing activity and subsequent video clip as a stimulus for enquiry.

*A further activity*. The following is based on an experience that A Square had subsequently and which convinced him of the existence of a third dimension. Ask students to close their eyes and visualize what is happening as you read the story out.

*Guidance*. Return to the *Flatlands* book and relate the reasoning of the grandson which is described in Section 1 below. Having done this move on to the events chronicled in Section 2. Ask students to pose their own questions for a community of enquiry or suggest the questions in the subsequent 'Philosophical questions and concepts' section.

## Section 1

The book, *Flatlands*, is written from the point of view of 'A Square' who has a grandson, 'a hexagon of precocious intelligence'. He is rather shocked when the said grandson starts questioning whether there might be a world beyond two dimensions. The grandson reasons as follows:

If a point by moving 3 inches makes a line of three inches represented by 3; and if a straight line of three inches, moving parallel to itself, makes a square of three inches every way, represented by 3 squared, it must be that a square of three inches every way, moving parallel to itself (but I don't see how) must make something else (but I don't know what) of three inches every way and represented by 3 cubed. (Abbott, 1987, p. 64)

## Section 2

The narrator in *Flatland* describes an event which, following on from his grandson's musing above, starts A Square seriously considering the possibility of other dimensions. Consider first what this event might represent and, further, consider questions it raises for you about our three-dimensional world.

A Square describes himself as a shape of some repute and standing, not given to fantasies or hallucinations of any sort, but goes on to relate a very strange occurrence that came about recently.

While gliding on the Salisbury Plain he noticed a point appear on the plane. On closer examination he noticed that it was not a point but a small circle, which started to grow before his very eyes. It continued to grow to attain a diameter of around three times his own, and then began to shrink. It continued to shrink until, momentarily, it assumed a point form and then suddenly disappeared. A Square claims to have always been a sceptic in matters of other worlds and life beyond this, the flat universe, but this incident has started him thinking about the mysterious beyond.

*Philosophical questions and concepts*

- Can we visualize in more than three dimensions and what is the status of the fourth dimension?
- Why might it be important to think about more than three dimensions?
- How is our understanding of the world limited by our senses?

## Activity 8: Chaos and complexity theory – new branches of mathematics

### Stimulus: Mandelbrot set

Chaos and complexity theory are associated with the use of computers. This relatively new area of mathematics captures the imagination through the use of graphic imagery, for example, computer-generated fractals. The internet has many images of fractals including the Mandelbrot set. (This can be located by entering 'Mandelbrot set' in your search engine.)

One starting point for understanding the concepts involved in this area of mathematics is to create a pattern which is self-similar at different scales, that is, repeated with minor variations as you zoom in. This in itself is a good starting point for enquiry about scale, production of the images and complex patterns that grow out of simple situations.

### Guidance

Drawing a 'snowflake' (see Figure 5.2) is a common activity in primary schools but is not often linked to possible reflection on ideas of pattern.

Repeat this activity at the next level, that is, the new crinkle shape will be reduced in size to fit the new straight lines on the snowflake. A new shape emerges. The length of the new perimeter of the shape could

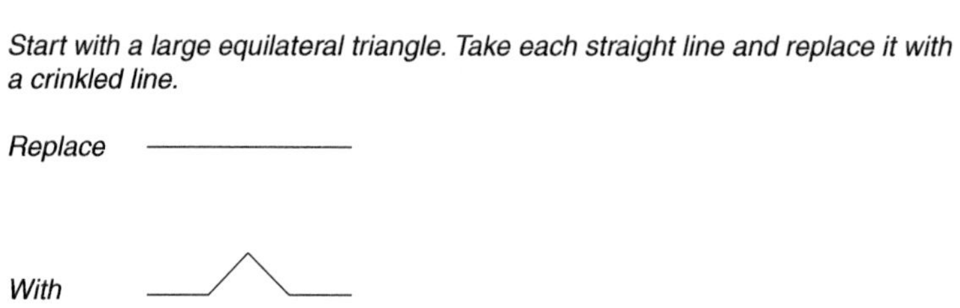

*Start with a large equilateral triangle. Take each straight line and replace it with a crinkled line.*

*Replace* ————————

*With* ————⌃————

**Figure 5.2** Rules for drawing a snowflake

be measured. What happens to the perimeter as successive versions of the shape are produced? What might the final perimeter be after a large number of versions?

### Resources
Students will require paper with triangular lattice paper, pencils and rulers for the activity above. They could use Logo programming or a graphics programme.

### Philosophical questions and concepts

- Even when our initial rule is simple, can we always predict the outcome after repeated use of the rule?
- How does this affect our view of 'prediction'?

### Notes
Jack Cohen and Ian Stewart (1994) use the phrase 'The Collapse of Chaos', as the title of their book and this phrase describes situations in which pattern emerges out of chaos. This phenomenon can be approached by considering weather patterns, economic cycles, and so on. There are a considerable number of references on the internet and a growing number of applications in all fields of science and engineering where classical mathematics and differential equations give way to a range of computer-aided techniques. For the keen student, reference could be made to 'strange attractors' and 'Complex Adaptive Systems'. Strange attractors are essentially signature patterns that are generated by complex systems (see images of turbulence in a fluid, for example,). The vast majority of real-life activity takes place in Complex Adaptive Systems. These involve continuous change and development through the activity of feedback mechanisms.

### A further activity
A key idea in complexity theory is that of 'Emergence'. A good way to think of this is of the whole being more than the sum of the parts. Think of times when what you observe happening seems to be at a higher level than the individual units that contribute to the activity and crucially, there does not seem to be any overarching control mechanism. Here are some examples:

- A top premiership football team scoring a goal
- Ants constructing and maintaining a nest
- A symphony orchestra playing
- A rock band performing at Glastonbury
- The internet
- A Mexican wave

Ask your students to think of some more.

*Stimulus*
Video clip – Starlings flocking in Somerset

*Guidance*
Put 'starlings flocking in Somerset' in your search engine and obtain a clip of this amazing behaviour or click on the link on the companion website. Show the clip and ask participants to consider what questions are raised for them. Common ones are, 'Why do they do it?' 'How does it happen when birds have such small brains?'

*Notes*
It seems likely that these birds follow very simple rules that might be put into words as follows: 'Fly at the same speed as those birds around me and try to move into the centre of the flock where I am safer from predators.'

But this doesn't explain or describe the overall result. It seems that we need language on a different level to do this. Talking about individual birds doesn't capture the bigger picture.

Try to describe the movement of the birds. Try to describe the emotions that watching this clip evokes in you.

## Activity 9: Observing a Mexican wave

*Stimulus: Mexican wave*
Another way of considering levels of description is to consider how you would describe a Mexican wave. The instructions for the participants might go as follows: 'Wait until the person next to you starts to stand up then do so yourself, raising your hands in the air, then bring them back to your side and sit down.' For someone viewing this event from

a distance, however, the description would be at the level of the overall effect.

### Guidance

You could try this sitting in a circle and performing a Mexican wave, getting some people to describe what each participant has to think about and have someone else outside the circle describing the overall effect.

### Philosophical questions and concepts

- Is the whole more than the sum of its parts?
- What about collections of humans? Is a society more than the sum of the individuals that make it up?

# Conclusion

Most teachers aim to develop approaches in their classrooms that encourage thinking and dialogue but evidence (a good summary of which can be found in Alexander, 2008) suggests that they are often absent. Many mathematics lessons have indeed earned a reputation as being lessons in which discussion was not encouraged and conceptual understanding was not prized highly. As a consequence, many students become disillusioned and frustrated with the subject at secondary school. The commitment to mutual respect and collaboration contained within P4C is an important prerequisite for this kind of work and provides a rich alternative to what can often become quite an instrumental task of promoting the development of mathematical skills. The large enquiry group can be alternated with paired and small-group work, linked by the aim of creating spaces for an open exchange of understandings, some examples of which are suggested above. The variety of lesson style this promotes should also be highly motivating for students and teachers. If students had been exposed to P4C elsewhere, teachers might capitalize upon this by extending the range of their questioning, involving students in reasoning and hypothesizing, setting up mini enquiries around mathematical concepts, persuading students to express themselves and argue for a position, and so on. Note that these are often the neglected and difficult areas of mathematics but they are essential if students are to attain higher levels. They are valuable too at every stage in harnessing students' curiosity and their abilities to pursue enquiries that appeal to them.

# Further reading

A number of useful books have already been mentioned in this chapter. Another book that would be useful as a starter with students in Key Stage 3 and might provoke some interesting ideas is J. Scieszna and L. Smith (1995) *The Math Curse* (New York: Viking Press).

# Further resources

A number of Julian Baggini's (2005) starters for enquiry have a mathematical theme, such as, 'Squaring the Circle' (p. 70) and 'Wheel of Fortune' (p. 16).

The Ultimatum Game: set up a few pairs with a sum of money, get them to play this game, watch how they react and use this as a stimulus for questions.

   http://en.wikipedia.org/wiki/Ultimatum_game

NRICH is a mathematical website posing open-ended questions

   http://nrich.maths.org/public

Bowland maths establishes problem-solving scenarios for Key Stage 3

   www.bowlandmaths.org.uk

Rokeby School – London, a specialist mathematics and languages school

   www.rokeby.newham.sch.uk

For general information about P4C at the school and the following for suggested mathematics links

   http://msmilki.com/p4c.aspx

   http://msmilki.com/Documents/Maths-related_stimuli.pdf

## Stimuli for enquiry: Images

Pictures such as the Chambered Nautilus, Escher Prints, Hubble telescope images and the Mandelbrot set can be used to stimulate enquiry.

   www.seasky.org/deep-sea/chambered-nautilus.htm

   www.mcescher.com/

   http://hubblesite.org/gallery/

The following combines fractal shapes with music by J. S. Bach

   www.youtube.com/watch?v=0CAmnl9JaAo&feature=fvwrel

## Stimuli for enquiry: Film

The following stimulate questions about the more extreme end of the spectrum of mathematical talent, as they feature this along with other themes:

- *A Beautiful Mind* (2001), director Ron Howard
- *Enigma* (2001), director Michael Apted
- *Good Will Hunting* (1997), director Gus Van Sant
- *Proof* (2005), director John Madden

## Stimuli for enquiry: Music

Music with a strong rhythmic line can be used to stimulate question generation about rhythmic structure. In particular, music such as that composed by Steve Reich ['Music for Hammered Instruments' is one appropriate piece] since the rhythm changes over time.

Bach's canons are mathematical in structure. Particularly fascinating is his 'crab canon' which is palindromic, that is it plays the same forward and backwards.
    www.youtube.com/watch?v=xUHQ2ybTejU
The Pythagorean scale is interesting for its mathematical structure.
    www.youtube.com/watch?v=ZaSwmZiL0d4.

# References

Abbott, E. A. (1987) *Flatland: A Romance of Many Dimensions.* London: Penguin Books.
Alexander, R. J. (2008) *Towards Dialogic Teaching* (4th edn). York: Dialogos.
Baggini, J. (2005) *The Pig That Wants to Be Eaten.* London: Granta Books.
Bird, M. H. (1991) *Mathematics for Young Children: An Active Thinking Approach.* London: Routledge.
Cohen, J. and Stewart, I. (1994) *The Collapse of Chaos.* London: Penguin Books.
Gravett, E. (2009) *The Rabbit Problem.* London: Macmillan.

# 6 P4C in Science

Lynda Dunlop

## Chapter Outline

Connections between science and P4C                                    92
Activities using science and P4C                                      94

# Connections between science and P4C

Secondary school science lessons are primarily concerned with describing and explaining the world as it is through the use of observation, experiment and study of scientific ideas. So what can philosophy and P4C contribute to the study of science?

In the first instance, philosophy is a search for truth and P4C brings the process of *doing philosophy*, through enquiry, to science. In common with science, P4C has enquiry at its heart. This enquiry process includes, but is not limited to, asking questions, creating hypotheses, justifying points of view and considering assumptions, implications and consequences. There is a clear connection between the type of thinking that is desirable in science and that cultivated through P4C.

In addition to the development of more effective thinking, philosophy helps us to understand what this thing called science is. The nature of science, or 'how science works' (essentially philosophy of science) has become embedded in secondary science curricula. It can therefore be argued that there already exists a place for philosophy in school science. This extends from national curricula and exam board specifications to post-compulsory science courses such as AS/A2 Science in Society, the Perceptions of Science unit for the BTEC Level 3 Nationals in Applied Science and Theory of Knowledge for the IB diploma. P4C can help students to understand how scientific knowledge is obtained, the strengths and limitations of science as a pursuit, and how science is differentiated from other ways of knowing.

Ethical awareness too has gained prominence in science curricula. Ethical exploration of issues arising from science is also philosophical in character, linking what is and what ought to be and enabling students to make connections between science and their wider world. Science-flavoured philosophical dialogue can also support students to reach a deeper understanding of scientific concepts and of the context in which science happens.

Furthermore, the process of working in a community of enquiry can make students aware of their own and others' ideas and of how to effectively challenge their own thinking and that of others by, for instance, listening deeply and considering and responding to ideas that are not their own, developing the sort of inter- and intrapersonal skills that are valuable in scientific research. The role of the teacher as facilitator enriches discussion as children are required to probe their own thinking and cannot simply rely upon the teacher to supply a 'correct' answer.

Likewise, question creation is fundamental in both P4C and science. P4C assumes that children are curious about the world and takes their questions as the starting point for enquiry. This gives students greater ownership of the learning, driving deeper engagement with science.

Finally, philosophical enquiry in the secondary science classroom makes space to exercise the imagination through an alternative approach to some elements of the curriculum. It enables students to be creative, to test their own ideas and to connect scientific ideas with the social context in which we live. It allows them to focus on the wonder and beauty of science.

This chapter will examine the connections between P4C and the natural sciences through four main themes: (a) the **nature of science**, (b) scientific **discovery**, (c) science **ethics** and (d) the development of students' understanding of science **concepts**. Each theme contains examples of stimuli that may be used to inspire philosophical questions for enquiry, many of which are applicable to several themes. Further examples of stimuli are found in the **resource list** at the end of the chapter.

# Activities using science and P4C

## P4C and the nature of science

Perhaps the most natural place for P4C in the science curriculum is in the exploration of 'how science works', as consideration of the nature of science is inherently philosophical. This section examines how, through P4C, students might come to a better understanding of what science is and aims to highlight some concepts in the nature of science that may be tackled effectively through P4C. These are **observation** and **experiment**, **hypothesis**, **theories** and **laws** and the relationship between science and **certainty**. The sequence in which these elements are considered is not to suggest that science proceeds in this orderly nature. For an introduction to the philosophy of science see Chalmers (1999).

### What is science?

Feynman (1999) describes science as 'sometimes, a special method of finding things out. Sometimes it means the body of knowledge arising from the things found out. It may also mean the new things you can do when you have found something out' (p. 5). This highlights two perspectives on science: as knowledge and as method. P4C can help students to gain a better understanding of the characteristics of scientific *knowledge* and of science as a *process*.

Recognition of a critical incident in the science classroom as an opportunity for philosophical enquiry can convert a frustrating episode into a productive learning experience. Incidents that may spark philosophical dialogue include practical activities that 'don't work' or which yield anomalous results, the use of models, the comparison of the electronic structure of the atom as presented in GCSE and A level textbooks and finding the best place for hydrogen in the periodic table. Philosophical enquiry may also be prompted by students' questions, news stories and emerging science.

As well as spontaneous enquiry, there are more structured means by which students can explore the nature of science through P4C. One way is through the use of discovery stories as stimuli for philosophical enquiry as discussed in the section 'P4C and scientific discovery'; another more explicit approach is to compare scientific activity and/or knowledge with that which is non-scientific (Activity 1). A comparison of science with a pseudoscience (astronomy/astrology; pharmacology/ homeopathy; evolution/creationism); with magic or alchemy (Sprod, 2001), or with prescientific activity (Activity 1, alternative warm-up) compels students to identify characteristics of science. Likewise, extracts from *Bad Science* (Goldacre, 2009), raises questions relating to how science works through true stories relating to medicine and healthcare, for example, vitamins, vaccination and the Placebo effect.

## Activity 1: How is science different to non-science?

### Stimulus
*Science Is Real* video by They Might Be Giants.

### Resources
Music video download (available from iTunes); index cards.

### Guidance
For a warm-up activity, print and laminate the statements below (you can download them from the companion website). Working in small groups, ask students to classify the statements as either science or non-science. During feedback, elicit from students what makes a statement 'scientific' and draw out the differences between science and other disciplines.

- God created the universe.
- There are eight planets in the solar system.
- George Orwell's *1984* is a great piece of literature.
- Atoms are mostly empty space.
- Water is made of molecules containing one oxygen atom and two hydrogen atoms.
- An acid added to a base makes a salt and water.
- Friendship is important.
- Being in love releases chemicals in the brain that make you feel good.

- The universe was created during a big bang.
- The Second World War lasted from 1939–45.
- The highest mountain on Earth is Mount Everest.
- Water boils below 100°C at the top of Mount Everest.

Following feedback, introduce the music video: *Science Is Real* by They Might Be Giants. A key idea contained in this song is that when you are seeking knowledge, science will give you the truth. To promote listening and reflection, ask students to write down the three most important messages from the song on an index card. Show the video twice, then ask students to pass their index cards around the circle before creating their questions.

### Philosophical questions and concepts

- What is science?
- Which statements are scientific/non-scientific?
- What makes a statement scientific?
- Are scientific statements true forever?
- Is the distinction between science and non-science clear-cut?
- How are scientific statements different to other types of statement?
- How are scientific 'facts' obtained?
- Is science real?

### Notes

An alternative warm-up activity focuses on scientific activity rather than knowledge. In this case, ask students to classify the following activities as 'scientific' or 'not scientific'. At the end of the activity, discuss whether all scientific activities share essential characteristics.

- Trying to turn lead into gold using alchemy.
- Hydrogen turning into helium by nuclear fusion inside stars
- Turning uranium into lead inside a nuclear reactor
- Making aspirin
- Chewing on willow bark to reduce fever and inflammation
- Testing aspirin on a group of people to see if it helps relieve pain better than a sugar pill
- Using leeches to help improve blood circulation during surgery
- Treating headaches and fevers by tying a patient's arm until the vein swells, then cutting it to drain blood

- A recent piece of practical work you have completed in science class

Another They Might Be Giants song *Put It To The Test* may be played at the end of the enquiry if the question selected has focused on the nature of science. This song highlights the importance of testing your ideas.

### Observation

While sense perception may seem unproblematic in science, the existence of illusions, selective observations, observer bias and technological ways of seeing mean that this area is ripe for exploration through philosophical enquiry.

Perception is more than just the impact of a stimulus upon our senses: it takes place in the mind. Sensory illusions that may be used as stimuli for P4C in science include optical illusions in nature (the sun appearing to move across the sky, the moon appearing larger when lower in the sky and a stick appearing to bend when dipped in water) and accounts of synaesthesia (Giles, 2011 and Sacks, 2008). The relationship between what one expects to see and what one observes can be explored through philosophical dialogue stemming from scientific stories and students' own experiences.

The distinction between novice and expert 'seeing' (for instance, students' own microscope or telescope drawings often differ significantly from more expert drawings such as their teacher's or those printed in textbooks) may be used for a spontaneous philosophical enquiry arising from an episode in classroom. Likewise, news stories provide an opportunity for students to explore philosophical dimensions of the application of scientific principles. For example, our bodies are increasingly observed inside and out using electromagnetic waves (e.g. X-rays, radio waves and visible light) and ultrasound for reasons including medical diagnosis and security screening. As well as raising ethical issues about the ownership of our body and image, these activities also present questions such as whether we can trust what we see, whether what we claim to observe is real and to what extent correlation indicates causation in a set of given circumstances (e.g. increased activity in some brain cells indicated by the detection of more intense radiation in a PET scan).

The use of non-visible frequencies of light can form the stimulus for an enquiry focusing on the nature of seeing (see Activity 2).

## Activity 2: Can the invisible be observed?

### Stimulus

Show pictures of the same object taken using detectors for different wave-lengths. Astronomical images are particularly rich as different wavelenths often expose different features of an object, for example, the sun, a nebula, the Earth. Figure 6.1 shows the Milky Way galaxy in different wavelengths.

### Resources

Image (Figure 6.1).

### Guidance

In groups, students could be asked to think about, describe and draw their present location if they could put on special glasses that let them see a different part of the electromagnetic spectrum (they must have an understanding of the sources of different electromagnetic waves as well as the opacity of different materials to these waves). This is in effect what scientists do when they use equipment such as radio telescopes and infrared detectors. This activity may be more interesting if completed outdoors. Present the stimulus (Figure 6.1) of our own galaxy viewed in different wavelengths.

### Philosophical questions and concepts

- Is there 'more to seeing than meets the eyeball' (Hanson, 1961)?
- Can we know what we see is real?
- Where does 'seeing' happen?
- Does reality depend on the way it is observed?
- Can it be said that an object has been 'seen' when the observation has been made using expert equipment?
- Can discoveries/measurements made using expert equipment be trusted?

**Figure 6.1** The Milky Way galaxy in (from top) radio, infrared, visible, X-ray and gamma ray wavelengths. Images courtesy of NASA

## Notes

Our eyes detect visible light, but all of the colours that we see are only one part of the electromagnetic spectrum. Other regions of the spectrum are radio waves, microwaves, infrared, ultraviolet, X-rays and gamma rays. Other images that may provoke philosophical enquiry include thermal (infrared) surveillance images, UV images of the Earth's atmosphere showing the Antarctic ozone hole and an image of the cosmic micro-wave background radiation.

The final aspect of observation considered here is the selection of data. In narrowing down the field of observation in a scientific experiment, it is possible to overlook important results and observations. The story of NASA's failure to discover the hole in the ozone layer over Antarctica in spring 1983 (Christie, 2000) may be used to stimulate philosophical enquiry while drawing attention to issues associated with the selection of relevant data. Visual awareness tests (e.g. Simons, 2010) also illustrate this point: in the midst of counting the number of passes between bas-ketball players wearing white, the observer frequently misses something surprising in the field of vision. While it may be argued that the way sci-ence is done, in particular the requirement for repeatable and reproduc-ible experiments, mitigates for the effects of observer bias, it is important to remember that science is a human enterprise and that claims of objec-tivity must be tested. The story of René Blondlot's 'discovery' of N-rays (Klotz, 1980) illustrates how the context of scientific activity can affect what a person believes they see. Blondlot was a respected researcher working in Nancy, France at the beginning of the twentieth century. X-rays had just been discovered and Blondlot reported a new type of ray that behaved differently to X-rays. Over 20 researchers corroborated his findings and more than 50 academic research papers were published in one year relating to N-rays. However, many reputable scientists were unable to reproduce his findings. One was Robert Wood who visited Blondlot's laboratory. The latter demonstrated his experiments to Wood, who remained unconvinced and during one experiment in the dark, sur-reptitiously removed a crucial piece of equipment. Blondlot claimed to see what his theory predicted despite the removal of the critical equip-ment. When Wood published his account of his visit to Blondlot's labora-tory, N-ray research around the world soon stopped, taking longer to die out around Nancy. Philosophical questions that might arise include:

- Was it right for Wood to behave as he did?
- What is honesty in science?
- To what extent can phenomena invisible to the naked eye be 'seen'?
- What is the relationship between what we believe and what we see?
- Can experiments confirm theory?
- Can scientists ever be considered independent, impartial or neutral observers?
- Is it better to design an experiment to confirm or to disprove an hypothesis?

### Hypotheses

A useful connection can be made between P4C and science by considering hypotheses and their relationship to experiment and observations.

A P4C session focusing on hypotheses may begin with an activity that asks students to consider what makes a good hypothesis (Activity 3).

## Activity 3: What makes a good hypothesis?

### Stimulus

Demonstration of floating, for example, the floating teabag or floating and sinking raisins (see notes).

### Resources

Six helium balloons.

### Guidance

Place six helium balloons, each containing a different hypothesis to explain why they float (Figure 6.2), in a different part of the room. Read the hypotheses together and ask students to reflect on which they think is the best, and why. After some thinking time, ask students to stand next to the balloon which they think contains the best hypothesis. Hear justifications from each balloon, then allow movement between groups. Record the reasons given as characteristics of a good hypothesis.

Share the stimulus (a demonstration of floating). During the stimulus, encourage students to focus on what they can see/hear/smell before creating questions.

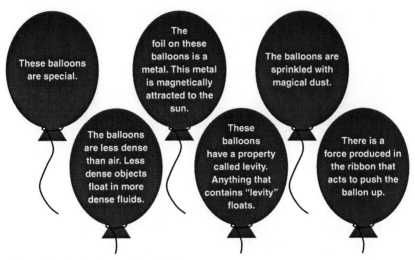

**Figure 6.2** Which is the best hypothesis?

## Philosophical questions and concepts

- Is it better to do an experiment to confirm a hypothesis or to refute it?
- What makes a good hypothesis?
- What makes a hypothesis scientific?
- What is the connection between observation and hypothesis?
- Is the simplest hypothesis always the best?

## Notes

To demonstrate the floating teabag, remove the staple and tea from a *Twinings* tea bag (other tea bags that are fastened with a staple may work) and arrange the empty tea bag as a cylinder on a heat proof surface. Ignite at the top using a match. The flame will burn down the tea bag and the remains will float towards the ceiling.

To demonstrate floating and sinking raisins, pour some sparkling water into a large beaker. Add a handful of raisins and observe them rise and fall.

These stimuli often generate questions that involve the examination of alternative hypotheses to explain the phenomenon observed. It may be useful to create a concept cartoon during the enquiry (Figure 6.3) to focus the dialogue on the examination of hypotheses suggested by the community.

**Figure 6.3** Concept cartoon created during an enquiry following the demonstration of the rising teabag

The exploration of hypotheses also can be developed by sharing a demonstration that provokes the 'wow' response, and asking students to generate questions that can then be explored through a community of enquiry. Examples include making (and playing with) a corn-flour suspension in water, adding Mentos to cola (outside!) or using smart materials such as ferrofluid (a magnetic liquid) or memory wire (it 'remembers' that it 'should be' straight). These stimuli may or may not raise questions of a philosophical nature: frequently the question selected asks why the phenomenon occurs. This type of enquiry can have philosophical characteristics, with students creating, sharing and analysing their own hypotheses and deciding what makes a good hypothesis, and what evidence would be needed, and be enough, to accept the hypotheses.

### Experiment

Linked to the creation of hypothesis is the means by which they are tested: experimentation. These interventions are empirical, deliberate and original and aim to determine how the world works. However, the features of experiments are characteristic of the field of study, for example, double blind randomized control trials are used to find out whether a new medicine works, while ALICE attempts to recreate the conditions of the big bang to find out how the particles that make up the universe were created.

Stimuli that focus on philosophical issues relating to experimentation include school practical work, the song *Put It To The Test* by They Might Be Giants and the story *ALICE and the Soup of Quarks and Gluons* (CERN, 2004). Questions that might arise include:

• What is the relationship between observation and experiment?
• Is it right to perform some types of experiment (e.g. those involving living organisms or the environment)?
• Which (theory or experiment?) should take precedent should an unexpected result arise?

The design of an experiment may also be the outcome of a P4C enquiry such as that relating to teabag hypotheses (see Activity 3). A philosophical approach encourages students to challenge assumptions and to explore consequences of experiments.

### Laws and theories

Ohm's law, the Ideal Gas law, Faraday's law, Hess' law, Avogadro's law, Boyle's law, Newton's laws, Kepler's laws, laws of reflection and refraction ... you could be forgiven for thinking that school science involves learning an array of laws, not least of all Murphy's law (if it can go wrong, it will!). What connections are there between P4C and the dimension of science that would appear to deal with 'the facts'?

P4C can promote creative thinking relating to scientific laws and thereby contribute to students' understanding of them. For instance, students may be asked to imagine what would be different if a law, for example, the law of reflection, could be broken. This activity could be done in small groups, each considering a different law and feeding back their ideas to the whole class. Questions could be used to stimulate thinking, such as what would you see if you looked at yourself in the mirror, or how would you see behind you when driving? Likewise, breaking natural laws may be explored using the example of miracles. Questions that might arise include:

- What is a miracle?
- Are miracles possible? In what sense?
- Are miracles evidence for the existence of God?

Philosophical enquiry can highlight the problem of induction in science: how many observations are needed before a relationship can be called a law? When can a generalization reasonably be made? To what extent is a law universal? Such an enquiry might be most opportune following a class practical which yielded unexpected results, for example, when students have found that a chemical reaction 'doesn't work', or when they have obtained anomalous results.

While laws pertain to empirical generalizations, theories explain and in doing so can be used to make predictions or hypotheses. The history of science, including ideas that students encounter in school science, reveals examples of theories that have been rejected in favour of new theories, for example, oxygen theory in place of phlogiston. Students may be asked to consider the fact (if it is a fact) that most scientific theories have been false. For further reading about competing paradigms and scientific revolutions, see Kuhn (1996).

An interesting role for P4C in science is to examine 'big' theories that interest young people such as the big bang theory, the theory of evolution and theories that account for the origin of life on Earth. Theories of origin (of the universe, of human life) can effectively be explored in a community of enquiry, not least because it provides a safe space in which students can question their own and others' beliefs about origins, the relationship between science and religion and whether we can ever know about our origins. Activity 4 focuses thinking on the origin of life on Earth.

## Activity 4: How did life on Earth begin?

*Stimulus*

The Urey-Miller experiment summary (Figure 6.4).

## Resources

### The Urey-Miller Experiment (1953)

**Aim:** To find out whether simple chemicals thought to be present in the early atmosphere could make the chemicals necessary to create life on Earth.

**Method:** Set up the closed system shown. Simulate lightning using electric discharges across electrodes. Leave running. Take samples from each place labelled S.

**Results:** Over 30 new chemicals were found in the system including formaldehyde, hydrogen cyanide, formic acid, urea and amino acids.

**Conclusions:** It is possible to create organic molecules from inorganic molecules.

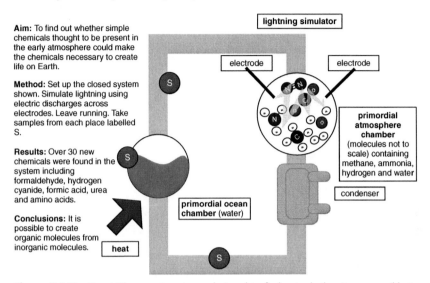

lightning simulator

electrode    electrode

primordial atmosphere chamber (molecules not to scale) containing methane, ammonia, hydrogen and water

condenser

primordial ocean chamber (water)

heat

**Figure 6.4** The Urey-Miller experiment was designed to find out whether it was possible to create organic molecules that are the building blocks of living organisms in the conditions that were thought to exist in the early Earth's atmosphere

## Guidance

Divide the room in two using a piece of string. One side of the string represents 'agree' and the other 'disagree.' Read out the following theories for the origin of life on Earth, and ask students to move to the side of the room corresponding to whether they agree or disagree with the theory:

- The building blocks of life were made in the early Earth's atmosphere/oceans.
- Life spontaneously generates from non-living materials.
- Building blocks of life arrived on rocks from space (the Panspermia theory).
- A divine creator made all forms of life in their present state.

After reading each theory, students are given time to discuss with others who share their opinion and asked to question those who disagree.

The facilitator may ask the following questions: Is the theory scientific? Does it explain/predict? What evidence exists for this theory? How could you disprove it? What experiments could you do to test it? Is it contradictory to other ideas or with evidence? Is the simplest theory always the best?

## Philosophical questions and concepts

- Is it possible to know about the past?
- Is it possible to accept scientific and religious ideas at the same time?
- How can theories about the origin of life on Earth be tested?
- What makes a theory scientific?
- Should scientific theories be given precedence over other theories?
- What is authority in science/religion?

### Notes

The questions created in response to this stimulus (and others related to origins) often raise issues sensitive to some students, for example, which question their religious beliefs. It is important for the facilitator to anticipate how they will address such issues in a community of enquiry.

Stimuli that can encourage students to explore other theories relating to origins include texts (extracts from Darwin's *On the Origin of Species*, the Scopes trial transcripts, recent newspaper articles), animation (the Big Bang Time Machine at http://resources.schoolscience.co.uk/stfc/bang/bang.htm), images (of the Cosmic Microwave Background following study of evidence for the big bang), music (the *Big Bang Theory* by Barenaked Ladies or Baba Brinkman's *Rap Guide to Evolution*), and film/drama (*Inherit the Wind*).

### Certainty

We often hear references in the popular media along the lines that science has 'proven' that love is blind (BBC, 2004), that acupuncture works (*Independent on Sunday*, 2009) and that time travel is impossible (*Daily Mail*, 2011). While scientists exercise more caution in describing their findings, there exists a misconception that science is certain, always providing us with the 'right' answer, and a concomitant lack of understanding about the role of doubt and uncertainty in science.

A common misconception is that scientific knowledge is definite, true forever, and uncontestable. It is important for students to understand the provisional nature of scientific knowledge that theories that have stood the test of time for hundreds of years will be rejected if there is evidence to do so.

Activity 5 encourages students to think about certainty in science.

## Activity 5: Certainty and science

### Stimulus
JJ's letter to Auntie Anna's problem page (Figure 6.5).

### Resources
Post it notes; Figure 6.5 printed and in an envelope.

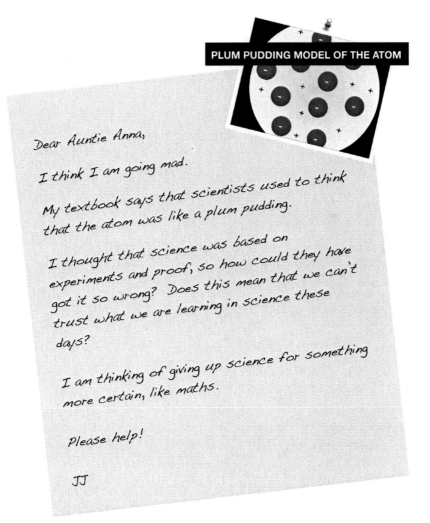

**PLUM PUDDING MODEL OF THE ATOM**

Dear Auntie Anna,

I think I am going mad.

My textbook says that scientists used to think that the atom was like a plum pudding.

I thought that science was based on experiments and proof, so how could they have got it so wrong? Does this mean that we can't trust what we are learning in science these days?

I am thinking of giving up science for something more certain, like maths.

Please help!

JJ

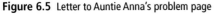

**Figure 6.5** Letter to Auntie Anna's problem page

### Guidance

An activity to provoke thinking about certainty may be used to introduce the enquiry. Students are given a post it note and asked to write on it one scientific fact of which they are certain, and then to attach it to their forehead.

They are then asked to mix with others in the room and to quiz each other on what makes them so sure, what evidence they have for it, what they would stake on that truth and what would make them change their mind.

At the end of the activity, students are asked to sit in a circle to feed back what they found out from the activity. Arrange for a colleague to deliver JJ's letter to the problem page towards the end of the activity.

 ### Philosophical questions and concepts

- Is scientific knowledge ever proven?
- Can science text books be trusted?
- How do scientists know about the atom?
- Is mathematical knowledge more certain than scientific knowledge?
- Is it possible to know something that cannot be observed directly?

### Notes

Students may be asked to respond to JJ's letter following their enquiry.

Another important connection that can be made between P4C, the nature of science and certainty is a consideration of the uncertainty principle. Although this is beyond the scope of school science it can give students a glimpse of some of the puzzling aspects of contemporary science. Where time, a trip or cross-curricular link allows, Michael Frayn's (2003) play (and film) *Copenhagen* (or excerpts) may be used as a stimulus for generating philosophical questions. The drama focuses on the question of what happened when Werner Heisenberg (a German scientist) went to Copenhagen to meet former colleague and friend Neils Bohr (a Danish Jew living in occupied Denmark). It raises questions about war and morality, the atomic bomb, uncertainty and reality, such as:

- What is more important than friendship?
- If it is not possible to measure/observe a system without changing it, can we ever really know about it?

- Did the use of the atomic bomb save lives?
- Can we be said to know something we are not certain of?

Issues related to certainty and scientific knowledge may also be investigated through stories of scientific discovery.

## P4C and scientific discovery

Discoveries of scientific ideas and phenomena and the associated human stories are a great source of inspiration for philosophical enquiry. Concepts that might be explored include imagination and serendipity, the connection between discovery and invention, how science works, the role of scientists who came before ('standing on the shoulders of giants'), risk taking, ownership of data, motivation for and funding of research, reward and recognition for scientific discoveries and the relationship between competition and community in scientific enterprise.

An enquiry relating to discovery might be based on a stimulus such as a film clip, a radio story or a book extract, some of which are suggested on the resource list. Presenting a discovery story as a stimulus for philosophical enquiry promotes deep engagement with history of science, scientific ideas and how science works. Discovery stories that are linked to topics in science curricula and that are potential stimuli for philosophical enquiry include the following.

The discovery of the psychoactive properties of lysergic acid diethylamide (LSD): Albert Hoffman was investigating potential pharmaceuticals when he accidentally absorbed LSD through his skin (Roberts, 1989). He recorded the effects it had and later dosed himself with LSD to further understand its properties. This discovery might raise philosophical questions related to perception and reality and the use of medicines/drugs, scientists' responsibilities for their findings and self-experimentation, for example:

- Are scientists ever justified in taking risks with their own and others' lives?
- What does someone experience in an hallucination?
- Can we discover anything about reality through drug-induced experiences?
- Does 'chance favour the prepared mind' (Pasteur)?

**Figure 6.6** Kekulé's structure of benzene: a ring containing six carbon atoms, connected to each other by alternating double bonds. Each carbon is also bonded to two hydrogen atoms

**The ring structure of benzene:** Some insight into the role of inspiration in scientific discovery can be gained from Kekulé's account of his discovery of the ring structure of benzene (Figure 6.6) containing alternating single and double bonds following a daydream involving an ouroboros and gambolling carbon atoms (RSC, 2011). Kekulé's structure has since been superseded by the idea that benzene contains a $\pi$ system of delocalized electrons.

This raises questions about representation and reality, the myth of discovery and creativity in science, for example:

- Are incorrect ideas useful?
- What can a model tell us about reality?
- Is Kekulé's idea scientific?
- How is it possible to know about something that can't be experienced directly?

**A process for obtaining ammonia from air and natural gas:** Ammonia is a gas used to make fertilizer and explosives and at the start of the twentieth century Europe's main source was sodium nitrate from Chile. Fritz Haber discovered a new way of making ammonia that released the First World War Germany from dependence upon trade with Chile ($N_2$ (g) + $3H_2$ (g) $\rightleftharpoons$ $2NH_3$ (g)). Today over half of the world's food production relies on ammonia made using the Haber process. Haber was also involved in the German war effort, producing poison gases such as chlorine, mustard gas and hydrogen cyanide. The latter was used by Nazi Germany in the Second World War to kill humans in gas chambers (including relatives of Haber). Haber's story is told in Einstein's Gift (Thiessen, 2003) and a short film by Daniel Ragussis. Philosophical issues that may be explored include:

- Can Haber be held morally accountable for the deaths of those executed with the gases he helped to produce?
- Are chemical weapons 'worse' than other weapons?
- Can we weigh the benefits of Haber's discovery against the lives of those killed?
- Is nationality more important than religion?

**The double helical structure of DNA:** Tales of discovery often focus on the contributions of one or two key scientists, for example, Francis Crick and James Watson in the discovery of the structure of the DNA molecule. An alternative approach to learning about discoveries is to look at the less well-known participants in a discovery. In this case it may be the role played by Rosalind Franklin. Crick and Watson obtained Franklin's X-ray photograph of DNA without her knowledge and used it to unravel the molecule's structure. They were awarded the 1962 Nobel Prize in Medicine along with Maurice Wilkins, Franklin's colleague at the time. Franklin died before the award was made. An enquiry on this theme, based on The Secret of Photo 51 or Life Story might focus on the following:

- Were Crick, Watson and Wilkins fair to Franklin?
- Is it ever right to use someone's work without their consent?
- What makes a contribution to science important? Was Franklin's contribution as important as that of Crick, Watson and Wilkins?
- Is recognition for discovery important?
- What makes a good scientist?

**Pulsars (the super-small, dense, spinning neutron stars left over when a huge star dies spectacularly in a supernova explosion):** In 1967, Jocelyn Bell was monitoring radio signals from space. She noticed a regular series of pulses coming from outside the solar system. The duration and frequency of the pulses (one 16 mm pulse every 1.3 sec.) suggested that it came from something the size of a planet. Was it possible that this was an alien communication? Students could be asked to imagine they are to send a communication to intelligent life elsewhere in the universe and to discuss in groups what information they would want to convey, how they could express the information so that it would be understood, and what the consequences may be if intelligent life existed and received the message. Philosophical questions that may arise include:

- Does it matter if we are alone in the universe?
- Is language universal?
- Are humans justified in exploring/exploiting space?
- Should humans try to contact extraterrestrial life?

**The immortality of HeLa cells:** The discovery of a human cancer cell line that could grow in vitro is one of the most important breakthroughs in contemporary biology. The first HeLa cells were grown by George Gey from a sample taken from the cervix of Henrietta Lacks who died that same year. The cells were taken without Lacks' consent, as was standard practice at the time. The HeLa cells are said to be immortal: they keep on dividing from the original sample. They have been used across the world to find out how cells work, to study viruses such as HPV and HIV, as well as to create clones, cross-species hybrids and the polio vaccine. Extracts from Skloot's *The Immortal Life of Henrietta Lacks* (2010) can be used to stimulate philosophical dialogue relating to, for example:

- What is life?
- What does it mean to be immortal?
- Who owns HeLa cells? Do you own your own cells?
- Should historical figures/actions be judged using today's standards?
- Can knowledge be owned?

There are of course many other discoveries that feature in science curricula that may form the focus for a philosophical enquiry. Popular accounts of scientific discoveries appear in Roberts (1989), Bryson (2003), Le Couteur and Burreson (2004) and Gribbon (2002).

## P4C and science ethics

It is important to recognize that science is not done in a vacuum: what scientists do, and the way they do it, has far-reaching consequences for society. There is an ethical dimension to many of the concepts that children are expected to understand in their secondary science education, and the exploration of such issues is increasingly prominent in national curricula (e.g. in Northern Ireland and Scotland). When tackling the ethical dimension of science it is necessary that students understand the differences between ethical and scientific reasoning and methodology.

Ethical issues in science are particularly engaging for students as there are many everyday yet complex issues that they find meaningful. An ethical dilemma presented as a stimulus for philosophical enquiry may involve exploration of what is right or good as well as the underlying scientific and technical details, not to mention issues related to the nature of science: what makes a good theory?; how hypotheses are tested; what evidence is 'good enough'; how/if one can 'prove it' and experimental design. Indeed, approaching dialogue through how science works via concrete examples of ethical issues relating to scientific advances may be more accessible and less threatening than beginning with the abstract concept in question. In facilitating the enquiry, assumptions relating to different ethical frameworks may be highlighted (e.g. utilitarianism, cost–benefit analysis, duty ethics, rights ethics, virtue ethics) and arguments tested for coherence and consistency, helping students to reason and argue more effectively. A useful introduction to ethical decision making is found in Levinson and Reiss (2003) and Warburton (2004).

This penultimate section on P4C in science provides sample stimuli for enquiry relating to the ethics of doing science in (a) biology, (b) chemistry and (c) physics.

### The ethics of doing science

Ethical issues which apply to the students in their school science laboratory and also to the practice of the experienced researcher include plagiarism, falsification and fabrication of results, record keeping, peer review, ownership of intellectual 'property', the use of animals and humans (including oneself) in scientific experiments, acceptable risk, whistle blowing, informed consent and conflicts of interest when doing research.

A philosophical enquiry can be inspired by practical work with ethical implications. This might include the use of human samples (such as students' own blood samples, cheek cells or urine), the use of animals, for instance, in heart and kidney dissections, the use and disposal of comparatively large volumes of reagents in the presence of alternative (microscale) techniques or the demonstration of the properties of α, β and γ radiation using radioactive sources.

As well as drawing on students' own experience of science, stimuli might include examples from professional research such as the way in which data was discussed and managed at the UEA's Climate Research Unit, and the way in which this was made public. Scientific ideas with ethical implications may also be explored philosophically: the book *What Is Your Dangerous Idea?* (Brockman, 2006) contains many examples from biology, chemistry and physics that may be used as stimuli for philosophical enquiry. Questions that may arise from a consideration of 'real' science include:

- When should the precautionary principle be applied?
- Which experiments go too far (the Stanford prison experiment; the trials in humans of TGN1412; genetic modification of plants and animals, military research)?
- Should researchers be allowed to use results from Nazi experiments?
- Can scientific ideas be dangerous?
- Does science deserve its authority?
- Does knowledge justify the means of acquiring it?
- Is all knowledge good?
- To what extent are scientists free to study their subject of choice?

### Ethical issues in biology

There is an ethical dimension to many of the topics in secondary biology, from the relationship between humans and other organisms in their environment (e.g. use of bacteria in metal extraction, genetically modified food crops, pharming), human health and fitness (e.g. clinical trials of new medicines, artificial hearts, the use of performance-enhancing drugs) to the manipulation of cells and genes (e.g. stem cell research, in vitro fertilization, cloning). Activity 6 demonstrates how contemporary research in biology can stimulate philosophical enquiry.

## Activity 6: Future foods

*Stimulus*
Priceco future foods advertisement.

*Resources*

Figure 6.7; heart and head cut-outs.

**Figure 6.7** Mock advertisement for stem cell meat

### Guidance

Begin with a game of Philosopher's Fruit Salad, during which children change seats with others if their answer to a question is 'yes'. Suggested questions for this topic include:

- Are you a vegetarian?
- Are you a vegan?
- Have you ever eaten quorn?
- Do you think it is morally acceptable to eat meat?
- Is it better to eat eggs from free range hens than battery hens?
- Do you think it is ever acceptable to eat humans?
- Is farming cruel?

After sharing the stimulus with the group, ask students to reflect individually on the stimulus, considering their emotional response (which can be recorded on a heart cut-out) and their initial thoughts or questions (recorded on a head cut-out).

### Philosophical questions and concepts

- Is the development of lab chops fair on animals/farmers?
- If I eat lab chops, can I be a vegetarian?
- Is this meat?
- Is the production of cultured meat more risky than conventional food production?

### Notes

This is a rich topic for enquiry as the idea of 'lab chops' contains many accessible scientific as well as philosophical ideas. Stem cells, cell specialization, cell multiplication, muscle growth and repair, food production and food chains as well as ideas about the nature of scientific enquiry can be taught as part of Key Stages 3 and 4 programmes of study for science. The topic also raises ethical issues relating to animal rights, the food industry, vegetarianism and veganism, as well as questioning the nature of meat, the scientific method, intellectual property rights and what is natural.

### Ethical issues in chemistry

The types of issue that can form the basis of an ethical enquiry in chemistry are what is good or right relating to chemicals in our bodies and in the environment. Common issues in chemistry are those related to the development of new molecules as solutions to problems, which are later found to be harmful to people or the environment, for example, Thomas Midgley's discoveries that leaded petrol resolved engine cracking and that chlorofluorocarbons (CFCs) are non-toxic refrigerants. The ethical issues that arise are often linked to what is an acceptable level of risk, when the precautionary principle should be applied, and where responsibility lies for dealing with the consequences of chemical advances.

Many ethical issues in chemistry can be addressed through case studies. Examples include the use of performance-enhancing drugs in sport and the production and use of pesticides. Other contemporary debates include the fortification of breads and cereals, antibiotic use and abuse, drug development and testing, the disposal of heavy metals and off-label use of medicines.

Activity 7 introduces some ethical issues related to the production of chemicals by humans.

## Activity 7: Wanted!

*Stimulus*
Wanted poster (Figure 6.8).

*Resource*
Figure 6.8.

*Guidance*
Begin the enquiry by encouraging students to think of a world without some key pollutants. The names of pollutants (e.g. dyes, carbon dioxide, methane, plastics (e.g. PVC, polystyrene, polythene), pesticides, flame retardants, medicines, CFCs, hydrocarbons) are printed and taped to an inflated beach ball. The ball is thrown around the room (one turn per child) and on their turn to catch, each student completes the sentence 'if there was no X . . .' where X is the name of the pollutant on the ball between their hands as they have caught it.

*Philosophical questions and concepts*

- Can a molecule be 'bad'?
- How can environmental problems be addressed fairly?

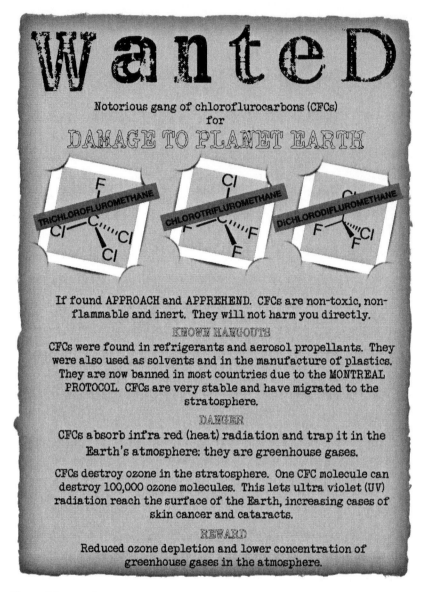

**Figure 6.8** Wanted poster

- Does it matter if the Earth's atmosphere changes?
- Do people alive today have responsibilities to the next generation?
- Should all nations be treated the same?
- Is it ever justified to release new chemicals into the environment?
- If CFCs could be 'caught', what should happen to them?

*Notes*

The wanted poster (Figure 6.8) format can be adapted and applied to many chemicals students encounter in the curriculum and can be used to stimulate philosophical enquiry.

### Ethical issues in physics

Philosophical enquiry can help students consider ethical issues associated with advances in physics from the very small scale (radioactive emissions from atoms in the context of nuclear power, nuclear waste and nuclear bombs) to the very large (communication across the world and exploration of the solar system). Many experiments in fundamental physics require the pooling of resources on a national or international scale. The resultant equipment gives rise to questions relating to the funding of science, fair access to equipment, and whether it is right to dedicate large amounts of money and effort to fundamental science when so many contemporary problems relating to human health and happiness remain unresolved. A stimulus that raises questions relating to money and science is a mock-up 'For Sale' sign on the surface of the moon. This relates to the practice of selling land in space and may lead to an exploration of colonization, exploitation of land, whether it is right to be able to buy land, air, water on earth, parts of the moon or whole stars and what ownership means in this context.

## P4C and concept development in science

One characteristic of philosophical enquiry is the scrutiny of concepts. Study of science requires students to understand many abstract concepts and specialized vocabulary including everyday words that have a specific meaning in science, for example, heat and energy. Philosophical enquiry can help students improve their understanding of key scientific ideas and processes through the analysis of these concepts. Stimuli for philosophical enquiry can be created around misconceptions in science, around classification systems, to develop understanding of nuanced ideas or to make explicit connections between science and everyday life. Activities 8 and 9 demonstrate how P4C might develop students' concepts in science.

## Activity 8: Understanding chemicals

### Stimulus

The act of opening the box to reveal a chemical that is important in the class' studies (e.g. a bottle of hydrochloric acid or ethanol, piece of copper or iron, a sample of crude oil, fuel or plastic, or an apparently empty box containing only air).

### Resources

A sealed box containing a chemical.

### Guidance

A sealed box placed in the centre of the room. Students are asked to imagine this box in the centre of the room contains a chemical. Individually, then in pairs and small groups they are asked to consider the questions:

- What question would you most want to know the answer to before the box was opened?
- What could it be that you would want to be around because it made you healthier/happier, and so on?
- What would you least want to be around because it harmed you?
- How does the concentration of the chemical affect how helpful/harmful it is?

After sharing answers as a whole class, introduce the stimulus by opening the sealed box to reveal the chemical in focus.

### Philosophical questions and concepts

- Is (insert name of chemical) the matter before you or something else?
- How can the benefits of a chemical be weighed against the harm it causes?
- Are some risks with respect to newly synthesized chemicals justified?

### Notes

The philosophical questions that will arise depend on the chemical that is revealed to them. Many children associate 'chemical' with something bad: poisons and pollutants, for example. However, everything is made of chemicals (for instance, water, oxygen, haemoglobin) which are 'good' or 'bad', harmful or helpful depending on the use to which they are put, their concentration and the people they interact with (adult/child, male/female, people who possess particular genes or who behave a particular way). Not everything natural is 'good'; not everything synthetic is 'bad'; indeed these value judgements relating to chemicals cannot be separated. Water is vital for life, yet deadly in some instances. This activity could reveal water or air and in doing so deal with a common misconception in chemistry.

## Activity 9: Defining species. What makes a good definition in science?

### Stimulus
Fossil(s).

### Resources
Four A4 pages with definitions of species written on; fossil sample.

### Guidance
Tell the class you are going to give them four definitions of species. The definitions might be

1. individuals that look alike,
2. individuals that mate to produce fertile offspring,
3. individuals that share common ancestors and have evolved separately from others and
4. species do not exist: labelling individual organisms is just classification according to random criteria.

Ask students to consider which they think is the best definition then to hold up the corresponding number of fingers, for example, three fingers held up if they think the third definition is the best. Group all students holding the same number of fingers up together, and tell them you would like one representative to justify the group's opinion. Allow students time to discuss, sharing their reasons with each other. Following group discussion, ask each group to justify their opinions. Allow students to swap group when each group has been heard.

Then, present each of the following examples in turn and ask students to reconsider their definition in light of this information.

- A bacteria made from synthetic DNA.
- A goat–sheep chimera (geep) made by mixing goat and sheep embryos: the animal has cells of goat and of sheep.
- Organisms that look alike but are genetically very different, and which cannot sexually reproduce with each other, for example, the African bush elephant and the African elephant.
- Butterflies that look very different but that can mate, for example, *helioconius himera* and *helioconius erato*.
- Species that reproduce asexually, for example, most species of bacteria reproduce asexually, many plants can reproduce asexually, as can some aphids.

Discussion might include problems with the concept of species and the utility of the concept, whether we pick out real distinctions in nature, or project our own distinctions onto nature.

Introduce the stimulus by passing the fossil(s) around the class, allowing each student to handle it. While students are handling the fossil, share the story of the fossil, for example, how long ago it lived, the conditions in which it lived, what it ate, how it moved, how the fossil was made and when the species became extinct.

## Philosophical questions and concepts

- What is a 'species'?
- Why do some species survive and others become extinct?
- Are fossils sufficient evidence for the evolution of species?
- Do all living organisms have a common ancestor?
- How can we know about fossils?

### Notes

The concept of species is one that students use in biology when considering variation, reproduction and evolution, and while the working concept of *a type of living thing that can reproduce to produce fertile offspring* may be useful, the concept of species is contested. This can be an interesting launch pad for a philosophical enquiry that explores the relationship between *homo sapiens* and other animal species in the age of genetic engineering and hybrid embryos. The definition of species can be further explored by considering what it means in light of a story in contemporary science that involves mixing the genes of two species. This may be related to pharming, hybrid embryos or xenotransplantation.

Concept development through philosophical dialogue helps students to develop their use of scientific vocabulary, to link curriculum concepts to contemporary scientific advances, to test their ideas among their peers and to learn from their contemporaries.

## Conclusions

Although philosophical questions (e.g. is it right to clone mammals?) and scientific questions (e.g. how can a mammal be cloned?) are answered in different ways, the skills of identifying assumptions, asking questions, generating hypotheses, selecting the best explanation, providing evidence and analysing consequences, which are developed through the community of enquiry, are central to both philosophical and scientific enquiry. The free flowing nature of a philosophical enquiry can very usefully expose students' misunderstandings and identify scientific questions that remain unanswered. The open nature of philosophical enquiry can also help children to think creatively about the science they are studying and reconnect with a sense of wonder about the world that many have lost by the time they reach secondary school.

Issues that the science teacher must consider before introducing P4C is how they are going to deal with factual errors, introducing new ideas and misconceptions during the enquiry. As with all good teaching the facilitator needs to assess, in the moment, the most appropriate response to further the learning and development of the students. The most appropriate action might be to assert something in the enquiry or it might be best left to be followed up in a separate lesson.

The following resource list contains potential stimuli for philosophical enquiry in a science context.

# Further reading

Brecht, B. and Rorrison, H. (1986) *Life of Galileo.* London: Methuen Drama New Scientist magazine (www.newscientist.com).

# Further resources

## Images

The Wellcome Library contains many historical and contemporary images relating to the biomedical sciences.

www.images.wellcome.ac.uk

World Press Photo features photojournalism in nature, sport and other contemporary themes.

www.worldpressphoto.org

The Science in Society picture library represents the visual collection of the Science Museum and includes images on the themes of chemistry, geology and space.

www.scienceandsociety.co.uk

Images of space including stars, nebulae and galaxies can be found on the website of the Hubble Space Telescope

www.hubblesite.org/gallery

Adbusters contains spoof advertisements relating to the sale of alcohol and fast food, the use of antidepressants and environmental issues.

www.adbusters.org/spoofads

Maps of the world distorted according to statistics relating to disease, pollution and fuel are available at

www.worldmapper.org

## Music

They Might Be Giants' *Here Comes Science* is an album of science songs for children on topics including evolution and electric cars.

Flanders and Swann's *First and Second Law* is a musical take on thermodynamics.

The track *The History of Everything* (30 seconds of which is the theme tune for the TV programme *The Big Bang Theory*) by Barenaked Ladies.

Baba Brinkman's peer-reviewed *Rap Guide to Evolution* covers sexual selection and natural selection.

www.bababrinkman.bandcamp.com

A list of music sent into space on the Voyager spacecraft in 1977 is available at

www.voyager.jpl.nasa.gov/spacecraft/music.html

The Voyager discs have travelled past the outer planets beyond Pluto.

## Films

*Apollo 13* (PG): based on the story of the Apollo 13 mission to the moon.

*Erin Brockovich* (15): based on a true story about water pollution and health.

*Gattaca* (15): fictional tale of genetics and determinism.

*Lorenzo's Oil* (12): based on the Odone's attempt to cure their son of a rare degenerative brain disorder.

*Outbreak* (15): fictional story about the transmission of a zoonotic viral disease.

*The Island* (12A): fictional account of cloning humans for organ transplants.

## Teaching resources

Information on ethics in science education is available through the BioEthics Education Project, Physics & Ethics Education Project and the AS/A2 Science in Society sites.

www.beep.ac.uk

www.peep.ac.uk

www.nuffieldfoundation.org/science-society

Smart materials and other thought provoking science resources are available from Mindsets.

www.mindsetsonline.co.uk

For teaching resources for P4C-based science lessons, visit

www.sciberbrain.org

www.ulster.ac.uk/scienceinsociety/forwardthinking.html

# References

BBC (2004) *Love is Blind* [online] Available at news.bbc.co.uk/1/hi/health/3804545.stm [accessed 19 August 2011].

Brockman, J. (ed.) (2006) *What Is Your Dangerous Idea? Leading Thinkers on the Unthinkable.* London: Simon & Schuster.

Bryson, B. (2003) *A Short History of Nearly Everything.* New York: Random House.

CERN (2004) *Alice and the Soup of Quarks and Gluons* [online] Available at aliceinfo.cern. ch/static/Documents/outreach/Cartoon/E_AliceBD.pdf Geneva, Switzerland [accessed 19 August 2011].

Chalmers, A. F. (1999) *What Is This Thing Called Science?* Maidenhead: Open University Press.

Christie, M. (2000) *The Ozone Layer: A Philosophy of Science Perspective.* Cambridge: Cambridge University Press.

*Daily Mail* (2011) *Scientists 'Prove' That Time Travel Will Always Be Impossible by Building a Toy Version of the Big Bang* [online] Available at www.dailymail.co.uk/sciencetech/article-1376736/Scientists-prove-time-travel-impossible-building-toy-version-Big-Bang.html [accessed 19 August 2011].

Feynman, R. (1999) *The Meaning of It All.* New York: Perseus Books.

Frayn, M. (2003) *Copenhagen.* London: Methuen Drama.

Giles, C. (2011) *The Man Who Can Taste Sounds* [online] Available at www.wellcometrust. wordpress.com/2011/05/26/the-man-who-can-taste-sounds [accessed 19 August 2011].

Goldacre, B. (2009) *Bad Science.* London: Harper Perennial. See also Sense about Science: www.senseaboutscience.org

Gribbon, J. (2002) *Science: A History 1543–2001*. London: Penguin.

Hanson, N. R. (1961) *Patterns of Discovery: An Inquiry into the Conceptual Foundations of Science*. New York: Cambridge University Press.

*Independent on Sunday* (2009) *Science Proves Acupuncture Is Sound Medicine* by J. Laurence [online] Available at www.independent.co.uk/life-style/health-and-families/health-news/science-proves-acupuncture-is-sound-medicine-1644893.html [accessed 19 August 2011].

Klotz, I. M. (1980) 'The N-Ray Affair', *Scientific American*, 242, 168–75.

Kuhn, T. (1996) *The Structure of Scientific Revolutions* (3rd edn). Chicago: University of Chicago Press.

Le Couteur, P. and Burreson, J. (2004) *Napoleon's Buttons 17 Molecules That Changed History*. New York: Penguin.

Levinson. R. and Reiss, M. (2003) *Key Issues in Bioethics: A Guide for Teachers*. London: Routledge.

Roberts, R. M. (1989) *Serendipity: Accidental Discoveries in Science*. New York: Wiley.

RSC (2011) *Chemistry in Its Element: Compounds. Benzene. Story of the Discovery of Benzene as Ring Transcript* [online] Available at www.rsc.org/chemistryworld/podcast/CIIEcompounds/transcripts/benzene.asp [accessed 19 August 2011].

Sacks, O. (2008) *Musicophilia*. London: Picador.

Simons, D. J. (2010) *Selective Attention Test* [online] Available at viscog.beckman.illinois.edu/flashmovie/15.php [accessed 19 August 2011].

Skloot, R. (2010) *The Immortal Life of Henrietta Lacks*. London: Pan.

Sprod, T. (2001) 'Building Scientific Thinking via Philosophical Discussion', *Teaching Thinking*, Autumn (5), 14–18.

Thiessen, V. (2003) *Einstein's Gift*. Toronto: Playwrights Canada Press.

Warburton, N. (2004) *Philosophy: The Basics*. Oxford: Routledge.

# P4C in Religious Education

Patricia Hannam

7

## Chapter Outline

| | |
|---|---|
| Introduction | 127 |
| Background and purpose of RE | 128 |
| Connections between RE and P4C | 129 |
| Activities using RE and P4C | 136 |
| Conclusion | 144 |

## Introduction

Effective philosophical enquiry in Religious Education (RE) needs teachers who can form their RE classes into communities of enquiry, to support students in raising and formulating significant and puzzling questions that are both of persistent human concern and also the subject of religion and faith. Planning for systematic conceptual progression deepens understanding of religious and philosophical concepts; integrating philosophical enquiry builds an awareness of and sensitivity to others' views which is an imperative for living in plural globalized communities.

This chapter presents a background and purpose of RE in a plural democracy, a rationale for an enquiring pedagogy for RE, models of enquiry in RE, an analysis of philosophical enquiry and its value for RE in adolescence alongside the Hampshire Enquiry model for RE.

# Background and purpose of RE

To appreciate the significance of philosophical enquiry for RE it is helpful to consider the unique history of this subject in the English school curriculum. The existence of RE in the maintained sector in England came as a consequence of an accommodation the government of the day made with different Christian denominations in order to fulfil the growing need for elementary education for all. Christian denominational organizations, already providing elementary education for the children of the poor, would allow the buildings belonging to the churches to be used by the authorities. The compromise for the state was that there would also be RE for all, even in the newly built county schools; RE would be locally determined, the local authority responsible for developing and implementing RE eventually through a Locally Agreed Syllabus which could respond to the needs of the local community. Over time the position of RE in maintained schools was strengthened, but discussions about its scope and purpose are ongoing. Whereas initially these discussions took place in the context of a fairly homogenous society, waves of movement, particularly after the Second World War, have radically altered the social and religious landscape of the United Kingdom. RE remains locally determined and still able to respond to local need; however, responding in terms of content may not be enough.

After 120 years of statutory RE in English schools we are torn between RE having a social or political purpose, related to the acquisition of knowledge needed for life in contemporary society and a more personal or moral purpose focused on the well-being of the individual child. This tension is reflected in the attainment targets used in most Locally Agreed Syllabuses in England. Separating 'learning about religion' from 'learning from religion' does little to help clarify the reasons either why young people should study this subject or help teachers understand an *educational* purpose for RE. Ofsted (2010) noted that lack of clarity of the core purpose which exists for RE may make for lively debate, but 'inhibits the effectiveness of classroom practice' (p. 41). This chapter outlines a congruent process for working in RE weaving together a vision for education itself with the practicality of what happens in the classroom. In this way we can ensure that classroom practice demonstrates clear educational purpose as well as offering a model relevant and meaningful for young people that takes the plurality of religion in British society today seriously.

# Connections between RE and P4C

## Why an enquiry pedagogy for RE?

We can identify two key reasons for advancing enquiry in RE. The first, drawing from John Dewey (1916), is that enquiry itself at the heart of good educational practice. John Dewey suggests that enquiry will always be a precursor to the acquisition of knowledge for there is always the troublesome business of engagement with the unknown when the individual is moving from the position of unknowing to knowing. Learning, if it is to be something more than just by rote, necessitates the young person opening up first to the *possibility* that there is something new out there, of being in the position of 'coming to know', which is a position not of unknowing but one of uncertainty. This requires a particular kind of thinking we call enquiry.

The second reason why enquiry is important in RE relates to the fact that we are living in increasingly uncertain times and must acknowledge that this has a great impact on the lives of young people. We are in a period of mass globalization, by which I mean the shifting significance of national boundaries and geographical distance as constraints on mobility of many different kinds of things, including people, goods and services. It includes the factors of production and their owners, financial capital, enterprises, technology, brand names, knowledge, ideas, culture and values; for all these things now move with increasing ease across national frontiers. The impact of this increased mobility can be seen in a number of ways: some positive and others less so. As products and services have increasingly begun to move, so have people and with them their explanations of the cosmos and humanity's place within it and formal belief systems and practices. Understanding the links between and consequences of these different events requires intelligent development of reasoning and thinking. Britain is now a plural society especially in terms of religion and belief. However, Hannah

Arendt reminds us that plurality has always been with us, indeed that, 'Plurality is the condition of human action' (Arendt, 1998, p. 7). The reality of the plurality within faiths is often not made clear enough to young people. In RE, we must assist our young people in making meaning for themselves from these different explanations of existential questions. Empowering young people to make a difference and to face the uncertainty of the times requires a different approach to education that goes way beyond knowledge transmission. Knowledge alone is insufficient to form young adults who are capable of reflected moral action and who have a clear sense of personal identity. In RE, in the secondary school especially, we need to make opportunities for deliberation and enquiry, where young people can dialogue with their peers, facilitated by teachers who themselves have skills to enable the young people to reason and think well.

Religious belief systems are complex frameworks for living in response to the existential questions that confront us. They invariably include an ethical code together with authoritative guidance for living well, not just as individuals but also as communities; religious traditions appeal to an authority for this justification. A concept such as 'authority' is an important one in different religious traditions; it is also an important concept for adolescents, challenge being a modern hallmark of this period of life. How would it be if we could model a kind of RE that enabled an exploration of concepts, which are key to the understanding of religion as well as key to young people making meaning of their lives: from both without and within a religious context?

## Models of enquiry in RE

The Ofsted 2010 report 'Transforming Religious Education', concluded that 'The most effective lessons were based on a clear model of how pupils learn that matched the nature of the subject.' And further that 'This was most evident in the schools that adopted a clearly defined enquiry-based approach to the subject. This had a number of benefits' (Ofsted, 2010, p. 45).

1. It provided a clear but flexible framework for structuring and sequencing activities that focused on the process of learning as well as on content.

2. It promoted challenge because it involves pupils in planning activities and enabled them to develop higher level skills such as investigation, interpretation and analysis.
3. It provided confidence among teachers without a specialist background in the subject because they were working with a structure and process of learning which they could understand and apply.
4. Assessment focused not just on what pupils knew but also on the progress they were making in becoming effective explorers of the world of religion and belief. (Ibid.)

In Hampshire, since 2004, a method for advancing enquiry in RE was embedded across the county through the well-developed use of the County Agreed Syllabus for RE, *Living Difference*. This was rooted in theory that Clive Erricker, County Inspector/Adviser for RE between 2003 and 2009, together with Judith Lowndes, General Inspector for RE developed for RE and called 'Conceptual Enquiry'. This way of looking at RE was formulated in order to rectify perceived problems in RE. These problems included the lack of clear pedagogical development which linked education and learning theory with the students' personal development and also a rigorous engagement with the study of world religions. The approach depended upon establishing a methodological approach to the development of conceptual understanding. Process-based syllabus enables young people to interpret the experiences of religious people and communities and relate these meaningfully to the realities of their own lives.

Since this time other County Agreed Syllabuses have begun to speak about 'enquiry'. Some now include the mention of P4C as 'one strategy for enquiry'. However, I argue that is not sufficient. This chapter is advocating a rigorous and disciplined use of the community of philosophical enquiry facilitated by well-trained teachers who have a good understanding of the consequences of their interventions: in other words how they facilitate an enquiry. Interventions need to be understood in terms of supporting the development of a deep understanding of the human purpose of the subject matter of religion as well as the development of the young person's self-understanding. The unity of these two purposes is reflected in the single attainment target for RE in Hampshire, where we aim to support young people to make progress in their ability to 'interpret religion in relation to human experience'.

## Philosophical enquiry and its value for RE in adolescence

Children grow up primarily concerned for the immediate practical questions of their own lives; for example, how to relate to siblings and parents, what to eat, or what to wear. For the child many of these things are determined in the first instance by their parents but this all starts to change with the arrival of adolescence. Parents gradually slide into second place and soon friends, peers and classmates become the most important points of reference. From around 12, adolescents must be given the opportunity to develop the capacity for making wise judgements with regard to the important decisions they will have to make in their lives, and in this stage of life the community of philosophical enquiry takes on a particular significance in giving young people the opportunity to experience thoughtful reflection with their peers (Hannam and Echeverria, 2009, p. 24). This can be an educational space where young people can learn to reason well, to think imaginatively, to take intellectual risks, be open-minded and reach some contingent resolutions to significant existential questions. Through skilled use of philosophical questioning, which develops the capacity for higher order thinking, we guide students to a critical reflection of the matters raised. The teacher needs to transform their own practice and become instead a facilitator of the young people's thinking and reasoning: modelling and encouraging the new thoughts and ways of thinking to be born into speech and new ways of acting into the world. This is important since the concepts we are working with in RE, especially those specific to a particular religion, are frequently complex and their subtlety as well as significance for human understanding are best explored through enquiry.

The facilitator's role is to push the students to go deeper into their thinking by asking for more reasons and better examples to support them. Young people can make progress with recognizing weaker and stronger arguments and develop logical, inferential as well as hypothetical reasoning in order to better recognize and enquire into concepts – both the familiar (more significantly as they move towards adulthood) and those with which they are not familiar. RE can be a significant educational space where young people can think about what matters to them and consider with their peers what kind of people they would like to become and what kind of a world they would like to live in.

## The Hampshire Enquiry Model as in *Living Difference Revised* 2011

The revised Hampshire County Agreed Syllabus *Living Difference Revised* 2011 builds on the work of *Living Difference* which came into use in all Hampshire schools in 2004. In his book, *Religious Education: A Conceptual and Interdisciplinary Approach for Secondary Level*, Clive Erricker (2010) examines many current debates surrounding RE and discusses in detail a 'conceptual enquiry' approach to the teaching of RE. This approach formed the basis for *Living Difference* (2004) and was developed further in *Living Difference Revised* 2011. It is in contrast with more analytical or epistemological approaches to RE such as that of Critical Realism of Andrew Wright (e.g. 2001, 2007a, 2007b) or the interpretative approach of Robert Jackson (e.g. 1997). In Hampshire, many secondary practitioners are now finding that working with philosophical enquiry in RE is congruent with, and builds on, the strong pedagogical foundations for RE which were embedded in the 2004 syllabus. Both *Living Difference* and now *Living Difference Revised* 2011 present a model for learning in RE which is innovative in several ways. First, it is based upon a clear enquiry methodology rather than a programme of curriculum content to be delivered and secondly it has only one attainment target: 'interpreting religion in relation to human experience'. The 2011 revision of the Hampshire Agreed Syllabus for RE acknowledges that developing the skills of enquiry in ourselves as teachers is essential in order to facilitate our students' engagement in skilful enquiry for themselves. 'Enquiry lies at the heart of the Hampshire, Portsmouth and Southampton Agreed Syllabus. Developing the skills of enquiry in children and young people is an important part of the work of the teacher of religious education' (p. 21).

## Using concepts

*Living Difference Revised* 2011 introduces pupils to a particular approach to RE which focuses students on investigating concepts.

Concepts are understood to be big ideas that have developed in human language enabling us to interpret and communicate human experience. They are tools for making sense of the world. The sense we make of the world is dependent upon our concepts. Within religious traditions people use distinctive concepts to express their experience and their understanding of the world. (*Living Difference Revised* 2011, p. 17)

To ensure progression and coherence in the programme for RE at Key Stage 3, the teacher develops a 'concept map' or overview of the concepts to be explored together with religious contextualizations of each concept. The careful planning of concepts across one religious tradition ensures that a coherent understanding of key religions required is formed. The crucial shift for the teacher is that from the moment they begin their planning they must think conceptually and follow this up by finding meaningful contexts for the concepts in order to support the development of students' understanding of the concept, rather than be driven by communicating knowledge of beliefs and practices alone.

In *Living Difference Revised* 2011 (Figure 7.1) we think of concepts as being in three broad groups.

Group A concepts are those which are common to all human experience, for example, love, community, beauty, charity, justice, fairness,

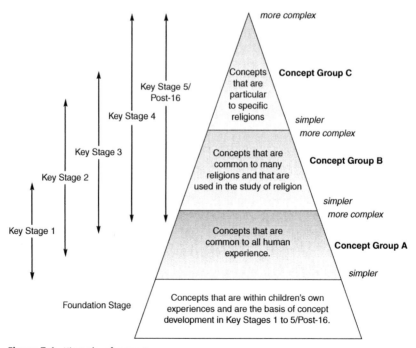

**Figure 7.1** Hierarchy of concepts

special – religious and non-religious people alike are concerned about these. The next group (B) of concepts we would say are religious concepts, but are used by all or some religions, for example, god, holy, sacred, worship, prayer, faith. The third group of concepts (C) are those which are distinctive of a particular religious tradition; these concepts are vital to understand if one is going to be able to deeply appreciate the distinctiveness of a particular tradition. For example, Umma, Sangha, Church, Khalsa, Atonement, Grace, Trinity, Islam, Brahman. Understanding the significance of the three groups of concepts, even if the placing of concepts is contested, is essential to ensuring rigour in the subject.

Although there is no restriction regarding the number of concepts covered for each religion over the key stage, the concepts which are included at Key Stage 3 will in the majority be Group C concepts. In every point in the cycle of enquiry in RE the teacher can use philosophical questioning techniques to deepen students' enquiry into the concept. Conceptual understanding is supported by the teacher's skilful use of philosophical questioning which encourage the students:

1. to make distinctions (e.g. 'In what way is the idea of power different from the idea of authority?') to search for criteria through encouraging students to look for good examples (e.g. 'What are we saying would count as "authority" then?')
2. to look for connections with linked concepts, which is assisted by encouraging good reasons and examples.

There are two starting points for the cycle (Figure 7.2).

The cycle can start at 'Communicate' or 'Enquire'. Whichever starting point is adopted for the cycle the students follow the enquiry by engaging with each of the five steps in turn. If starting at Communicate in the cycle (as is especially the case with a Group A concept for which at least some in the class will have personal experience) students will be invited to make a response to the concept before the next element, 'Apply', where students could be asked to reflect on their view of the concept in different situations. At this point students are nudged to see the potential challenges for the concept when placed in different situations. For example, the facilitator may ask for the concept 'community'. *Can you think of a time when you did not want to be part of a community? What difference did it make? What would it be like if there were*

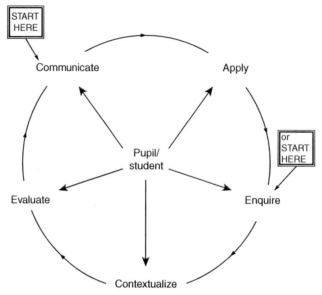

**Figure 7.2** A methodology for enquiry into concepts

*no community?* The aim at this point is to encourage students to relate the concept to their own experience. It is at this point that the concept begins to be problematized and be ready for further examination in the context of a philosophical question.

# Activities using RE and P4C

## Activity 1: An enquiry into the concept of respect

*Stimulus*
Images.

*Resources*
Photographs that raise the concept of 'respect'.

*Procedure*
Display a photograph for the community and ask them to reflect on their personal reactions. They then share these thoughts with others in small groups before generating questions together such as those listed below.

*Philosophical questions and concepts (generated at 'Enquire')*

- Why should we respect people who have committed a crime?
- If you're giving respect to get it, who is going to give it first?
- How exactly do you give to earn respect?
- If you want respect do you have to give it?
- How do you earn respect?
- How do you judge who you respect?
- Would you respect anyone even if you don't like them?

### Notes

'Contextualize': GCSE work related to reasons why Christians believe all life deserves respect. The 'Enquire' stage of the cycle, especially when working with a Group A or Group B concepts, lends itself to a full community of philosophical enquiry. The core concept for the questions is determined but a further 'stimulus' can be presented before the formation of philosophical questions to create further discongruence of the concept. The important thing is for the students to develop questions which they own and to agree a question which they can explore and interrogate in the class community to bring greater appreciation of the three dimensionality of the concept before it is studied in a religious context.

## Activity 2: An enquiry into the concept of god

### Stimulus
Philosophical questions.

### Resources
Questions as illustrated below presented on a screen or on cards.

### Guidance
Facilitating the enquiry: Questions such as 'Does God exist?' contain immense concepts, such as existence, and can therefore be very hard to facilitate. The first step in such an enquiry is to encourage the students to seek some clarification of what existence means. One way to begin with this is to look for examples and counter-examples:

Can you give an example of something that exists for certain?
Can you give an example of something that does not exist?

Another helpful way to seek clarification is to look for concepts which are close to the idea of existence in order to enable distinctions to be made:

**Exist/real**
If something exists is it the same as being real?
Can you think of something that is real but does not exist?

**Exist/alive**
Is existing the same as being alive?
Can you think of an example of something that exists but is not alive?

A further move is to look for hypothetical examples.

Can we think of an example or imagine anything that does not exist?

This will help problematize and expand the community's appreciation of the complexity of the idea or concept of existence. We then need to do some conceptual clarification of the concept of God/god.

### Notes
Following such work with the community, all the while encouraging contributors to agree and disagree with good reasons, building and thinking critically, creatively and collaboratively; it will be possible to develop some sound inferential reasoning in the community.
  Dialogue like this may follow:

**Jane:** I think that for something to exist it must be an idea in someone's mind.
**Facilitator:** Can you give us an example?
**Jane:** errr . . . well . . .
**Facilitator:** Can any one else help Jane here?
**Luke:** I think that when I have a dream it exists because I can remember it.
**Tara:** I disagree with Luke because sometimes I remember things that did not happen, for example, when I remember that my mum said she would give me extra pocket money and she says she didn't promise anything like that.
**Jack:** I think that something exists when it is real because something that is not real can't exist.

**Sophie**:    I disagree with Jack because I don't think fairies are real, but they exist in my imagination.

**Jade**:    I kind of agree with Sophie because other things exist in my imaginations which are not real – I mean they don't exist in the real physical world. Also I agree with Tara because sometimes we can be mistaken about what we remember.

**Facilitator**:    Does that mean that something that is not real in the world could exist in another kind of way, for example, in our imagination? Could there be other ways of existing? How could this idea help us answer the question?

**Jack**:    Well I think we need to go back to our discussion on what you think God is like. If God is like a dream then I suppose God could be said to exist in a kind of way to them. We need to look at the two concepts together.

**Facilitator**:    Does any one agree with Jack? That if you think God is like one particular thing and you decide existence is another, thinking about the relationship between the two is important in order to answer the question?

**Jane**:    In one way I agree, we can argue that God can exist in my mind. But is that enough for a religious person? Doesn't a Christian or a Muslim want to say that God exists in reality too?

**Facilitator**:    OK I think we have reached a point where we need to learn something about what Christians and Muslims say about God and how they argue for God's existence.

### *Philosophical questions and concepts generated at 'Enquire'*

- Does God exist?
- How can we know God exists?
- If there is a God why does he allow bad things to happen?
- What kind of a God would allow children to be harmed?
- Can God interfere with human action?
- Who says that God is good?

At 'Contextualize' the teacher enables the students to examine the application of this concept to a specific religious situation. For example, with the concept of God students may investigate two contrasting belief systems about God – for example, a Christian view or Hindu view. Sometimes a double 'Contextualize' is possible as, for example, in a GCSE course where comparison is required. The activities of a local religious community, Christian, Muslim, Sikh, and so on could be relevant as could the inclusion of non-religious material if it enhances the cycle of enquiry. Effective contextual material allows the enquiry to deepen. The context may be a case study, news article, scenario, and so on. It enriches understanding of the concept by placing it in a real, precise situation which raises issues and questions. This enables pupils/students to appreciate alternative viewpoints and see how the concept informs certain beliefs and practices of the religious group or tradition, for example: *What issues about community are raised in this context? How is the Salvation Army's, or other religion's, idea of community different from or similar to our own? What questions and problems might this raise about different interpretations of the concept of community?* The context needs to be chosen carefully and it must ensure that the faith tradition is represented accurately. However, students also need to grow over time in their appreciation that members of any one faith tradition may have several different ways of looking at a particular concept. They may become more aware that their original view was limited or mistaken or even wrong. Also there will be a growing awareness of contingency, that this is the answer that I have for now but with other information my response may change. These qualities, which develop through the work of the community of philosophical enquiry, are helpful habits of mind to bring to learning about religion and are helpful ways of looking at others' beliefs in order to advance interfaith understanding. It is important that the specific situation in which the concept is placed will raise issues and promote discussion. Furthermore, the context should open up how the concept affects beliefs and practices and how the concept impacts on the way someone really lives their day-to-day life.

I felt that philosophical enquiry (at 'Enquire') really helped lay the foundations from which we could contextualise, and later evaluate and finally communicate and apply the concept.
Rebecca Costembeys Head of RE Costello College Basingstoke and County AST RE (first published in *Secondary RE News* Summer 2011)

A unique element of the Hampshire Agreed Syllabus is the element of 'Evaluate' where students are asked to make informed, evaluative judgements about the concept in two ways: first, from the viewpoint of a believer – 'Evaluate' within; then by giving their own point of view – 'Evaluate' without. This should involve collaboration and dialogue prompted by questions ('Evaluate' within) such as: What would a member of the Salvation Army (or Sikh or Buddhist, etc.) argue is the significance of the concept of community? Or what do you think about the significance of community for a member of the Salvation Army ('Evaluate' without) we are finding that a community of philosophical enquiry may sometimes fit very well at this step of the process? Here we can use a philosophical enquiry to help the students to weigh up the significance of beliefs and arguments that they have explored through the whole cycle. Philosophical enquiry, as we have discovered, already has an aim of enabling formation of reflective judgements, which is exactly the purpose of the 'Evaluate' step of the Hampshire enquiry model. This is highly significant for RE since it is in the formation of judgements that we begin to reveal what kind of people we are, and it is in being enabled to act on our judgements that we can participate in forming the kind of world in which we would like to live.

## Activity 3: Philosophical enquiry in RE at 'Evaluate'

*Stimulus*
A school letter.

*Concept*
Democracy.

*Resources*
Mock school letters from the headteacher.

*Guidance*
The school letters are distributed to the students.

'Communicate' and 'Apply': The sequence of lessons starts with the distribution of an official school letter, explaining that, by decree of the headteacher, summer holidays are now one-week long. Students then explore and communicate their views about, and experiences of, democracy.

'Enquire': Students explore the meaning of democracy.

'Contextualize': The concept is contextualized, for example, by examining democracy in Apartheid South Africa. Students could be introduced to Nelson Mandela and Desmund Tutu and the religious and non-religious arguments for democracy.

'Evaluate': 'Evaluate within' the context is undertaken and then finally, pupils evaluate the concept of democracy in their own lives through a piece of writing.

*Now is an opportunity for a community of philosophical enquiry (P4C).* At this point of the cycle, pupils can be asked to create 'glossary cards' of all the beliefs and ideas that had been touched upon through the cycle. Students then place these on a spectrum of importance, selecting the issues they find most interesting at the top, and these are shared with the class. The pupils build a philosophical question around the concepts they find most interesting, resulting in the election of the class question.

### Philosophical questions and concepts

Pupils might come up with ideas such as 'justice', 'equality', 'protest', 'murder' and 'terrorism' or a question such as: *Is terrorism ever justified in the search for democracy?*

### Notes

In this case the whole process of the Cycle of Learning, the investigation and contextualization of the concept, might become the stimulus for the P4C enquiry.

Gary Green, Fernhill School, Farnborough (first published in *Secondary RE News* Summer 2011)

Sometimes it will be more effective to begin the cycle at 'Enquire', for example, if the concept is beyond the experience of the students such as is likely for a Group C concept. If the cycle of enquiry starts at 'Enquire' with a 'C' concept it will be hard to have a philosophical enquiry since the students do not really have much informed experience to bring to the discussion. Here the teacher's role is to enable the students to engage with the range and depth of different understandings of the concept at the outset, paying particular attention to how the students respond to the concept before contextualizing in the usual way. For example, Umma could be well contextualized by teaching about Ramadan. A community of philosophical enquiry could really come into its own at 'Evaluate'. In such an example the cycle would continue on to 'Communicate' and this would give the students the opportunity in small groups to develop an installation, a film or podcast to communicate their understandings of the significance of the concept for the faith believers. This could well include a reflective judgement based on the findings of the community of philosophical enquiry at 'Evaluate'. Further a community of philosophical enquiry may also be appropriate at a final stage 'Apply'. Here the students are given the opportunity to consider how the learning could apply to their own lives. The whole experience of the cycle can be brought into the enquiry; the previous 3–5 lessons becoming the stimulus for the enquiry.

I have no doubt in my mind that working with the students in a community of philosophical enquiry (P4C) at the 'Enquire' stage of the cycle in RE is a powerful pedagogical tool that can be inclusive but also challenging for all members of the community. I have seen pupils in a short space of time grow in confidence and become effective participators. This has taken time and practice but after the third enquiry I felt we were really making progress.
Nikki Jeffery, Head of Department, Mountbatten School (first published in *Secondary RE News* Summer 2011)

This approach lends itself to interdisciplinary enquiry. An example of this is where in the RE classroom the teacher begins with 'Communicate' with the concept of 'martyrdom'. The pattern of 'Communicate', 'Apply' and 'Enquire' is followed by a philosophical enquiry at 'Enquire'. The 'Contextualize' could be included as an history enquiry into the question 'Was St Thomas a Becket a Martyr?' and in RE the contextualization being the life of Archbishop Oscar Romero in El Salvador. What we can be sure of is that the historical understanding of whether Thomas a Becket was a martyr will be greatly extended with an appreciation of the Christian understanding of 'martyrdom'. The students being able to develop an understanding of the historical significance of Thomas a Becket's death will in turn inform the 'Evaluate' and also perhaps second 'Communicate' and 'Apply' steps in the concluding phases of the enquiry.

## Conclusion

This chapter has discussed a developing method for embedding philosophical enquiry with rigour; where progression is planned against staged level descriptors together with an appreciation of what it means to make progress in philosophical enquiry and where the teacher understands the educational purpose of their work.

Religious education lends itself to an enquiring and philosophical approach. In a world where truth is contestable, young people need skills to debate, discern and engage with difference confidently. Religious education conducted through enquiry can help young people develop their own sense of identity, belonging and personal world view. The young person will gain confidence in coming to appreciate the plurality of religious and non religious belief. Forming classrooms into communities of enquiry offers a safe framework for children and young people to explore both common and contestable areas of expression. The teacher is the guide for the journey. (*Living Difference Revised* 2011, p. 23)

## References

Arendt, H. (1998) *The Human Condition* (2nd edn). London: University of Chicago Press.

Dewey, J. (1916) *Democracy and Education: An Introduction to the Philosophy of Education.* Free Press. New York.

Erricker, C. (2010) *Religious Education: A Conceptual and Interdisciplinary Approach for Secondary Level.* Abingdon: Routledge.

Hannam, P. and Echeverria, E. (2009) *Philosophy with Teenagers: Nurturing a Moral Imagination.* London: Continuum.

Jackson, R. (1997) *Religious Education: An Interpretive Approach.* London: Hodder and Stoughton.

— (2004) *Rethinking Religious Education and Plurality: Issues in Diversity and Pedagogy.* London: Routledge Falmer.

*Living Difference Revised* (2011).

*Living Difference* (2004).

Ofsted (2010) Transforming Religious Education.

Wright, A. (2001) 'Dancing in the Fire: A Deconstruction of Clive Erricker's Postmodern Spiritual Pedagogy', *Religious Education*, 96 (1), 120–35.

— (2007a) 'Critical Realism as a Tool for the Interpretation of Cultural Diversity in Liberal Religious Education', in M. D'Souza, G. Durka, K. Engebretson and R. Jackson (eds), *International Handbook of the Religious, Moral and Spiritual Dimensions of Education*, Volume One. Dordrecht: Springer, pp. 333–47.

— (2007b) *Critical Religious Education, Multiculturalism and the Pursuit of Truth*. Cardiff: University of Wales Press.

# 8 P4C in Personal, Social and Health Education (PSHE)

Roger Sutcliffe

## Chapter Outline

Connections between PSHE and P4C                                     147
Activities using PSHE and P4C                                       152

The phrase 'a curate's egg' has its origins in a Punch cartoon of 1895, in which a Bishop, hosting a curate for breakfast, says: 'I'm afraid you've got a bad egg, Mr Jones' – to which the Curate replies: 'Oh, no, my Lord, I assure you that parts of it are excellent!'

The cartoon was titled 'True Humility', and perhaps one should indeed approach PSHE with humility. It is neither a simple matter nor a slight one, and excellence in every aspect of teaching it may be beyond ordinary mortals.

That said, P4C offers a purpose and a process – a proven pedagogy – for PSHE teachers that will be useful to them at least, and vital to them at best.

Through this chapter the initialism PSHE – Personal Social Health Education – is used as the simple catch-all for the various forms it takes, for example, Personal Social Health Economic education.

# Connections between PSHE and P4C

## P4C aims

The purpose might be summed up in two quotations from Matthew Lipman:

The aim of P4C is to help children become more thoughtful, more reflective, more considerate and more reasonable individuals. (Lipman, 1980, p. 15)

P4C is not about prescribing any one philosophy to children but about encouraging them to develop their own philosophy, their own way of thinking about the world. (Lipman, 2008, p. 166)

For many teachers these statements represent the very essence that made them enter the profession – to contribute to the fulfilment of young people in themselves, and to their flourishing in society.

By definition PSHE focuses more than any subject in the curriculum on the development of self-knowledge and understanding of others, and P4C provides the perfect framework and approach for this task – enabling the sort of meaningful dialogue that teachers want to have in their classes.

It does this first by aiming beyond knowledge and understanding – towards good judgement – and then by modelling a process for attaining that goal.

## P4C process

Initially, the teacher will herself model the desired qualities of thoughtfulness, reflectiveness, consideration and reasonableness, probing pupil responses and offering more questions or even arguments to consider. But before long, pupils will start questioning and developing each other's ideas, and then they will be well on the way to forming their own community of enquiry.

Partly it is the pull of philosophical questions themselves that leads pupils on – and PSHE is full of potential for such questions, as will be highlighted shortly. But partly it is the deliberate attempt to create a 'safe' community that gives the pupils the confidence to play (seriously) with ideas.

So, for a start, PSHE lessons could be routinely conducted in a circle – and better still labelled as a circle, if not a community, of enquiry. The very set-up would indicate that every member of the class has equal and autonomous access to the group activity, while the emphasis on enquiry would signal the purpose of examining life (as Socrates would have put it).

Parents, indeed, remark that PSHE, and particularly P4C, sessions precisely address aspects of their children's development that they know are important for their lives beyond school, but which can so easily be ignored in the drive towards better grades in that other sort of examination.

And students who have the benefit of enlightened PSHE/P4C lessons, find them an oasis in a world which presses ever more heavily on them (to the extent that Guy Claxton in his 2008 book, *What's the Point of School?* heads his first chapter, 'Stress: The Children's Epidemic?' – and sadly proceeds to give strong reasons for answering his question in the affirmative).

In response to these and other signs of stress and strife, the body politic (or perhaps society at large) seems to place ever more unreasonable expectations upon teachers, especially PSHE teachers, to solve its growing problems.

But before looking a little more closely at how P4C might help in this regard, there is a need for just a little more 'big picture' thinking about the very concept of PSHE.

## PSHE rhetoric and reality

The first thing to say is that PSHE, even more so than the National Curriculum itself, is a social construct – that is, an idea whose meaning and application reflects the particular society, or societies, in which it is used.

The very fact that in Wales, for example, the usual initialism is PSE (Personal and Social Education), whereas in England it is, currently, PSHE(e) – standing for Personal, Social, Health and Economic (education) – indicates a different focus, or indeed a different way of approaching such common ground as there is.

In the framework for PSE published by the Welsh government for implementation in 2008 (p. 4), schools are expected to provide experiences for learners to:

- develop learners' self-esteem and a sense of personal responsibility
- promote self-respect, respect for others and celebrate diversity
- equip learners to live safe, healthy lives
- prepare learners for the choices and opportunities of lifelong learning
- empower learners to participate in their schools and communities as active responsible citizens locally, nationally and globally
- foster positive attitudes and behaviour towards the principles of sustainable development and global citizenship
- prepare learners for the challenges, choices and responsibilities of work and adult life.

That is quite a specification, even when set in a context that the Welsh framework (p. 5), calls 'holistic' – interpreting PSHE as 'everything that a school or college does to support and promote the personal and social development of its young people. It comprises learning opportunities within and beyond the classroom.'

Dedicated PSHE sessions might contribute significantly to this holistic vision, but PSHE teachers, however dedicated themselves, might be among the first to remark how far short the reality falls from the rhetoric. Many timetables barely schedule an hour a week for PSHE, and not surprisingly such sessions can have an all-too-limited focus.

In England the Schools White Paper (DfE 2010, p. 46 para 4.30), stated that: 'Children can benefit enormously from PHSE education. Good PSHE education supports young people to make safe and informed choices. It can help tackle public health issues such as substance misuse and support young people with the financial decisions they must make.'

The phrase 'safe and informed choices' *could* cover a wide range of life choices, both present and future. However, the specification of issues around substance misuse and finances suggests a narrower focus, quite possibly reflecting adult (political?) anxieties about social practices and economic possibilities – a perceived 'sex, drugs and pay as you (l)earn' culture.

In short, the rhetoric around PSHE often does not match the reality. The notion that it helps young people to 'fulfil their potential' or that it has a significant role to play in their 'personal and social development' is undermined by the minimal time given to it in the formal timetable.

Realistically, this problem will never be solved unless there is a rethinking about the relationship between PSHE and the rest of the curriculum, and indeed about the nature of teaching within it.

## Reconfiguring PSHE

Some schools actually began this task when they located Personal, Learning and Thinking Skills within a broader PSHE framework, and such reconfiguration should still be possible, regardless of any new, minimum, requirements for PSHE.

Schools which take personal and social development seriously – with a proper emphasis on educating the whole person – will reap benefits not only in better interpersonal relations but also in terms of better thinking and learning across the curriculum.

A regular session of open, philosophical enquiry as part of such a reconfiguration would almost certainly develop not just good skills but good habits for life – intellectual curiosity and tenacity, for example, to add to Lipman's thoughtfulness, reflectiveness, consideration and reasonableness.

So, how might such a session be planned, beyond setting up a circle?

## Skills and habits

For a start, the focus should be far more on building **skills** and **habits** than on any prescribed content.

You could, for example, focus on one or two particular skills during each PSHE session. It might be desirable, then, to spend a little while at the start of the session discussing the nature and value of the chosen skills, especially how they relate to personal and social development.

There are various lists of such skills – sometimes called 'moves' – in P4C, of which the following is just a sample:

Engaging in dialogue (personal skills)

- Listening carefully
- Waiting to contribute
- Noticing who else wants to contribute
- Responding encouragingly to others

Practising critical thinking (Thinking Skills 1)

- Seeking clarification
- Seeking examples
- Checking evidence
- Checking assumptions

Practising creative thinking (Thinking Skills 2)

- Drawing conclusions
- Imagining consequences
- Connecting ideas (with each other, or with experience)
- Making alternative suggestions

Reviewing (learning skills)

- Remembering (a sequence of ideas)
- Connecting ideas (with prior knowledge or experience)
- Recognizing relevance (to question or subject in mind)
- Reconceptualizing (organizing information and interpretations)

Simple reflection at the end of the session on how the skills came into the enquiry is usually enough to consolidate their use, but some skills may benefit from practice with tailored exercises. Exercises such as those presented below improve reasoning skills, which are vital to the ultimate objective of PSHE, helping young people make good, reasoned judgements. But they also point the way to more reflective habits of mind, such as being sceptical or inquisitive.

These habits might be particularly worth encouraging in the context of the world beyond school, which seems increasingly to be trying to persuade young people of one thing or another – whether in regard to comparatively trivial things such as clothing brands, or in regard to more important life choices. PSHE is probably the best opportunity to help young people reflect critically on such matters, and indeed on controversial issues such as pregnancy or obesity – and the community of enquiry is the most thoughtful environment for this to happen in.

More generally, it is a common observation that participating in a community of enquiry helps develop a wide range of good thinking **habits** and attitudes, of which any of the following could equally be chosen as a focus for a session – though, again, there are many such lists:

- Seriousness (taking people and their ideas seriously)
- Open-mindedness (being open to other perspectives and ready to change one's mind)
- Courage (being ready to stand up for oneself or others, or go against the flow)
- Reasonableness (being ready to give and to seek reasons)
- Accuracy (being concerned to establish the facts where possible and appropriate)
- Tenacity (sticking to the question or to the point, or even to one's principles)
- Empathy (being ready to see, or even feel, that others have different experiences and emotions)
- Sense of humour (to balance the seriousness!)
  o Information for consideration

But PSHE does, of course, have important 'content', and a P4C approach is not inimical to the introduction of information to young people in regard to drugs, alcohol, sexual health, and so on. What it urges is for such information to be presented not only in a balanced way, but also in such a way as to present a challenge of judgement to young people.

It is recognized as unwise simply to tell them how to react to the information. But it is also unwise to suppose that statistics or stories carry their own obvious message. What is needed, above all, is to stimulate some philosophical questioning around the basic concepts and values at play in these matters.

Below, there are examples of how such questions can be prompted by the use of real-life situations, stories and issues.

# Activities using PSHE and P4C

## Activity 1: Inferring (concluding) and implying (suggesting)

### Stimulus
An exercise, taken from Newswise (2006) based on a news story about a couple who had a baby in their early sixties.

### Resources

Newspaper article and exercise.

## Guidance

The activity below can be done in pairs or as a whole-group discussion.
NB You might find it simple enough to separate the **conclusion** from
the **reason(s)**, but the challenge is to make an **assessment** of how good
the reasoning is.

## Questions for the students

Clarify the **inference** (conclusion) in each of the following cases, and
then make a judgement as to whether the reasoning behind it is sound
or strong.

1. One baby boy, born in early July, received more attention than
   usual . . . because his mother was 62 years old, far older than the
   average woman having a baby.
2. A member of the public commented: 'She may not be too tired at
   62 but the next 16 years or so may be a different story to deal with
   a teenager's tantrums.'
3. An estimated one in ten British schoolchildren experience serious
   depression, due to factors such as divorce, bullying, exam pressures, drugs, and so on. So the government is experimenting with
   the idea of having 'happiness' lessons.

## Philosophical questions and concepts

*Questions*

- Does the birth of a baby always demand attention and celebration?
- Are the births of some babies more significant than the births of
  others?
- Why might it be a matter of concern that a mother is well above
  average age for giving birth?
- When might it be important to be close to the average?

*Concepts*
Celebration, reproduction, age, mother(hood), average(ness).

*Questions*

- What is public business?
- When does tiredness begin to affect one's judgement or capacity?
- If age brings wisdom, might that make for better parenting?

- What is the difference between a temper and a tantrum?
- Are teenage tantrums natural or are they social constructs? How could one best deal with tantrums?

*Concepts*
Public, comment, tiredness, parenting/upbringing, temper/tantrums, self-control

*Questions*

- What counts as depression, and when is it 'serious'?
- Is depression an 'experience' or state of mind, or what?
- What counts as bullying, and what are we to think and do about it?
- What do examinations examine, and what should they examine?
- Should we examine less, or more?
- Could people be examined without being put under pressure?
- Is all pressure on people bad for them?
- What counts as 'drugs', and what do we think and do about them?
- Is it the government's job to promote happiness, especially in young people?
- Can happiness be taught in 'lessons', and if so, how?

*Concepts*
Depression, experience, mind (changing), bullying/abuse of power, examination, pressure, drugs/medicines, government, happiness, learning (lessons)

### Notes (to be shared with the class before the exercise)

Some people confuse these two ideas, but they are different. To infer is to draw a clear conclusion on the basis of reasoning or evidence. To imply is to make a statement that suggests a conclusion without actually stating it clearly. (The conclusion, we sometimes say, is *implicit*, rather than explicit. We also use the noun *implication* for the conclusion that is *implied* but not stated.)

The next activity is also best done in pairs or as a whole-group discussion. NB You might try to agree on a statement beginning: 'This line of reasoning **suggests** that . . . .' But, of course, there may be different ways of starting or ending such a statement.

See if you can draw out an **implication** or conclusion from each of the following cases:

1. The couple had gone to a lot of trouble to get the medical treatment they needed to have the baby. But now they could not have been happier. (It might help to focus on the words 'trouble' and 'happier'.)
2. Spokesperson for CORE (Comment on Reproductive Ethics): 'I don't think it's an example to be followed.' (Consider how the mother might respond to this.)
3. The mother's doctor said she would provide the wisdom and strength to help him meet life's challenges and find his own happiness. (Concentrate on the little word 'to' – what is being implied about the relationship between what comes before and what comes after it?)

## Activity 2: Reasoning

### Stimulus
A newspaper article on obesity.

### Resources

An article around the subject of obesity and specifically another 'reasoning' exercise from Newswise (2004), which encourages critical questioning of public statements, in this case the subject of obesity in Australia.

### Guidance
You might start by discussing the questions suggested with the students, but that could very well give rise to further questions of your own. Or you could just find your own ways of 'critiquing' the statements, for example, questioning the **meaning** of what is said, or the **truth** of what is said (or what is assumed), or the **validity** (i.e. strength) of the argument, or the **value** (i.e. importance) being placed upon it.

### Critical questioning for the students

1. '*Sport is meant to keep people fit and lean. Australia is considered the most sporting nation in the world. So, how come Australia has a problem with obesity?*'
   What possible weaknesses can be found in the use of 'meant', 'considered', or 'sporting nation'?

2. *'The Australian government is giving extra money to schools that encourage children to eat healthier foods. With 1 in 4 Australians under 18 counted as obese, that seems reasonable enough.'*

   Schools may encourage children to eat healthier, but how likely are they to succeed? (Could some forms of 'encouragement' be more effective, and therefore more 'reasonable', than others?) Would this argument still apply if it were shown that the 1 in 4 obese youngsters were overeating at home?

3. *'One of the MPs argued that if MPs had a "puritanical" attitude about food, then people would ignore what they said.'*

   What assumption is this making about people's attitude to 'puritans'? Does the MP, or anyone else, have an agreeable definition of 'puritanical', since it clearly no longer means being a member of the 'puritan' Christian sect? Even if the definition includes some sense of being unpopular, does it follow that if what you say is unpopular, it will necessarily be ignored?

4. *'Obese people are not so easy to persuade into exercise. Perhaps food manufacturers should be persuaded to make less fattening foods cheaper.'*

   Does the second sentence follow from the first? Even if it does not, is it stronger if the first sentence is true than if the first sentence is not true?

5. *'Between the World Wars there was a real problem that children were underweight because of poor nutrition. Is it such a big problem, then, if only 8.5% of 6-year-olds and 15% of 15-year-olds are obese? Let's get the argument into proportion.'*

### *Philosophical questions and concepts*

- Someone might respond, 'Two wrongs don't make a right'. What would that mean in this case?
- Are being underweight and being overweight exactly comparable?
- Is it not right for expectations to rise over time?
- Does the word 'only' prejudice the argument?

## Activity 3: Dialogue

### *Stimulus: The Olympics*

Sadly, before every Olympics, the thorny issue of use of performance-enhancing drugs arises anew. But this can become a platform for serious consideration not only of the wider role of drugs in our society (including prescribed 'medicines') but also of what makes for human satisfaction and dissatisfaction (including honour and dishonour).

*Resources*

A dialogue from Newswise (2007).

*Guidance*

Below is a dialogue from Newswise (2007) that touches on these and other issues, and a range of philosophical questions that could be drawn out of the dialogue. Share the dialogue with the students, either in pairs, groups or as a whole class.

**A:** I see exam results are better, yet again.

**B:** *Yes. That's good news for those who sat them this year, but rather depressing for those who will be trying next year.*

**A:** Why depressing?

**B:** *Oh, well, there'll just be under even more pressure, won't they?*

**A:** Perhaps not. After all, if results get better year by year, perhaps that just means it gets easier to pass every year.

**B:** *Of course, that's what some people say. But it's not the only way to interpret the results.*

**A:** So, what's your theory, then?

**B:** *Well, there could be several. One is that the students are working harder every year. Another is that the teachers are preparing them better each year. Another is that the students are naturally more intelligent every year.*

**A:** Well, I heard that playing on computers could actually make you more intelligent.

**B:** *How did they argue that one?*

**A:** Oh, the idea was that your brain is having to process more information, more quickly, so it is getting more exercise. And just like physical exercise improves your fitness, so mental exercise improves your brain power.

**B:** *Could be. But I guess there are many ways of exercising your brain. And playing with computers doesn't seem to me much like exercise.*

**A:** Me neither. But perhaps that's just the point – we're used to lots of things happening around us, and so maybe we just cope with them better than older people.

**B:** *Mm. Tell that to my dad! Anyway, I do believe that most teachers are teaching students better.*

**A:** What makes you think that?

**B:** *My teachers are always coming up with new things to see and do in my lessons, whereas Mum tells me, in the old days, they just used to read books or lecture to the class, and everyone had to be very still and quiet.*

**A:** Nothing wrong with being still and quiet!

**B:** *No, so long as your brain is turned on. But if it isn't . . .*

**A:** Okay. I take your point.

**B:** *Besides, I heard a teacher on the TV news point out that people are always breaking records and pushing limits, in all sorts of ways, and why shouldn't that be happening in children's learning?*

**A:** Mm. I'm not so sure about that argument. Firstly, it's not everyone who is breaking records – that may be just for a few. Secondly, you've got to ask how they come to be doing it. Is it from their own efforts and abilities, or is it, for example, that they have better tools and technology? I'm thinking of climbing mountains, say, or deep-sea diving.

**B:** *Good points. And then, when you think about it, maybe some of the sporting records are gained through cheating. There seem to be lots of sports where the competitors are taking drugs – like the Tour de France, even. That's not just one man and a bike any longer.*

**A:** Agreed. But if we come back to exams, that is still one person and a pen, isn't it?

**B:** *Mm. You'd think so. But, another thing I heard is that students at some universities are now selling each other drugs that are supposed to help their brains work better in exams, just like some athletes take drugs to help them in their races.*

**A:** Really? Why don't the examiners ban them?

**B:** *Easier said than done, for one thing. For another, maybe it's not so bad after all – perhaps we should all take drugs to improve our brains. Why not? And thirdly, exams aren't everything. If they're not caught cheating at exams, they'll probably be found out later in life. Either they'll have what it takes to succeed in life, or they won't. Exams grades aren't everything.*

## *Philosophical questions and concepts*

- To what extent is life a competition, especially between young and old?
- How good (as distinct from effective) is competition in life?
- Can pressure lead to depression? Can it have the opposite effect? In either case, what exactly is going on?
- Are there degrees of pressure or depression, and if so when does either become 'real' or 'too much'?
- Which explanation of improving exam results seems most plausible? Might there be yet other theories? (Why) is there a need to explain it?

- Does 'intelligent' have one meaning or several? In any case, is it always desirable?
- Is processing information really exercise for the brain? What other forms of brain exercise might there be? Is exercise good in itself or only as a means to improve?
- Are more things happening now than in the past, and, if so, are older people not as able to cope with them as younger people?
- Is using better tools in sport a sort of cheating? Even if not, is it less admirable or satisfying than using worse tools, or no tools at all?
- Is a good diet likely to enhance performance in sport? If so, why shouldn't performance-enhancing drugs be counted as part of a good diet? Could this apply in the future to performance in studies as well as sports (e.g. a 'memory' drug)? If so, *should* it?

### Notes

These questions are mostly ethical, though in some cases they simply invite classical philosophical analysis, for example, the exploration of the concepts of 'depression' or 'intelligence' (which might also be located in the Philosophy of Mind).

Ideally, they would be drawn out of the dialogue by the pupils themselves in a deliberate exercise of critical questioning. But some stimuli provoke immediate discussion by pupils, and then the teacher might more naturally note questions as they arise, or perhaps help crystallize what question is being discussed.

In any event, it is by challenging pupils to clarify their own meanings, to corroborate their own claims, and to justify their own sense of value (good or bad, right or wrong, beautiful or ugly) that the facilitator brings the discipline of philosophy to bear on the issues.

## Citizenship and ethics

Of course, many issues have both personal and social, even ultimately political, dimensions, and so even if citizenship ceases to be a headline in the curriculum or timetable, there will still be questions of 'citizenship' to deal with in PSHE.

P4C, and Newswise in particular, contributed greatly to the appreciation that many such questions, if not all, were in effect philosophical questions. The grand concepts related to citizenship, such as democracy and decision making, freedom and authority, rights and responsibilities, fairness and exclusion, unity and diversity, individuality and community, crime and punishment, and even wealth and economy, all have their origins – and their continuing meanings – rooted in philosophy.

This is not to say that every PSHE teacher needs a philosophy degree, but it should encourage them to develop their own interests, if not their pupils', in the moral and political perspectives articulated in classical philosophy. The three most significant of these are probably Utilitarianism ('The Greatest Happiness Principle'), Deontology ('The Duty Principle') and Virtue Ethics ('The Good Character' approach).

There are several good, short introductions to these and other moral and political perspectives by modern British philosophers such as Simon Blackburn and Nigel Warburton, or Julian Baggini and Stephen Law, both of whom have written specially for the teenage market.

(But, for example, any discussion/enquiry in which the idea that 'you are free to do what you like with your own life' would be the better for some acquaintance with John Stuart Mill's short 1869 classic 'On Liberty'.)

Here are two enquiry plans from Newswise (1999), examining stereotyping and racism, in the wake of the murder of Stephen Lawrence – but, sadly, they remain issues for our society, and need to be addressed with our young citizens, whether we have 'citizenship' in the curriculum or not.

## Activity 4: Stereotyping

### Stimulus
Stereotyping – Newswise article.

### Resources
Quote from Duwayne Brooks.

### Guidance
The quote from Duwayne Brooks, below, is taken from the Newswise article and should provide sufficient stimulus in itself for the activity. But by all means give your own account, or present others, of the notorious murder.

In any case, it is suggested that you preface the activity itself with the explanation of the origin of the word 'stereotype'. Then present Duwayne's quote, and use the questions after it to help the students clarify their understanding of the word.

The word 'stereotype' originally had to do with printing. A stereotype  was a copy made using the same metal plate. Nowadays, the word is used more to mean saying (or thinking) that all people of the same TYPE or group are pretty much the same as each other, if not exactly copies or 'clones'.

It is possible for a stereotype to be 'positive', for example, to think that all nurses are good people, but most often stereotypes of other people are negative, and result in treating them badly. This is what Duwayne Brooks, a witness to the murder of his friend, Stephen Lawrence, accused the police of after the crime:

At the scene the police treated me like a liar, like a suspect instead of a victim, because I was black and they couldn't believe that white boys would attack us for nothing. They tried at the police station to get me to say that the attackers didn't call us nigger. They described me as violent, uncooperative, intimidating. They were stereotyping me as a young black male.

Which of the following are examples of stereotyping?

- Those Irish people must be good at music. They are always winning the Eurovision song contest.
- Women should have babies. All the women in my family have them.
- Only women have babies. No men in my family have them.
- Britain is a nation of television watchers.
- A boss tells a tall man he hasn't got a job because, 'tall people get too angry to be good with customers.' Then the tall man gets angry with the boss. Would the boss have been proved right?
- I thought the black youth who crossed the road to my side was going to attack and rob me so I ran away.
- It's obvious the police are racist from what Duwayne said about them.
- My dad had the same teacher as me and says he used to treat him just like he treats me.

*Notes*

Discussion of the above could be followed by a written activity, as below. It begins as a paired activity, but you could open it to the whole group whenever you like.

There is a big difference between the words 'all' and 'some' when it comes to making judgements about other people. In pairs, write a list of true statements about groups of people beginning with the words 'some'. Then write a list of true statements about groups of people beginning with the word 'all'. Compare your lists and give reasons for your choices. Then discuss whether it is possible to judge people **as they are**, and not by comparison with other people of the same type or group.

### Treating people the same and differently

Note to teacher: The following activity could also start with paired discussion, but each example could be also opened up for whole-group discussion.

Is anything wrong with what the following people say? Could they treat those they talk about the same but in a better way? Explain your thoughts.

- A boss said: I know some of my staff don't eat pork, but I want to treat everyone the same. I'll invite them all to a pork supper at my house.
- The gas man said: I warned everyone in the street to leave their homes because of the dangerous gas leak. I know some of them didn't speak English but I didn't do anything special for them. I treated everyone the same.
- A teacher said: You're all going to stay in at break time because some people were noisy. I want to treat everyone the same.
- A shopkeeper said: I'm bad-tempered with everyone, black and white. I treat everyone the same.

(These are fictional examples. There is no intention to stereotype the kinds of people mentioned.)

*Philosophical questions and concepts*

- Is it possible for someone to think they treat everyone the same when, in fact, they don't? Explain your thoughts.

The Stephen Lawrence Inquiry report says racism means 'using conduct or words or practices that advantage or disadvantage others because of their colour, culture or ethnic origin.'

- Is this different from saying we should treat all people the same?
- Could we treat people the same but disadvantage some of them? If so how?
- Can ignoring someone be a 'practice'? If so, then every time you ignore someone, does that mean you are being racist?

The main focus of such enquiries is on practising and developing *good judgement* – so that, whatever situations young people are in, and whatever changes they face (which will be many), they can set about making their choices and decisions in a serious and systematic way.

## Conclusion

### *Being open to complexity*

To conclude, there are many issues that young people have to face as they enter the adult world, both personal and social, some comparatively small or some comparatively large. Most people agree that the range and complexity of these issues continues to grow, and that is why it was right for the 2010 government to review the PSHE curriculum in England and Wales.

It was also welcome that they said:

There needs to be room in the life of the school for an exploration of wider social issues which contribute to the well-being and engagement of all pupils. It should be for teachers, not government, to design the lessons and the experiences which will engage pupils. Different schools may want to cover different life skills, reflecting their pupils' interests and local circumstances.

The P4C approach has always been one of openness – not only to address the wider issues in the lives of young people but to do so through open enquiry, rather than through closed worksheets.

By this approach even the dullest of issues deemed necessary to be addressed, such as health and safety, can be brought to life – or, one might say, life can be brought to the enquiry. The process would be to problematize the very concept of safety, asking – not assuming – what it is, and how much it is to be sought. It is not exactly 'safe' for young people to start questioning their parents' values, but there comes a time when it is natural, and perhaps even necessary for personal fulfilment, for that to happen. What teachers can best do at such a time is 'scaffold' the intellectual journeys of the young people in their charge, modelling and motivating thinking that is constructive and compassionate.

### PSHE as practice – in self-management – rather than a 'subject'

The route needs to be reconceived, not as a subject or 'study' in the conventional sense but as an intellectual journey or 'exercise' in which well-managed talking and thinking leads to better self-management and judgement.

As the PSHE Association briefing paper (2009) by Dr Jenny McWhirter, put it:

The aim of PSHE education is not to determine how people should behave or what lifestyle or financial choices they should make. PSHE education is about the provision of information and the development of skills and attitudes which enable children and young people to make effective choices and take opportunities which will help them to live happy, successful, healthy lives, now and in the future.

### Philosophy: A School of Freedom

P4C provides a model, methods and materials for conducting such a journey. If all aspiring teachers were educated into facilitating philo-sophical enquiry and dialogue, they would be ready for the challenge of PSHE teaching.

Meanwhile, for those who are already meeting that challenge, P4C provides the simple reminder that good PSHE teaching *is* philosophical teaching. It is putting aspects of life into question, and using all one's intellectual and other resources to come up with the best answers one can to that questioning.

It is to follow the spirit of the UNESCO publication of 2007, *Philosophy: A School of Freedom*, – a study 'dedicated to the young spirits of today, bound to become the active citizens of tomorrow' advising the teaching of philosophy as 'a fertile guarantor of liberty and autonomy'.

To conduct PSHE education without such a moral framework and without the discipline of philosophy that makes sense of such a framework is to put such citizens – and all our futures – at too much risk. (There again, 'risk' is an important concept to problematize!)

# Further resources

## Websites

Newswise was a series of news stories specially adapted and developed by Steve Williams and Roger Sutcliffe between 1999 and 2009. Those of perennial interest for PSHE can now be accessed by subscribers to www.p4c.com, the online resource and collaboration website, where there are many other resources and exercises written by a variety of authors.

Many other websites, of course, contain or point to materials fit for philosophical enquiry in the social field, particularly that of Global Citizenship, and the following Development Education Centre sites are particularly recommended because the centres have incorporated P4C in their work with schools.

www.cdec.org.uk/content/view/54/57/

www.cheshiredec.org/

www.decsy.org.uk/default.asp

In general, there are few resources purpose-written for philosophical enquiry in the field of PSHE. This is partly because the spirit of P4C is towards open enquiry based on either 'real life' or on narratives or art that reflect the human condition without trying to limit the philosophical response. There is, however, a set of hard-hitting video resources produced in Australia for upper secondary students that not only raises issues ranging from the interpersonal to the international, but also provides fascinating teacher notes that track some philosophical approaches to those issues down the ages. This is the website: www.ethicsonline.net/index.html

# References

Claxton, G. (2008) *What's the Point of School?* Oxford: Oneworld Publications.

Department for Education (2010) *The Importance of Teaching: Schools White Paper 2010.* London: HMSO, www.education.gov.uk [accessed 1 October 2011].

Lipman, M. (1980) *Philosophy in the Classroom*. Philadelphia: Temple University Press.

— (2008) *A Life Teaching Thinking*. Montclair: Institute for the Advancement of Philosophy for Children.

McWhirter, J. (2009) *Personal, Social, Health and Economic Education: From Theory to Practice.* London: PSHE Association.

Mill, J. S. (1869) *On Liberty.* London: Longman, Roberts and Green.

UNESCO (2007) *Philosophy: A School of Freedom.* Paris: UNESCO.

Welsh Government (2008) Personal and Social Education Framework for 7 to 19-Year-Olds in Wales – Ref: AC/GM/0828, ISBN: 978 0 7504 4432 3, available from www.wales.gov.uk/personalandsocialeducation

## Chapter Outline

Connections between history and P4C            167
Activities using history and P4C               174
Conclusion                                     177

# Connections between history and P4C

The study of history has moved on from what some might see as an overemphasis on the acquisition of facts in traditional history lessons. There is an increasing understanding with both teachers and students that this is no longer enough; instead more and more, history is focused on the selection and interpretation of these facts and more importantly the concepts, such as nationalism and diversity of cultures that underpin them.

In the modern world we have all the information we need and access to it is becoming increasingly easy. The challenge now is to process this wealth of information which can be overwhelming, and apply it for our needs by making considered responses and good judgements. The challenge is the ability to 'see the wood for the trees' in the school context but becomes more important in the outside world and we look to develop the skills students will need in the twenty-first century. How students face up to this increasing challenge of how to make discerning and well-reasoned judgements is supported by philosophical enquiry, as we endeavour to answer more complex questions that arise. As a subject, history is about interpretations and opinions; students need to be able to analyse and assess these interpretations to fully involve themselves in its study. To achieve this we look to our students not only to recall important facts but to skilfully apply them to reach a supported conclusion, or to investigate the different interpretations before coming to an answer. P4C offers an excellent approach to this process of interpretation. Through a community of enquiry students are challenged to question what they believe as they search for clarity in their reasoning.

P4C supports the teaching of the key concepts such as 'interpretation'. As outlined further a P4C teacher will look to spot and act on the opportunities for a community of enquiry when they arise in the study of a topic as well as planning for discrete P4C sessions.

## Philosophical skills and concepts in history

Therefore, in this chapter I aim to show how the implementation of P4C and the infusion of its habits and skills cannot only enhance the teaching and the learning experience of students but also have an impact on their success in the study of history. It is no longer sufficient for a student to say 'William the Conqueror won at the Battle of Hastings' without saying why. The use of P4C does not allow for this level of response as it pushes students for more considered and extended responses to challenging questions.

Issues and concepts such as 'significance' in history are not, and should not be, straight forward. For example, if we take the skills highlighted in *Thinking through Philosophy* (Cleghorn, 2002, p. 2) who can argue that these do not underpin good history teaching?

• Information handling
• Enquiry
• Reasoning
• Evaluation

Or if we take the skills highlighted in the *SAPERE Level 1 Handbook* again the connection to the teaching of history is clear.

• Reflecting on ideas from all sources
• Connecting

- Identifying different perspectives
- Using examples

Not only do these examples of skills and dispositions, which are the focus of P4C, sit at the heart of a historians' approach to historical material, but they are also reinforced by the structure and application of P4C. In a community of enquiry, students know that they cannot make unsupported claims without clear reasons or evidence. They also have the expectation that their claims will be challenged in the first instance by the teacher as facilitator, who with skilful questioning techniques, delves deeper into the students' thinking. As the community grows in its skill and confidence, this role will be taken up by other students. These skills also sit at the heart of public exam mark schemes. For example, the Aims and Learning Outcomes of the OCR History B Modern World GCSE specification (OCR GCSE B, 2009) includes:

- develop the ability to ask relevant questions about the past and to investigate them critically using a range of sources in their historical content
- organize and communicate their historical knowledge, understanding in creative and different ways and reach substantiated judgements

If this clear connection were not enough there is also proof of the link within the mark schemes, as we can see from this extract from the OCR mark scheme.

This marking scheme has been designed to assess candidates' understanding of the **key concepts** of the course, and their ability to use source material to illustrate their understanding. These concepts, and the ability to **interpret** and **evaluate** source material, are central to GCSE history, and it is, therefore, upon these that the marking scheme focuses. The candidates' factual knowledge is important, but it is only rewarded if it is used to back up the **demonstration of understanding** of these concepts.

An example of this is the exam question 'Explain why Franz Ferdinand was assassinated?' (OCR GCSE History B A971 Aspects of International Relations, 2010, Question 5B) and the mark scheme – Level 5 explains three or more reasons or develops two explained reasons. The emphasis on explanation and developed reasons matches well with the habits and skills the students should develop through the use of P4C. There are almost no marks for a purely factual answer but for explaining where the answer came from. The evaluation and selection of evidence that leads students to the conclusion, 'informed by evidence', is what is rewarded and the ability to do this well is developed in the habits of philosophical enquiry. This can also be seen as the result of 'good' history teaching but for students and teachers well versed in P4C it will come more naturally and continue to support the development of the habits that are at the centre of the community of enquiry.

It is not just in public exams that there is the focus on key concepts and skills highlighted by P4C, but also in the National Curriculum where the underpinning key concepts, such as '**Using Evidence . . .** evaluate the sources used in order to reach reasoned conclusions'. Therefore, this focus at all key stages makes the role of philosophy in our teaching not only welcome but necessary.

## Language and questioning in history

In our teaching we often reflect on the need for clarity and focus. How many times have you told your students to answer the specific question asked or challenged the relevance of evidence and detail in answers? The habits and facilitation of the community of enquiry reinforce the need for this. Philosophy with constant reflection and focus on the chosen question and knowledge that contributions must be both clear and supported by relevant evidence is excellent preparation for the thinking required to produce not just oral answers but also written answers of a similar ilk. The students internalize the philosophical skills and dispositions that they practice collaboratively with their peers, something that is very much a result of the P4C approach and would not be as explicit in other approaches to teaching history. The self-reflection required in a community of enquiry is embedded in the structure and so students are challenged to internalize and formulate their answers before sharing them.

The language of philosophy also sits neatly with the language of history, for example, our use of the words – evidence, judgement, explain, clarity. For students the constant reinforcement through the use of such language and the application of it in different situations from philosophical enquiries to formal assessments will help further embed understanding of both its meaning and application.

For example, read this short dialogue:

**Student**: 'I think Hitler was misunderstood.'
**Teacher**: 'What **evidence** do you have for this idea?'
**Student**: 'He provided jobs for German people and eased the problem of unemployment.'
**Teacher**: 'Can you **clarify** what you mean by German people?'
**Student**: 'Ah, that's difficult to **explain** as in this context it's what Hitler believed but many others would also consider themselves to be German despite him saying they were not.'
**Teacher**: 'Did Hitler help these *German people*'?
**Student**: 'The difficulty is what is meant by people; are we meaning those who are in the country of Germany or in the wider sense?
**Teacher**: 'What do you think constitutes a German person?'

From here a deeper enquiry develops as we struggle with the concept of nationalism and belonging. It is the application of the questioning techniques and the habits that have developed in the student from their experience of community of enquiry that result in such a dialogue as the students hone in on the wider concept of 'people'. A further activity following this dialogue might be to investigate the concept of 'nationalism'. You might ask the students to

list five things we would mention when describing Britain to someone else
list five things that makes Britain different to other places

or present the following philosophical questions:

'What makes us, us?'
'Do we have common beliefs?'
'Do members of a nation need to be the same?'

Not only would this enquiry support investigation into the concept of nationalism but also bring in such concepts as diversity and multiculturalism into the lesson.

The P4C approach works because issues in history are not straight forward but need to be thoroughly investigated and questioned. Central to this are the questioning skills of the teacher. Therefore, it is important that we model good questioning. The questioning techniques highlighted by P4C are an excellent tool to deepen the students' thinking as addressed in an earlier chapter.

Do you have any evidence for that?
How do you know that?
Not sure I understand that, can you give me an example?

These go beyond the community of enquiry and again right into supporting the search for clarity and more thoughtful and rigorous responses in history. Through this approach we are embedding the historical skills needed, such as the need for evidence to support what you say in the search for clarity of ideas. As 'co-enquirers' our questioning and philosophical skills develop alongside our students who become more able to respond at a deeper level and to ask searching questions. This is supported by awareness that reasoned interpretation is an accepted and valued response. As this becomes a permanent expectation in our interactions with students, they will aim to reach it. This wish to develop certain student behaviours through the application of philosophy in our lessons has a clear pay-off.

## Dispositions and reasonableness

Who would not want a student and therefore a class that can wait its turn, show respect and tolerance for other conflicting ideas? These dispositions and behaviours are taught, modelled and built upon through the use of community of enquiry. As we seek to develop more 'reasonable' students, not just in thought but also in behaviour, the study of history is well placed to explore and develop both meanings of 'reasonable' here. Taking examples from the past, such as the use of the bomb over Nagasaki, the students can investigate whether this was a 'reasonable' response to the situation. This is a significant change to the more traditional approach of 'was it the right thing to do?' as the enquiry is taken out of the subject matter and into a more philosophical realm of 'what is a reasonable response?'

As history teachers look to relate their lessons to current events this becomes an increasingly interesting area to develop. For example, the

Western intervention in Afghanistan could be interpreted as both a 'reasonable' and 'unreasonable' response to the 9/11 attacks. History is often involved with the concept of 'reasonable' and P4C allows students to explore it in depth and apply their understanding not just to the subject matter but their own behaviour and responses to situations in their own lives. The benefits of using P4C are then taken out of the classroom and into the lives and education of students. Students investigate and come to an understanding of what 'reasonable' means and this affects the wider disposition that society seeks from the education of young people. The highlighting and investigation of dispositions are central to the P4C approach. It is relatively easy to source a stimulus that would generate questions around concepts of thoughtfulness or reasonableness. The ability to link the concepts studied in history to everyday or current situations certainly supports the engagement of the students and their enjoyment of the subject.

There are many other concepts that can be explored by taking a P4C approach to the teaching of history. For example, the National Curriculum highlights concepts such as '**Cause and Consequence** and **Interpretation**'. The exploration of these key concepts through a community of enquiry will not only lead to a deeper understanding but allow the students to arrive at their understanding through a more collaborative and engaging approach. The highlighting of causes is an underlying theme of history teaching. As we investigate profoundly significant events such as the First World War there will be multiple causes. A more philosophical approach might generate questions such as:

When does rivalry turn to war?
If we join a war does that make us as bad as the enemy?
Why are people not satisfied?
Why do people always want more?

Exploring historical scenarios with a philosophical perspective leads us to examine words and concepts such as war, enemy, rivalry and motivation. In seeking to answer these questions through a community of enquiry we have made the concepts both accessible and engaging. For many, history can be seen as a dry subject but in an enquiry the concepts are ones the students can relate to and find meaningful. Students can also work on their understanding in a more collaborative way. A community of enquiry is not debate but allows all to throw ideas into the 'melting pot' and therefore build a shared understanding and response to the question the students have generated.

# Activities using history and P4C

## Activity 1: War

### Stimulus

Cards with facts and topics about World War.

### Resources

Quotes or facts such as:

'The war to end all wars'
'Lions led by donkeys'
'20,000 killed on the first morning'
'The Great War'

### Guidance

Present a selection of facts or quotes about the topic about to be studied in pairs or in small groups. In pairs, students are asked to generate five questions they would like to ask. The pairs are then challenged to narrow this down to one question.

### Philosophical questions and concepts

- How can it be the war to end all wars when there are still wars now?
- In war, who is innocent and who is guilty?

### Notes

The concept of innocence as well as war is likely to be explored. The nature of innocence lends itself well to the wider concept of 'interpretation'. In this way we can develop a student's understanding of historical concepts. We stimulate the students' sense of 'wonderment' as the open-ended nature of the stimulus allows them to 'wonder' at the meaning of such concepts and so are able to understand their impact on cause and effect in history. To support this, as the facilitator of the enquiry, a good question that stems during the question generation is 'What are you wondering about . . .? which reinforces the openness and personal connection of the activity.

A further extension of this method of students generating questions can also be used to personalize the history. Not only will this help support their engagement in the subject but also their sense of enjoyment as this is enhanced by making connections with the people involved in the events.

The relationship between students' initiation of philosophical ideas and questions in response to the delivery of historical information can form a cycle of enquiry. Information can arouse questions and enquiry that then leads to further investigation and research of historical material. Taught history combined effectively with philosophical enquiry creates a very clear and structured model for students to engage with the subject matter in a deeper and more effective way as the community of enquiry is designed to promote opportunities to generate philosophical dialogue within clear and understood guidelines.

## Activity 2: Reflections on being a soldier

*Stimulus*
Photograph of a soldier at the end of the First World War.

*Resources*
Photograph displayed on IWB or copies for small groups.

*Guidance*
The students are challenged to formulate a question, in pairs, that they would like to ask an individual in a photograph or illustration.

*Philosophical questions and concepts*

- Was it worth it?
- If you could go back would you make the same decisions?
- Is anything worth fighting for?

*Notes*

We can take the opportunity to explore wider concepts such as fate and value by selecting one of these questions for a community of enquiry.

## Activity 3: The Holocaust

*Stimulus*

A photograph of victims of the Holocaust.

*Resources*

A photograph of victims of the Holocaust.

*Guidance*

Ask the students to decide first to whom they would ask their question if they were able to. Again this provides an opportunity for the students to 'personalize' the history.

*Philosophical questions and concepts*

- Would you seek revenge?
- Is it wrong to seek revenge?
- Can people really forgive?
- When should you forgive others?
- Should you hide your faith?

The concepts that maybe highlighted by student questions are revenge and forgiveness, faith and culture, and these can form the basis for questions and enquiry.

*Notes*

These examples for generating the questions are fairly straightforward and easily applied. As we increasingly incorporate the use of P4C in our teaching, opportunities for an enquiry will present themselves. It is important that we can spot and therefore run with these as often the impetus will come from the students.

## Activity 4: Slavery and identity

In the context of studying slavery you may consider with the students the impact of having your name changed and the importance of names in general.

## Stimulus
Activity on names.

## Guidance
Ask the students to list all the names that they have been called, for example:

Doug
Douglas
Mr Paterson
Mr DWL Paterson
The odd nickname

then to compare and discuss these in small groups.

## Philosophical questions and concepts

- Is your name important to you?
- Does the name you are called change your behaviour?
- Why do we have different names for different situations?
- Whose name is it (from the idea that different people assign differ-ent names to you, for example, parents, school friends)?

## Notes
Once again the subject matter creates an opportunity to investigate an underlying concept, that of identity and personality. The outcome of an enquiry is likely to be a better understanding of the impact of forci-bly changing someone's name and this will impact the students' further study of slavery. The personalization of the subject matter not just to a single person as shown in earlier examples but to ourselves and our own experiences can support the connection with the subject and allow the students to pursue the concepts at a deeper and more personal level.

# Conclusion

I would argue that P4C can and does enhance the enjoyment and chal-lenge students gain from the study of history. It also reinforces the habits and dispositions we want for and from our students. The respect and tolerance that community of enquiry can build is an important part of the teaching of history as we explore different cultures, events and times. Again it is not the recall of the facts surrounding the events that counts but our deeper understanding and learning about concepts such as diversity and interpretation that makes the combination of P4C and history such an exciting one. Especially at a time when the teaching of history is high on the political agenda and more schools look to put history back into their Key Stage 4 Curriculum with the arrival of the Baccalaureate, it is important that we take this opportunity to enhance our teaching to support the development of students who can think more deeply and widely than before. P4C may not be the only approach to build these skills and habits but to my mind for the reasons outlined in this book it is one of the best.

# Further reading

*Dilemma-Based Learning in the Humanities* (with Phil Wood and Deborah Michel; London: Chris Kington, 2007).

# Further resources

Intelligent Learning: The Dialogue of Active Minds – A Video Based Training Course to Promote Curiosity, Independent Learning and Thinking Skills [DVD].

## Websites

http://firstworldwar.com
www.historytl.com
www.ocr.org.uk
www.philosophy4children.co.uk
www.redcross.org.uk/What-we-do/Teaching-resources/Teaching-packages/Robots-in-war/Autonomous-robots
www.unicef.org.uk

# References

Cleghorn, P. (2002) *Thinking through Philosophy Book 4*. Great Britain: Print Publishing.
OCR (2009) OCR GCSE (Full Course) in History B J417.
— (2010) GCSE History B A971 Aspects of International Relations.
*SAPERE Level 1 Handbook* (2010) (3rd edn), Great Britain, Fairprint.co.uk

# P4C in Geography `10`

Dick Palfrey

## Chapter Outline

Connections between geography and P4C                    179

Activities using geography and P4C                      184

Conclusion                                              196

# Connections between geography and P4C

For geography teachers, P4C offers the opportunity to engage young people with a wide range of perspectives on the world: the ethical, aesthetic, political and logical questions that underpin the discipline of geography. If students can engage with the subject in these ways they will be more able to respond well to the challenging questions that they encounter in this subject.

## Geographical enquiry

Secondary school geography's main pedagogical method has for long now been encompassed in the term 'enquiry', handed down from the original '16–19 Project' to GCSE, and the National Curriculum, as a sequence of questions followed by essentially scientific investigation. Enquiry in geography is, however, often neglected, not least because it can be difficult to engage in, particularly in short lessons in a crowded syllabus. Margaret Roberts (2003, pp. 44–6) identifies a framework for enquiry learning at Key Stage 3 which uses a variety of enquiry approaches. Introducing philosophical enquiry to geography can diversify the enquiry, helping learners become more critical, and to delve deeper into subject material. In relation to Margaret Roberts' framework, philosophical enquiry moves it forward from a sequence of question, data collection, analysis and reflection to one which starts from the questions and quickly identifies and focuses on the key concept embedded in the question. (The contrast between these two approaches is further explored in Rowley (2006).)

The following examples (taken from key processes of geography for Key Stage 3) illustrate the appropriateness of developing enquiry skills with students. (NB some subsections are omitted as less appropriate.)

In geographical enquiry students should be able to:

1. ask geographical questions, thinking critically, constructively and creatively
2. identify bias, opinion and abuse of evidence in sources when investigating issues
3. draw and justify conclusions
4. find creative ways of using and applying geographical skills and understanding to create new interpretations of place and space
5. plan geographical enquiries, suggesting appropriate sequences of investigation
6. solve problems and make decisions to develop analytical skills and creative thinking about geographical issues.

In terms of graphicacy and visual literacy we may consider the question: 'How important are maps to geographers?' It could be asserted that maps and *mapping* don't feature strongly or centrally enough in many secondary geography lessons. If they don't, then the lesson is in danger of not being 'geography' at all, but science, or citizenship, and so on. Where maps *are* used, it may only be for the purpose of 'location', when so much more sophisticated demands can be deployed through a map or other spatial diagram, whether on-screen GIS, or paper-based. The curriculum also refers to 'geographical communication' with which students should be able to communicate their knowledge and understanding using geographical vocabulary and conventions in speech.

## Why philosophy in geography?

Geography has much to benefit from using philosophical enquiry and indeed has a long history of questioning not only what it teaches and how it teaches, but also the nature of the subject itself. A first, very important, and often neglected question 'what is geography?' is sometimes reduced with younger secondary school students to sifting systematic branches of content into 'Physical', 'Human' and 'Environmental'. There is much more scope than this in exploring the nature of this rich subject, which is steeped in philosophical changes itself.

In fact, the epistemology, or theory of knowledge, in geography has a very rich and varied history, and as we perhaps pride ourselves on leading the school curriculum in taking alternative multicultural 'world views', we are, at the same time, perhaps purveying the subject itself as rather 'mono-philosophical' and one that is dominated by a scientific approach.

Our subject has evolved and matured through different historical phases and emphases: geography as content, geography as skills and geography as (a particular) philosophy. The content approach gave rise to the world regional 'capes and bays' (geography as facts). As this body of knowledge became organized, geographical concepts, skills and 'models' began to be distilled from it, and, by the late 1960s, with the subject becoming ever more influenced by science, the 'quantitative revolution' developed more abstract approaches, often models based. Unfortunately, the core of the subject, real places, was often forgotten in the process (despite earlier excellence displayed in the field of regional description).

The 1970s saw the birth and growth of two major critiques to what had been identified as 'positivist' geography, both based on opposing philosophies of the world: humanistic and radical geography, the former based on unique personal feelings associated with place experiences, and the latter emerging from a Left/Marx-inspired critique of the capitalist system itself (which scientific geography had taken as an assumed unstated assumption). Johnson (1983) described and contrasted these three ways of seeing geography.

To apply these to, for example, the recent tsunami in Japan the following questions could be posed, each to represent of the three philosophies:

What was the distribution of destroyed settlements? (positivist)
How might it have felt like to be in Japan at the time of the disaster? (humanistic)
Why was a Nuclear power station built by the sea in an area known for its earthquakes and tsunami's? (radical)

Young people need to consider all three types of questions, but often the latter two are neglected. Although critiques of positivist geography emerged strongly in the 1980s, they had less influence on schools than might be expected. The National Curriculum, introduced to schools at the end of the decade, had the effect of restrengthening the scientific approach for the next couple of decades, producing an imbalance, represented in the following Venn diagram (Figure 10.1), that is still sometimes evident in school geography.

Any geographer looking to review the balance of philosophies in their teaching could benefit from looking at *Thinking on the Edge* (Rowley and Lewis, 2003), a visually-attractive guide to landscape fieldwork

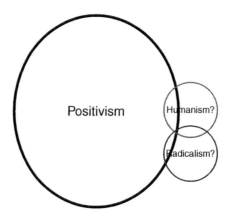

**Figure 10.1** A Venn diagram to depict the suggested imbalance in school geography philosophies in the National Curriculum

around Morecambe Bay, but which is far more widely applicable as a ubiquitous challenge to our involvement of learners into key landscape concepts. Some of the concepts included in that book – sacredness and beauty, boundaries, change and classification – are all contestable concepts. The importance of concepts in deepening geography cannot be overestimated. As a result the following examples of stimuli for philosophical enquiry are related to the key concepts of National Curriculum geography.

## Values

Geography abounds with instances of not just facts and concepts, but also questions of values and interpretation, that is, whose interpretation is this? This values awareness is essential to most geographical questions. If we ask a question such as 'Should we build a Severn barrage to tap tidal power?' philosophical enquiry is essential for students to get to grips with what the underlying issues are in order to make a reasoned judgement.

When considering value judgements about standards of living across the world students may perceive that there has perhaps been an over-emphasis on economic measures reflecting a Western business culture. More recently, social and environmental measures have gained more parity with economic measures such as the degree of freedom from light pollution at night. There is current UK government interest in studies of 'happiness' and 'well-being'. A BBC news report features the concept of happiness being discussed by the United Nations:

Bhutan has put the politics of happiness on the UN's agenda. This week the General Assembly adopted a non-binding resolution that aims to make happiness a 'development indicator'. Bhutan's ambassador Lhatu Wangchuk told the BBC the next step was to help UN members better understand the concept. (www.bbc.co.uk/news/world-14243512 [accessed 22 October 2011)

Geography offers opportunities for students to ask rich questions and to examine their own value judgements in relation to others and the world.

# Activities using geography and P4C

## Concepts in geography

The 'key concepts' in the National Curriculum are place, space, scale, interdependence, physical and human processes, environmental inter-action and sustainable development, cultural understanding and diversity. The examples to follow show opportunities for tackling complex philosophical ideas and concepts in a community of enquiry.

### Place

Geographers have experienced some difficulty in agreeing, and communicating, what they mean by the concept of 'sense of place'. At a basic level, there is the 'guide book/text book' sense of 'objective reality' of 'place'. Then, at another level, there is a more subjective, selective, remembered, personal or emotive space, in which reality has been individualized. This involves seemingly insignificant details which become more real for me/you as a memory than 'facts', that is, it *is* part of Aberystwyth, it *is* there, but only for me. This sense of place is reflected in the National Curriculum for geography as the students' personal experience of place. The following questions illustrate the kinds of philosophical concepts that students will address:

What is geography?
What does bringing a geographical focus contribute?
What do we understand by 'a sense of place'?
How important are maps to geographers?
How important is it to visit a place being studied?
What is a region?

Later in the chapter there is a case study of a field trip (the Uffington White Horse) that raises questions about landscape.

## Activity 1: Landscape

### Stimulus

Photograph of landscape (Figure 10.2), a scrap heap on the south side of the Colne Valley, west of Huddersfield, looking northwest over Slaithwaite towards Marsden, from High House Edge.

**Figure 10.2** Photograph by Dick Palfrey

Images in geography can be very powerful. In this landscape photograph note the typical hallmarks of a stimulus as containing some contradiction or puzzlement.

### Resources
An image of the photograph displayed for the whole class.

### Guidance
Ask the students to consider their personal responses to this image, then share and discuss them in small groups. Each group then creates one philosophical question that they would like to discuss.

### Philosophical questions and concepts

- How far should the landscape be managed?
- What do we understand by 'sense of place'?
- Why do I like this place more than that place?
- Are some places more favoured than others?

### Notes
There are many good examples of film footage available on the internet. One example is walking 'El Camino del Rey' in El Chorro, Southern

Spain. This is a supposedly closed, dangerous traverse of a high level rock gorge, along rickety pathways, but which attracts adrenalin junkies like a magnet, to not only cross it, but film it in a blasé style.

### Space

Radical geographers have challenged questions of space in the context of the way we deal with power, finance and 'justice', with consideration of the alternatives. Authors in geography who analyse 'space' from a critique of the way world capitalism moves money investments across space are David Harvey (*Limits to Capital, The Enigma of Capital: And the Crises of Capitalism, Spaces of Global Capitalism: Towards a Theory of Uneven Geographical Development, The Condition of Postmodernity: An Enquiry into the Origins of Cultural Change*, besides many, possibly more accessible, lectures, interviews and readings available online) and Roger Lee (*Geographies and Moralities: International Perspectives on Development, Justice and Place*, with David M. Smith (RGS-IBG Book Series), and *Geographies of Economies*, with Jane Wills).

## Activity 2: Emotions map

Doreen Massey (2005) examines our position in the crossroads of time and space. She talks of 'Thinking Space' and challenges the dominant notion of maps as representing only the connections of a horizontal surface. Philosophy offers us the opportunity to use stimuli that challenge our views and uses of maps. Using, for example, the 'Emotional Map of Greenwich' (Nold, 2006, http://emotionmap.net and Ordnance Survey 2006) a class could be involved in producing their own 'emotions map'.

Emotion Maps encourage personal reflection on the complex relationship between oneself, the environment and one's fellow citizens. In a group, people commented about their experiences and left annotations on the map. To create the communal Greenwich Emotion Map all the individual walks were aggregated to visualise a shared landscape of emotion. The map contains particular arousal hotspots reflecting many of the local discussions about regeneration of the Peninsula. (http://emotionmap.net/ [accessed 22 October 2011])

## Stimulus

Emotional Map of Greenwich.

## Resources

Copies of the map or access to the website.

## Guidance

Students may simply reflect on this stimulus or create their own emotion maps as suggested above before generating philosophical questions.

## Philosophical questions and concepts

- What makes us feel safe in some places and not others?
- Why are there differences in how we 'see' places?
- Is 'happiness' something that we can measure?
- How does experience influence how we feel about a place?

## Notes

This activity needs to be carried out in the context of work on how we feel about places. Prior work might include consideration of which places make us feel 'happy' or 'unhappy' and different aspects of 'happiness', or what characteristics make places 'special'. We might also consider different ways of mapping feelings and emotions.

## Scale

Concepts of scale involve appreciating different scales – from personal and local to national, international and global and making links between scales to develop understanding of geographical ideas. One of the distinctive facets of a geographer's eye is the tendency to zoom in or out in scale, as adeptly as a driver changes gear. This ability develops through constant use of a range of representations of place.

# Activity 3: Home, using air photographs as a stimulus

## Stimulus

The images of Yann Arthus Bertrand, or his film *Home* is a resource that offers a wealth of stimuli for questioning how we see the world.

### Guidance

Introduce the context of the film *Home* and watch the clip 'Home . . . The adventure of Yann Arthus Bertrand'. Yann Arthus Bertrand says the film needed to 'create a question'. Ask the students what questions they think he wanted to create?

### Philosophical questions and concepts

- Can we see beauty in all we see?
- Do films like this change how we think about the world?
- Is it OK to film people from the air?
- How does 'knowing something' change how we act?

### Interdependence

This involves exploring the social, economic, environmental and political connections between places and understanding the significance of interdependence in change, at all scales. There are often excellent stimuli in news items, particularly in relation to the 'global commons' such as ocean resources. An example which draws on ideas of interdependence, strongly linked to the section on 'Cultural understanding and diversity' (p. 191), is the complex background to the thorny and persisting geographical issue of Kashmir. Various maps and cartoons are available on this topic (see excellent multi-solution map-based presentation/enquiry titled 'The Future of Kashmir?' at http://news.bbc.co.uk/1/shared/spl/hi/south_asia/03/kashmir_future/html/)

This raises many ethical questions for students:

'[How far] Should the British hand in creating issues in the past, still trouble us [Brits] today?'

'Should the cold war between India and Pakistan over this region, each still controlling a part of Kashmir today, interfere with a resolution in which the majority of Kashmiris today appear to want independence?'

'Would it be irresponsible for the international community to help create a new land-locked state, whose economy would be dependent upon trade and transport links through and with India and Pakistan?'

'Would this at least remove the artificial North–South divide between Pakistani-controlled and Indian-controlled Kashmir, allowing significant East–West movement, for tourists and locals, along the natural valleys of the Himalayas?'

'What is the right thing to do?' 'Who should decide? And how?'

## Activity 4: Fishing rights

*Stimulus*

News article: 'African fishers tell EU fleets: Stop stealing our fish!'

*Resources*

Copies of the news story or access to the article online.

*Guidance*

A range of research might be undertaken on this topic to inform questions raised by the students. This could be used in the context of work on a West African locality or on ocean resources. It requires some prior knowledge of fishing, the scale of fishing, the distances fishers travel and the influence of the Common Fisheries Policy on both European and non-European fishers. This is a short article and could be read in class or as homework prior to raising questions. What are the ethical questions raised, for example, by the issue of British fishing boats off Senegal, one of the poorest countries dependent on protein from the sea?

*Philosophical questions and concepts*

- Who owns the sea?
- How do we decide how much of the resources to use?
- Are British fishers stealing from Senegal?
- Who should decide what fish can be taken from where?

*Physical and human processes*

In trying to understand how sequences of events and activities in the physical and human worlds lead to change in places, landscapes and societies the concept of change offers real opportunities. Goethe said of Nature:

She is ever shaping new forms: what is, has never yet been; what has
been, comes not again. Everything is new, and yet nought but the old.
(T. H. Huxley, first edition of Nature 'Aphorisms on Nature')

The last line could be interpreted as 'Everything is new yet also old.' Could something be both new and also old? To understand physical processes it is not simply a case of knowing the process but also of being able to recognize the way that systems operate together through feedback. The resource *Thinking through Geography* (David Leat) offers strategies, such as mysteries, to encourage precisely this type of thinking.

## Activity 5: Change

*Stimulus*
Images of beaches.

*Resources*
Images can be presented in a range of ways. As mentioned previously images need to be selected carefully and whether or not you choose to provide contextual information can influence the thinking of the students.

*Guidance*
Ask the class to consider how they might represent the change that is represented by the tide: as a circle, two opposing arrows, a dot, a graph. All are possible depending upon how you visualize the process that is happening, and the different responses offer real opportunities for philosophical questions around the nature of process.

 *Philosophical questions and concepts*

- Could something be both new and old?
- Is the beach always there?
- Should we control the changes on a beach?
- When is a change 'natural' and when is it 'human made?'
- How important are beaches to us?

## Activity 6: Reflecting on values in the environment

This topic involves understanding that the physical and human dimensions of the environment are interrelated and together influence environmental change. This also involves exploring sustainable development and its impact on environmental interaction and climate change.

The concept of sustainable development involves issues such as uncertainty and precaution. The notion that we 'might be wrong' raises further questions about whether we should act anyway on the basis that the consequences of inaction are so great. Philosophical enquiry is also founded on a principle of the possibility, indeed the likelihood, of 'being wrong' and having to reassess our position on a range of issues.

*Stimulus*
A short film by Phil Traill *Dangle*.

*Resources*
Film clip shown to the whole class.

*Guidance*
This short film from the British Film Institute has been used with a range of age groups and each will raise very different questions depending on what they 'see' in the actions of the film and based upon their own experiences. Used in the context of other work on our influence on the environment we might anticipate questions such as those that follow.

*Philosophical questions and concepts*

- To what extent do we control the environment?
- Do we have a responsibility to act differently when we know the consequences of our actions?
- Does having power change how we act?

*Cultural understanding and diversity*
Students are expected to appreciate the differences and similarities between people, places, environments and cultures to inform their understanding of societies and economies and to appreciate how people's values and attitudes differ and may influence social, environmental, economic and political issues, as well as developing their own values and attitudes about such issues.

A number of Development Education Centres in the United Kingdom use P4C to engage people with issues around culture, diversity and inequality. There are websites and resources listed at the end of the chapter.

## Activity 7: Challenging our preconceptions

*Stimulus*
Images of solar panels in Kenya.

*Resources*
Online search facilities for small groups or pairs of students.

*Guidance*
A Google image search for solar panels in Kenya brings up some stunning photographs of solar panels used in villages and on low-tech houses. These images are useful for challenging a view of low-technological and high-technological differences between the Global North and South. The beauty of these images is that they challenge our preconceptions of both technology and its use and to consider issues of sustainability.

 *Philosophical questions and concepts*

- What role does technology play in sustainability?
- Is it wise to use high technology in places where the means to repair and maintain it may be absent?
- Who is living the sustainable life, those who live without electricity or those who use technology to acquire it?

*Fair trade and food miles*
This area teems with ethical considerations. On the one hand we are encouraged to buy 'fair trade' products while on the other products with low 'food miles'. As consumers, how do we make reasoned decisions about the products we buy? While there are many activities available online for both fair trade and for food miles some tend to promote a perspective rather than encouraging the philosophical consideration of the underlying personal and social moral dilemmas that arise.

## Activity 8: The banana trade

*Stimulus*
Role-play.

*Resources*
Cards with the statements below.

*Guidance*
The students represent different players in the banana trade such as: a buyer, a wholesaler, a banana importing company, a shopkeeper, a

grower. Each can be fleshed out with more human details. The task involves them deciding how they would rank the following list of factors in importance from their roles' point of view. Factors to rank from 'most' to 'least' important:

Cheap bananas
Healthy working conditions for banana growers
High banana productivity
Healthy bananas, no pesticides
Bananas are a standard size

After presenting their views, possibly in the form of 'line-ups' in which they stand according to the priority they give each factor, the whole class can stand in a circle of groups each representing their role. As teacher you can then ask for suggested 'connections' between groups and pass a ball of string between them to represent those.

### Philosophical questions and concepts

- Are connections more important than differences?
- What is fair?
- Do we have an equal responsibility to everyone in the supply chain?

(Thanks to Donna Hurford for this activity, which is based on resources available from Oxfam and from the Fair Trade Organization.)

## Case studies

Field excursions can offer opportunities for raising philosophical enquiry questions also. Each of the examples below involve the teacher using short periods in which he or she goes into role. This technique is used to create points of tension, or dispute, which help to stimulate questioning.

### Case Study: The Uffington White Horse – questioning about landscape

The actual field run of this stimulus involved a visit to the White Horse, on the chalk downs above Uffington in Oxfordshire. It was decided that 'teacher in role' (a powerful, but greatly underused method, especially in secondary humanities) would be part of the stimulus at the site, from two leaders. One leader moved slowly from 'field trip organizer' mode to 'tourist guide', as he instructed the party to stand in a line, above the Horse, and, imagining each stride to be a century, we strode up the hill, still in a line, away from the 'date' of the carving of this, England's oldest white horse, at around 2,000 BCE. The 'tourist guide' began commenting that we should pause, to recollect what was happening at these different times in history. As we did so, we heard a cry behind us, and found, far below on this cold and windy February day, that the other leader had by now taken his shirt off, and in role as a Bronze Age boy, was shouting 'We carved the horse!', which had quite an alarming effect on the group. There developed some interesting questions around how people saw the Horse 4,000 years ago, and this links to how we 'see' landscape, according to when, and where, we are born.

### Philosophical questions and concepts

The follow-up philosophical enquiries harnessed this single landscape feature to open up really deep thinking about our identity, our relationship with the land (core geography in itself), the differences (and similarities) between us and our ancestors, our license to change the landscape, and so on, all things that 'conventional' geography is in danger of passing off as a 'mere' tourist antiquity landmark?

### Case Study: Cherbury Iron Age camp, Oxfordshire – questioning about location

'Cherbury Camp', just a mile north of the village of Charney Bassett, Oxfordshire, is unusual in that, unlike most of the other similarly aged forts nearby, such as those near the White Horse on the Chalk Ridgeway; it is not a hillfort, so its site is immediately curious. It is like a hillfort, minus the hill, sitting in fairly level low ground. From the geographer's point of view the location of this fort raises many questions concerning access, food supply, defence and suitability for building, all issues that surround most town and village locations.

Again teacher in role (TIR) stimulates questions. In this case the teacher could take the role of a tourist information officer or even an individual who 'appears' from the past to put their perspective, rather as in the White Horse example above.

Through carefully thought-out situations the group can be prompted to ask philosophical and geographical questions such as:

- Would it be right to build an interpretation centre here?
- Should tourists be encouraged to visit a place like this?
- Would the people who lived here have been living 'sustainable' lives?
- Do we see the landscape differently now to how it was seen then?

### Mysteries as a stimulus

By structuring the initial enquiry through use of 'Mysteries', popularized by David Leat, an advocate of thinking skills (Leat, 2001), new layers of complexity and depth can be accessed. Mysteries are small-group enquiries using themed cards, where a 'big question', apparently with some contradiction, problematizing or puzzlement, need to be linked and related. Through discussion about the stimulus (in this case the 30 or so cards), this acts to bring out high-level thinking and evaluation of philosophical dilemmas and concepts.

A mystery for introducing climate change to younger secondary students is titled 'What have polar bears, the tropical Maldive Islands *and you* got in common?' which deals with Arctic Ice melt and sea level rise globally. It is possible that the Maldive Islands, the lowest country on earth, will become the first submarine nation, possibly offset only by personal action taken by all of us to help reduce our collective $CO_2$ emissions. This takes the important step of connecting local actions and lifestyles with global outcomes, becoming known as 'glocal' for short.

This is also the case with Fair Trade where the learning focuses on questions such as 'How should we live?'

## Activity 9: Fair trade and food miles

### Stimulus
Bag of groceries.

### Resources
A large world map on screen – for locating known countries.

A distance calculator for places found – there are some good online ones available.

Transport mode cards – ship, plane, lorry.

A large rectangular space – outdoors would be better.

A selection of food wrappers with the country of origin identified, and distance and probable mode of transport ascertained (select groceries produced from as near the school as possible, for example, 2 km – and some from as far away as possible, for example, New Zealand – 27,000 km). You also need a selection of blankets with a range of thicknesses.

### Guidance

Give pairs of students a product to study from wrapper details. Students report back on their grocery item, then decide the distance (using a conversion to paces in the room, placing, for example, apples from NZ in the far SE corner) and direction from the school/United Kingdom, and deciding the planetary impact of the method/distance travelled on the warming effect. If high, they select a thick blanket or quilt from a pile of choice materials, and wrap it around the shoulders of a few volunteer 'planet Earth' students sat in a small circle at the front. If a local product that has travelled fairly sustainably, a thin sheet or nothing at all may be added. This way, the volunteers become covered in more and more layers of 'warmth', and the impact of our simple shopping on the planet is illustrated.

### Philosophical questions and concepts

Many philosophical issues arise from this. For instance, if we are faced with buying oranges from Chile or South Africa, there may not be a great deal of difference in the already considerable impact. When the choice is between oranges from South Africa and those from Spain, then the Spanish ones appear to have less impact from food miles travelled. However, the South African oranges are fair trade products, whereas the Spanish ones are not. How, then, do we resolve the choice between less miles, therefore climate change impact, and buying oranges which contribute a fair trade premium to the (poor) growers?

# Conclusion

Geography offers so much scope for wonder, marvel and mystery about the Earth, its patterns and features, both natural and human, with opportunities everywhere for taking deep and 'alternative' pauses for reflection on what we encounter. 'Enquiry' is already established as the prime investigative method, in all its myriad of forms, and P4C, applied to such content, offers the chance to add variety to this further, by occasionally selecting to deepen the meaning of the thinking through a judiciously placed philosophical enquiry. The danger is that if we have this option available now, but don't take it, the subject could become the victim of more 'content coverage', syllabus-chasing and timetable squeeze, to turn this mature subject's time clocks back to a version of glossing over spatial facts and skills in a rather indigestible form for the student. We surely want geography to remain an 'open' subject, where there is not always a clear answer (that the teacher knows).

Philosophical enquiry has also been shown to increase confidence, powers of oracy, literacy and critical thinking, while encouraging respect for others' (alternative) views in a diverse society, and schools are right to expect geography departments to contribute significantly to these aims too.

# Further resources

Desia, A. (1982) *Village by the Sea*. London: Penguin.

## Websites

A short film by Phil Traill *Dangle*
   www.tes.co.uk/teaching-resource/Teachers-TV-Reading-Film-at-KS1-Dangle-6048756/
Emotional Map of Greenwich
   http://emotionmap.net/
Jann Arthus Bertrand (2010) The video 'Home' is available on the internet as well as numerous short clips both from it and from the making of it.
   www.yannarthusbertrand.org
Goodplanet website
   www.goodplanet.org/en/
Geoworld: Further exercises using the strategies developed in Leat's *Thinking through Geography*
   www.geoworld.co.uk/pupilresources.htm

# References

Johnson, R. (1983) *Philosophy and Human Geography: An Introduction to Contemporary Approaches*. London: Edward Arnold.

Leat, D. (2001) *Thinking through Geography*. Cambridge: Kington.

Massey, D. B. (2005) *For Space*. London: Sage.

Nold, C. (2006) *Greenwich Emotion Map*. www.emotionmap.net/map.htm

Roberts, M. (2003) *Learning through Enquiry: Making Sense of Geography in the Key Stage 3 Classroom*. Sheffield: Geographical Association.

Rowley, C. (2006) 'Are There Different Types of Geographical Enquiry?' in H. Cooper, C. Rowley and S. Asquith (eds), *Geography, 3–11*. London: Fulton, pp. 20–2.

Rowley, C. and Lewis, L. (2003) *Thinking on the Edge*. Kendal: Living Earth.

## Chapter Outline

Connections between art and P4C                                    199

Activities using art and P4C                                       202

# Connections between art and P4C

Matthew Lipman, the originator of the P4C programme, was very interested in aesthetic matters. His first book was titled *What Happens in
Art* (1967). Aesthetic concepts are discussed here and there in his philosophical novels but always from the philosophical point of view, in the
abstract. Lipman was also an able draughtsman – his ink drawings deco-
rate several publications he was associated with – yet there are no illus-
trations in his novels. He believed that the inclusion of images would
restrict children's imagination when they were considering the texts by
directing it down a specific path.

The thinking in the P4C community has come a long way since. A
significant step in the inclusion of visual materials was the addition
of picture books to the resource base of P4C, a trend associated first
and foremost with Karin Murris and her collaborator Joanna Haynes
(2000). In the picture books there is often a dual narrative – the pictures either tell a slightly (on occasion, radically) different story from
the words, or greatly amplify the story told in words. The narrative as
gleaned from the pictures can become an independent stimulus for

enquiry. Going a step further, the pictures in picture books can serve not only as a general stimulus but as a specific source of aesthetic analysis. The images can be described in terms of their moods, messages, styles. Criteria can be sought for such analysis. The identification and negotiation of aesthetic criteria that enable deep analysis of the pictures can contribute to subsequent general philosophical enquiries about the nature of art. Hence it is but a small step from picture books to 'free-standing' images as starting points for philosophical enquiry. But what have picture books, usually intended for young children, especially non-readers or early readers, to do with the teaching of art in the secondary school? In fact, the outstanding quality and wide range of the art work makes picture books both rich and appropriate resources for aesthetic enquiry with secondary students. They are easily available, durable (copies of) works of art. Unlike a single image, they offer a ready-made context for an artist's work: each picture can be considered both on its own and in relation to all the others in the book. Books like *The Red Tree* (2001) and *The Arrival* (2006) by Shaun Tan, *Voices in the Park* (1998) and *Changes* (1990) by Anthony Browne, *Varmints* (2007) by Helen Ward and Mark Craste, *How to Live Forever* (1995) by Colin Thompson or Jeannie Baker's collaged images can provide material for many deep discussions. Jane Doonan has written an entire book titled *Looking at Pictures in Picture Books* (1993), based on her work with secondary school students – a useful resource, even if not written from the P4C angle. These resources are listed at the end of this chapter.

Taking a general perspective, secondary school students today tend to possess high visual awareness – even though most of this awareness may not be conscious. Their world operates with, and by, visual communication to an extent that older people – who might be on the fringes, rather than in the centre, of the unprecedented explosion of visual communication – tend to find it far from easy to keep up with.

First, how can art be taught effectively to a generation whose casual knowledge about deciphering and manipulating images is likely to outstrip the comparable expertise of their art teachers all the time?

Secondly, art education in the secondary school offers students plenty of opportunities for exploration as well as directed and self-directed making. However, reflection on and evaluation of the works created – as well as on the questions raised and concepts emerging – would benefit from being more profound and systematic, as well as more driven by the students' own aesthetic concerns.

P4C is an effective tool for addressing both these issues. It raises pupils' expectation of the breadth and depth of learning they can achieve while also letting the 'teacher as the universal and ultimate expert' off the hook. With the P4C approach the teacher no longer has to see him/herself as responsible for bringing order to the cacophony of unceasing visual stimuli in the students' world; the breadth and depth of learning does not have to be circumscribed by the teacher's own limits of understanding and experience. Instead, the teacher's task is to encourage and challenge students to constantly question the images, depictions, signs and symbols that populate their environment, and to create repeated opportunities for them to discuss their perceptions, discoveries and experiences, to identify concepts, uncover meaning, draw conclusions, compare, analyse, and so on, in communities of enquiry. Experience shows that, taught in this way, students become more discerning and appreciative as well as more discriminating and critical of the imagery that bombards them from all sides.

In other words, teaching the P4C way is being constantly alert to the wider – aesthetic, sociological, historical – connections and possibilities of the work on the one hand while consistently questioning the students and facilitating debate on the other.

Questions that should be regularly revisited include:

What is and isn't art? In whose terms and in what context is the answer given? To whom and to what does and doesn't it apply?

What is an image? How do we know what we are seeing? What clues do we use to decipher pictures? How do we cope with ambiguity (exemplified, for example, in the work of Keith Haring)?

What questions and concepts arise from the problem of depicting a 3-D world on a(n effectively) 2-D canvas?

What is the function, intention, message of the image before us? What would need to change about it for the message to change? How can we come to trust what we see?

What is the difference between a sign, a symbol and a (secular) icon?

The same philosophical, concept-driven, attitude can be applied to the historical study of art, for example:

How have ideas about the painting of nature changed from, say, Giotto to Howard Hodgkin?
What has been the role of portraiture: how have its concerns changed from the Middle Ages to our times?

An exemplification of philosophical enquiry in the art lesson can be found in a teachers' guide and resource for Key Stages 2 and 3 titled *Ta(l)king Pictures*. With photography as its point of departure, this publication shows the way into a virtuous cycle of aesthetic enquiry followed by students creating their own art work, which leads to further aesthetic enquiry.

In the following section, starting points are suggested for philosophical enquiries in art lessons. These can be used in a variety of ways: as warm-up activities at the beginning of a lesson, as thinking games on the subject of art, as exercises to raise awareness of various issues or to introduce concepts, or as stimuli for full enquiries, that is, going through the ten steps from preparation and the presentation of the stimulus to the review of the enquiry.

# Activities using art and P4C

## Activity 1: Which way up?

### Stimulus
Abstract paintings (such as Abstract Painting 780–1, 1992, oil on canvas by Gerhard Richter) by twentieth-century masters such as Paul Klee, Kandinsky, August Macke, Howard Hodgkin.

### Guidance
The teacher hands a copy of the same image to each group of students and asks them to decide what the right orientation of the image is. The students discuss the question in groups and present their interpretations to the whole class with justification from details of the image. Some students are likely to seek clues on the back of the card (if information is available there), for example, the title of the picture and the orientation of the printing.

*Philosophical questions and concepts*
*Questions*

- How can we tell what is on a picture?
- Does it matter, and in what way, if the artist gave it a title?
- Are other interpretations valid? Why or why not?
- Would the answers change if the paintings were representational?

*Concepts*
Abstract and representational painting, similarity/likeness, recognition, projection, copy (of nature), imagination, interpretation, naming/titles, identity.

*Notes*
Greeting card size or bigger is best, enough copies of each painting to have one between four or five students. I often use Gerhard Richter, Paul Klee, Kandinsky, Miro. This is a good activity with a new class. The range of interpretations opens the mind to new possibilities, develops flexibility of thinking and makes it obvious that there is no single right interpretation.

## Activity 2: Abstract self-portraits

*Stimulus*
Abstract images (such as *One Year the Milkweed*, 1944, oil on canvas by Arshile Gorky) and any of the images used in the previous activity. This is a version of the previous activity with a different thinking focus.

*Guidance*
The teacher places several abstract images in the middle of the circle, informing students that these are all self-portraits by different artists and asking for (detailed) interpretations of the personalities of the artists as gleaned from their pictures.

*Philosophical questions and concepts*
*Questions*

- Which artist(s) would be good to befriend and why?
- How do the images convey complexity of character?
- Do all students agree about the personalities 'depicted'?

- How can differences of interpretation be explained?
- Do students concentrate on the overall impression or on the details? Why?
- Do different students focus on different aspects of the pictures?

*Concepts*

Identity, personality, depiction, representation, interpretation, abstraction, (human) nature, rigid, organized, flexible, imaginative; tone, colour, shape, structure.

*Notes*

Initiated by the discovery of a genuine abstract self-portrait (titled *Laycock* by Kevin Laycock), this is another good activity for students to get to know each other. In the course of justifying their interpretation of the personalities by referring to aspects or details of the pictures students are 'forced' to use appropriate analytical vocabulary. The teacher can scaffold by offering terminology as and when required. The activity could be followed by students constructing their own abstract self-portraits, which could be subjected to similar analysis.

## Activity 3: Where does one draw the line?

*Stimulus*

A blank piece of flipchart paper.

*Resource*

A flipchart with two to three pens.

*Guidance*

There are two versions of this activity; the students or the teacher might devise several others.

**Version 1:** Start a group/class drawing with a single line, that is, a mark on the paper, which can be straight, curved, a zigzag, a dot. Ask students to take turns adding a line. If a student sees a picture emerging he/she can add a title instead of a line. At this point either a new drawing is started or the old one is developed further.

**Version 2:** Each student starts a drawing with one line and passes his/her drawing on. As the drawings are passed around everyone gets to add one line to each, or most of them. The final contribution to each drawing is a title. When the activity ends there are likely to be some unfinished drawings (i.e. without titles).

## Philosophical questions and concepts

*Questions*

- What makes a picture?
- How do we decipher an image?
- What are the sources of our visual understanding?
- How do we know we can rely on our interpretations?
- Are the finished pictures coherent?
- Is there one main element in them or are there decipherable details, too?
- Are there different interpretations of the finished pictures?
- What is the difference between a finished and an unfinished picture, that is, one to which we can give a title and one to which we cannot?

*Concepts*

Image, constituents, interpretation, projection, recognizing things known or experienced before, coherence, depiction, abstract art, title.

## Notes

This is a good game for simply and enjoyably raising fundamental issues about the nature of depiction and images in general and can easily turn into a full enquiry. Inspired by two drawing games described by Robert Fisher.

In yet another version of this activity students are asked to draw a recognizable object with one continuous line. After sharing and discussing their drawings the teacher can introduce Picasso's line drawings of a variety of animals, which can lead to further discussion.

# Activity 4: How do you know what you are seeing?

## Stimulus
Ambiguous images.

## Resource
Ambiguous images, for example, by Keith Haring (a selection of his pictures published under the title *I Wish I Didn't Have to Sleep!* in Prestel's *Adventures in Art* series is ideal).

*Guidance*

In this activity, whose thinking focus is similar to 'Where does one draw the line?' the teacher presents an image and asks for descriptions of it. It will soon transpire that students have different interpretations. The teacher asks for detailed justifications of each interpretation from elements of the picture. Different scenarios, 'back-stories' can be proposed. It is likely that degrees of ambiguity remain.

 *Philosophical questions and concepts*

*Questions*

(In addition to relevant ones from Activity 3: 'Where does one draw the line?')

- What is ambiguity?
- How is it manifested in pictures?
- Is the ambiguity in the picture or in our interpretation?
- Can we guess at the artist's intention?
- Does the artist's intention matter?
- Are there more or less convincing narratives or contexts for the pictures?
- Who decides?

*Concepts*

(In addition to relevant ones from Activity 3: 'Where does one draw the line?')

Ambiguity and ambivalence, clues, narrative, tension or confusion caused by ambiguity.

## Activity 5: Permanence and works of art

*Stimulus*

Sculptures and/or reproductions of conventional and unusual sculptures.

*Resource*

A reproduction of the sculpture of David by Michelangelo/*The Thinker* by Rodin (or other well-established work) contrasted with photographs of pieces by Andy Goldsworthy, for example, ice sculptures or a piece made with leaves.

## Guidance

This stimulus lends itself to the full enquiry treatment which, following the presentation of the stimulus, includes the construction and consideration of questions by students and facilitated dialogue about the students' chosen question.

### Philosophical questions and concepts

*Questions*

- What is a work of art?
- Can both kinds of work be considered sculpture? Why or why not?
- How are the two historical periods that gave rise to the two kinds of sculpture different from each other?
- How is this reflected in the art works?
- Are they appropriate reflections of their era? How?
- What values does each of them embody?
- What is the status of the artist as implied by the two kinds of work?

*Concepts*

Sculpture, permanence, impermanence, ephemeral art, land art, art materials, symbols, social value, social status, recognition, ecological concerns.

# Activity 6: Where is the art?

## Stimulus

Can a piece of writing be regarded as visual art?

## Resource

A copy of a written piece by Richard Long describing one of his walks (available from most volumes of his work).

## Guidance

The teacher presents the piece (ideally projected on a screen) and proceeds to a full enquiry with student-generated questions.

### Philosophical questions and concepts

*Questions*

- What is visual art?
- Can text be visual art? Under what circumstances?

- Is the piece by Long poetry?
- Is it a different, possibly new, art form?
- Where does the work of art reside usually?
- Where does it reside in this case? Is it in the text, 'out in the world' or in the viewer's/reader's imagination? If the latter, does each viewer/reader have a different version?
- Can a walk be a work of art?
- Can a description of a walk be a work of art?
- Does it make a difference if there is photographic record of it?
- Can the idea of the walk be art? If so, what is the relationship between Long's piece and conceptual art?

*Concepts*

Text in visual art, record(ing), representation, trivial and special, the choices made by the artist, the nature of art, photography as art and as record keeping, oneness with nature, the artist as a person with a special vocation in contrast with the artist as 'one of us'.

## Activity 7: What is female beauty?

*Stimulus*

Sculptures of female nudes from European art from Ancient Greece to Marc Quinn.

*Resource*

Reproductions of sculptures by Marc Quinn depicting disabled female nudes; of female torsos from classical Greek and Roman sculpture, and other, conventionally 'complete' sculptures of female nudes, for example, by Maillol and Degas.

*Guidance*

The presentation of the images can be followed by a full enquiry.

 *Philosophical questions and concepts*
*Questions*

- What is female beauty?
- What is similar and different between the classical sculptures and Quinn's pieces?

- What are social perceptions about physical disability? How do these relate to perceptions of female beauty?
- What is the role of the female nude in the history of sculpture?
- How do traditional perceptions of female beauty influence the social environment of today?

*Concepts*
Beauty, perfection, imperfection, ideal, depiction, femininity, sexual attractiveness, disability, hiding and displaying, the male gaze, convention, social acceptability, equality, power, fashion, manipulation by the media.

## Note
If you work in a coeducation school just light the touch paper and stand well back!

# Activity 8: Do portraits tell the truth?

## Stimulus
A variety of portraits (examples provided below).

## Resource
Reproductions of a large range of portraits, for example, ancient Egyptian mummy's mask, wall painting of a couple from Pompei, a Greek Orthodox icon of the Madonna, portraits by Titian, Velazquez, Durer, Watteau, Rembrandt, Renoir, Cezanne, Picasso, Modigliani, Stanley Spencer, Francis Bacon, Frank Auerbach, and so on or compare different portraits of Queen Elizabeth I, Queen Elizabeth II or Velazquez' and Francis Bacon's portrait of Pope Innocent X.

## Guidance
The students are asked for detailed descriptions of each image presented – as if explaining them to a blind person. The descriptions should extend to the mood of the images. Next students could be asked to speculate about the character of the sitters (or subjects of the portraits) and relate this to their understanding of the stylistic conventions each artist was working under.

*Philosophical questions and concepts*

*Questions*

- What is a portrait?
- What is its role or function?
- What is each artist trying to convey?
- What clues are there in the pictures to the personalities of the subjects?
- What is the artist's opinion of the sitter?
- What is the artist's (power) relationship with the subject?
- Can the students distinguish between the characters of the sitters/subjects and the artists' commentary on them?
- Can they detect any ambiguities in the portraits?
- Do any of the subjects appear to look better or worse on the portraits than they might have done in real life? If so, why?

*Concepts*

Likeness, a record, memento, portrait as status symbol, idealized portrait, 'official' portrait, public and private persona, artist as employee, artist as apologist, power, dependence/independence, hierarchy, social value.

## Activity 9: Did I buy that?

### Stimulus

Images from advertising.

### Resource

A selection of visual advertisements from a range of newspapers and magazines.

### Guidance

The teacher presents the advertisements without revealing their source. The students, in groups, are asked to guess (and justify) what type of publication each advertisement comes from and who it is aimed at. After the groups have shared and discussed their justified guesses and the teacher has revealed the sources, the whole-group discussion can focus on how each advertisement achieves its aim.

*Philosophical questions and concepts*
*Questions*

- How does advertising work?
- What is it in, or about, the images that is designed to attract us?
- How is it geared to different groups (gender, age, interest, environment, location, social class)?

*Concepts*
Selling, attraction, desire, appetite, peer pressure, fashion, status, wealth, ideal, perfection, lifestyle, fantasy, manipulation, humour, juxtaposition, subliminal messages.

## Activity 10: Form and function

### Stimulus
A selection of cups.

### Resource
A selection of cups: earthenware, porcelain, plastic; manufactured by specialists (e.g. Wedgewood, Villeroy & Boch), mass-made and individually made by studio potters and by the students themselves; originating from different traditions – twentieth century (e.g. Leach or Clarice Cliff) and contemporary British, Chinese, Japanese, Mediterranean, and so on.

### Guidance
Students are asked to describe, compare and contrast the pieces in terms of their material, form, function, style and other aesthetic qualities.

*Philosophical questions and concepts*

*Questions*

- What makes a good cup?
- How are the slightly different functions of different kinds of cup expressed?
- How do the pieces reflect the culture they originate from?
- Do the students have, or know of someone who has, a special cup?

- What makes it so?
- What is the difference between a mass-made and an individually made cup?
- How do the student relate to the vessels they made themselves?
- What is the difference for the owner between an inexpensive special cup and an expensive object (e.g. a piece of jewellery)?

*Concepts*

Form and function, individuality, relationships, importance, symbols, one-off, creating, self-sufficiency, celebrating, emotional attachments, ecological considerations.

## Activity 11: How do they connect?

### Stimulus

Images and music.

### Resource

Two images and two pieces of music (I often use *Lily Pond* by Monet and *Starry Night* by Van Gogh; Ravel's *Une barque sur l'ocean* and another twentieth-century, usually more 'disturbed' or 'anxious', piece of music, for example, a film soundtrack).

### Guidance

The students view picture 1 and describe its content and mood. Then they listen to the two pieces of music and try to make connections between them and the picture. Next they view picture 2, listen to the two pieces again and make connections anew, justifying them from elements of the pictures and of the music. The process up till this point can function as a stimulus, leading to full enquiry.

 ### Philosophical questions and concepts
*Questions*

- Can either of the pieces of music be connected with either of the pictures? What is the connection?
- Does everyone make the same connections?
- Has anyone been persuaded to change their mind between pictures or under the influence of other students' explanation?

- What makes a connection between an image and music?
- Do the connections relate to the whole picture/music or to details?
- Has anyone's perception of either the music or the pictures changed as a result of the juxtaposition? How and why?
- Does the picture or the music come first in the connection-making?

*Concepts*

Connections, distinctions, relationships, contrast, similarity, mood, tone, atmosphere, narrative, reconceptualization.

*Notes*

It is advisable to choose both pictures and pieces of music that are fairly similar to each other to avoid very obvious connections. Experimentation with different combinations usually pays rich dividends in the increased complexity and subtlety of the connections made.

As an alternative stimulus, Bryn Harrison (born 1969) British composer's *Six Symmetries* (2004) is a response to six panels by Bridget Riley.

# Further reading

Bosch, E. (2001) 'A Philosophical Approach to Contemporary Art: Looking Out Aloud', in T. Curnow (ed.), *Thinking through Dialogue*. Oxford: Practical Philosophy.

Carter, F-C. (2007) 'Developing Communities of Inquiry in the Creative Arts Classroom', *Thinking*, 18 (3), 43–8.

Elwich, B. and Lagodzka, A. (1999) 'Visions and Words: Exercises for Thinking', *Thinking*, 14 (2), 41–7.

Liptai, S. (2005) 'What is the Meaning of This Cup and That Dead Shark? Philosophical Inquiry with Objects and Works of Art and Craft', *Childhood & Philosophy*, 1 (2) (July/December), online at www.filoeduc.org/childphilo/n2/SaraLiptai.htm

Santi, M. (2007) 'How Students Understand Art: A Change in Children through Philosophy', *Childhood & Philosophy*, 3 (5) (January/June), online at www.filoeduc.org/childphilo/n5/marinaSanti.htm

Turgeon, W. (2001) 'The Mirror of Aesthetic Education: Philosophy Looks at Art and Art Looks at Philosophy', *Thinking*, 15 (2), 21–31.

Wilks, S. (2001) 'Aesthetic Education: A New Reflection in the Mirror', *Thinking*, 15 (4), 34–44.

— (2005) 'The Visual Arts as a Thinking Tool', in S. Wilks (ed.), *Designing a Thinking Curriculum*. Camberwell, Victoria: ACER.

# Further resources

Andersson, A., Fehily, C., Liptai, S., Newman, K., Sutton, R., and Williams, S. (2003) *Ta(l)king Pictures: Thinking through Photography*. Birmingham: Imaginative Minds.

Baker, J. (1988) *Where the Forest Meets the Sea*. London: Walker.

— (1991) *Window*. London: Random House.

— (2004) *Belonging*. London: Walker.

— (2010) *Mirror*. London: Walker.

Fisher, R. (1997) *Games for Thinking*. Oxford: Pollock Nash.

Kastner, J. and Wallis, B. (1998) *Land and Environmental Art*. New York: Phaidon.

The students' own artwork can, and should, be discussed in enquiry whenever possible.

Postcard size and larger reproductions of paintings, sculpture, ceramics, and so on are available from most museums. Bookshops also sell many suitable greetings or postcards.

There are several websites that display downloadable images, for example, Google Images. Photographs and advertisements in newspapers and magazines can also be used.

# References

Browne, A. (1990) *Changes*. London: Julia MacRae (Random House).

— (1998) *Voices in the Park*. London: Doubleday.

Doonan, J. (1993) *Looking at Pictures in Picture Books*. Stroud: Thimble Press.

Haring, K. (1997) *I Wish I Didn't Have to Sleep!* Munich/New York: Prestel.

Lipman, M. (1967) *What Happens in Art*. New York: Appleton Century Crofts.

Murris, K. and Haynes, J. (2000) *Storywise: Thinking through Stories*. Newport: DialogueWorks.

Tan, S. (2001) *The Red Tree*. Melbourne: Lothian.

— (2006) *The Arrival*. Sydney: Hodder.

Thompson, C. (1995) *How to Live Forever*. London: Julia MacRae (Random House).

Ward, H. and Craste, M. (2007) *Varmints*. Dorking: Templar.

## Chapter Outline

Connections between music and P4C                     215
Activities using music and P4C                        224

# Connections between music and P4C

## Introduction

At a superficial glance music education does not readily lend itself to the philosophical enquiry. We use music to relax with, to be cheered by, to help us feel our sorrow (as at a service of remembrance), to demonstrate and relish our unity with others (when singing a football song) – so what does philosophy have to do with any of this? In the life of many secondary schools, music is often seen as a 'light' subject, a break from the 'serious' learning of English, maths, science and the humanities.

In fact, music is a particularly rich topic for philosophical discussion. It is full of concepts, and controversial ones at that. For example, the question of what does and does not constitute music can lead to varied and thoughtful responses and further students' understanding of the concept of music as well as of themselves as musical beings.

Music is a multifaceted phenomenon that tends to play an important part in the lives of most secondary students. It is generally an important social marker. These two reasons alone make it an obvious focus for philosophizing that leads to cognitive and social, as well as aesthetic, development.

The educational establishment has offered varying degrees of acknowledgement of music as a potent source of intellectual, as well as emotional and social, engagement, even though music educators have consistently argued that music is a holistic source of learning and it should be seen as a subject that is worthwhile for its own ends and its own terms. Experience of philosophical enquiry is bound to enhance this perspective.

The National Curriculum music provision at Key Stage 3 allows for students to get a taste of a wide range of musical idioms – for example, the classical music of Europe and other parts of the world, such as, India; folk or folk-inspired and other indigenous styles from many different cultures, both 'pure' and 'fused' versions – and music teachers have generally offered a rich and varied diet of musical material to students, fundamentally from the point of view of the teacher as expert and the students as learners. Philosophical enquiry does something different: it co-opts students as co-enquirers, by empowering them to pool and clarify their existing knowledge of the topic and its social, historical, geographic, and so on, contexts. Students have a great deal of general and specific musical understanding, most of which is latent (probably because of having been acquired partly without the mediation of language), but is capable of explication, given the right circumstances. Philosophical enquiry is an ideal forum for the explication of such knowledge and, through this, the construction of a conceptual and contextual framework for musical understanding. An important aspect of the students' aesthetic development through philosophical enquiry is their evolving ability to articulate their musical experience in language (or other media).

P4C also has the potential to link the two musical worlds inhabited by the students – the world of school music and the world of what is often seen by them as 'real' music outside school – to each other. An obvious feature of school music is that its learning agenda is set by the educational establishment whereas the main attraction of the out-of-school musical world of students is the freedom to choose the musical styles and idioms they want to immerse themselves in. Philosophical enquiry in the music lesson can eliminate this divide by inviting students to bring their knowledge, understanding, experiences, concepts – that is, their freely chosen musical worlds – into the classroom and make these available for other students to experience and learn from. Such collaboration between teachers and students has been seen to lead to a host of positive outcomes: all participants, including the teacher, being enriched by the experience; the build up of trust and professional respect between students and teacher causing barriers to meaningful learning to come down, some formerly disaffected students finding their educational engagement strengthened and, perhaps most importantly, students displaying a new readiness to open their minds to whatever new musical idiom has been presented to them, be it Mozart, Miles Davis or Birtwistle.

## How is philosophical enquiry in music different from conventional teaching of music?

To the untrained eye teaching music through P4C might look like nothing more than good music teaching. No self-respecting skilled professional would expect to be teaching without regularly making the space for the students to think about the issues raised; to question them and expect thoughtful answers to the teacher's questions.

Philosophical discussions in all areas of learning focus on the many and varied concepts that underpin the subject. One list of key concepts in the study of music is provided in the National Curriculum programme of study. These concepts – integration of practice, cultural and critical understanding, creativity and communication – are extremely broad. They are explained in the curriculum document in terms of somewhat more specific concepts which, in turn, are further explained in terms of other concepts. This list of concepts is prescriptive: the expectation is that students will have made progress towards understanding them in the course of their music education. The contribution of P4C to concept clarification in music is

- to focus on and problematize the concepts identified by the students and to discuss these concepts in a philosophical framework and
- to empower students to contribute significantly to this process of problematization, thereby giving them a degree of autonomy about their learning agenda.

The concepts that students want to discuss are likely to encompass the affective aspects of music – an area of discussion that is less likely to emerge in non-arts subjects.

## What are the outcomes of P4C in music?

Teaching music through P4C leads to the development of thinking but it does more than this: by guiding the students to decipher musical works in a way that is meaningful for them individually and in a community it fulfils two functions at the same time:

- it teaches students how music as a cultural phenomenon works and
- it empowers students to articulate their own personal experience of pieces of music.

These attainments should open the way to the students becoming more thoughtful and discerning consumers of culture as well as generally more articulate, more subtle and enriched persons. The regular, cognitively challenging, discussions should also make them better at creating their own music by turning them into more reflective musicians. An obvious big issue for a teacher could be: how can students decipher pieces of music without having first been given the tools for this – how could they run before they can walk?

Students understand much more than they can articulate. The P4C process helps them in two ways here: by giving them the opportunity to make conscious that which had been unconscious in their understanding and by giving them the tools of musical concepts and vocabulary through which they can articulate their new and/or newly conscious understanding.

## How can this be done without direct teaching?

The articulation of questions and ideas within a philosophical community of enquiry is a productive process for deepening understanding of music.

As music is a non-verbal response to the world, discussions about it automatically assume and necessitate *translation*. This in itself inspires hard thinking. Further, music as a stimulus unfolds over time, that is, it is not instantaneous, unlike an image, and the response to it also happens over time. In this way music is like a narrative but it is also different from a story in that its complexities are structured in a different way. Most stories operate with one continuous narrative (and when this is not the case the novel is often seen as being reminiscent of music, as in Joyce's *Ulysses*), which can be explored, teased apart, revisited, to decipher its meanings. In a piece of music all the sounds, that is, the raw material of meaning making, is delivered in one go. Even if this can subsequently be analysed into its constituents, these units of meaning are never quite separate from each other. A multilayered analysis of a complex musical work – that is, analysis that goes beyond technical criteria such as structure, texture, dynamics, and so on, and probes the meanings of the musical work as well as its place in the history of its genre – is a mammoth undertaking that is not generally seen as being the task of ordinary schools to prepare students for. However, addressing complex stimuli with collaborative and focussed effort is an obvious way of developing complex thinking: philosophical enquiry in music goes quite some way towards grappling with the many facets of a great musical work.

Music is like mathematics in that a newly acquired tool, technique or understanding becomes readily applicable to new aspects of the discipline. Thus, learning about, say, the compositional tools of late nineteenth-century European Romanticism (e.g. Wagner, Mahler and Richard Strauss) leads to a better insight into the twentieth-century phenomena of film music and pop music; understanding the functions and moods of the different *ragas* of Indian classical music helps with deciphering the significance of different scales and keys in European Renaissance and Baroque music. Such 'big picture' insight is reached through the analysis of specific pieces, which yields understanding about how those compositional tools are used by a particular composer in a particular musical idiom. It also teaches students about musical features that have some degree of universal validity: for example, loudness and softness, static and flowing qualities, thick and thin textures in music tend to carry similar kinds of messages in all musical idioms, for example, loud music is never used as a lullaby.

By constantly making connections between detail and context, style and function, the individual voice and the social expectation *in the terms and through the concepts that they find meaningful*, students develop an increasingly thorough and sophisticated understanding both of the workings of particular pieces and of music as an aspect of culture.

## The stimulus for enquiries

Just like in other subjects, the stimulus for philosophical enquiry in music should be

- complex – provide a range of possible starting points for discussion
- intriguing – offer a puzzlement, a problem, something that arouses the students' curiosity.

All musical idioms can provide appropriate stimuli for musical enquiries. The choice of stimulus materials will depend on the teacher's own passions and on curriculum considerations. However, the idiom of European or Western classical music is a particularly strong candidate for deep exploratory discussions as American musicologist Lawrence Kramer explains:

This music provides as much insight as it invites; thinking and writing about it gives me a means of pondering the big questions of culture, history, identity, desire, and meaning. . . . This music stimulates my imagination and my speculative energies while it sharpens my senses and quickens my sense of experience. (2007, pp. 4–5)

He counters the perception that classical music is too difficult and that it is a preserve of the few:

Its rewards, I'm convinced, have nothing to do with the elitism and esotericism too often associated with this music. They are accessible to anyone with open ears and a sense of adventure; they require no mysterious rites of initiation. To find them out it is necessary only to talk about musical experience with confidence and precision. (Ibid., p. 5)

Kramer contrasts classical music with pop and folk music, suggesting that while in popular music the whole piece centres around the expression of one single emotion and tends to 'suggest fulfillment in the fullness of emotion', classical music tends to 'seek fulfillment by going beyond emotion without losing or diluting it' (ibid., p. 30). This difference needs to be taken into consideration when choosing music for enquiry.

## Three different ways into musical enquiries

Depending on the starting point, students can be guided towards a more overtly philosophical, more obviously aesthetic or sociological approach to musical enquiries.

(a) The philosophy of music
(b) The articulation of musical experience through deciphering musical meaning or the aesthetics of music
(c) The place of music in society

The distinction we make between (a), (b) and (c) is that the philosophy of music interrogates questions about the nature of music in relation to other phenomena, that is, not music. Conversely, taking the existence of music as a particular art form for granted, discussions about the aesthetics of music look at how music achieves its effect: what tools it uses for expression and how it uses them; how it refers, or does not refer, to physical or emotional reality; how it conveys thought. The sociological theme interrogates what kind of music tends to belong to different social, cultural, ethnic, and so on groups in society; how these tendencies came about and how they have been, or might be, transcended; it considers the social value or recognition afforded to different musical idioms and their representatives.

We approach (a), the philosophy of music, through the presentation of problematical musical stimuli – for example, pieces that have no obvious musical pitch structure or possess an indeterminate rhythmic structure or consist of unconventional sounds. In order to clarify whether, and how, the stimuli might fit into musical categories the students need to construct sets of criteria for 'musicness'. They are likely to find that different people have different sets of criteria, which need to be clarified, classified and negotiated. The music of the twentieth and twenty-first centuries provides a vast array of good stimuli for such problematization. 'What is and what is not music?' is a philosophical question.

Our approach (b) involves making connections.

The most straightforward exercise is *comparison* between two or more pieces of music. Comparison is a greatly underused pedagogical tool. When there is more than one piece under consideration the difficult business of describing music with words can be made considerably easier by establishing categories or criteria for comparing the pieces. Students are usually good at both proposing these and detecting their presence or absence in the pieces in question. The listing of various features absent or present in the pieces can be followed by consideration of how each of the features, and their combination, affects the meaning, mood and effect of the music.

Another way of making connections is *relating a piece, or pieces, of music to something outside music*. This 'something' may be implied or suggested in the music, for example, in the title, 'The Swan' or 'Music for 12 Trees', or it can be arbitrary: for instance, let's suppose that the two pieces of music are about buildings/animals/pieces of furniture/ modes of transport. What kind might they be? How do the two compare? Which features of the building/animal/furniture . . . match which detail of the music? Could there be a better match? If so, how should the building/animal/furniture . . . be changed to achieve this? How might the music be different to give a better match?

A variation on this approach is as follows: which piece of music out of the presented 2–4 is most suitable *to fit a specific scenario*, for example, a holiday by the sea, sitting under a tree in the meadow, sitting on top of a big hill we have just climbed, a wedding or a funeral. The scenarios should include both public and private occasions and the difference between the two in terms of the musical conventions and expressions discussed. Compare, for example, the music suited to a royal wedding and to celebrating an individual achievement, like completing a gruelling run.

The objects or scenarios are kept deliberately vague or general enough to leave a lot of room for individual interpretation: this is where the students' specific storehouse of experiences is brought into play; but they also represent matters that are common and central to all our lives – that is, everyone will have had experiences of it and there is a general understanding about the overall nature of the experience. When the students have responded to the question or challenge the teacher can ask them to justify their replies by reference to specific elements or aspects of the music. As they do this they have started to articulate their experience of the music. The teacher's follow-up questions impel them to make finer distinctions and to articulate details of the connections between the material of the music and the extramusical association.

Examples of teacher questions: How did you make the connection? What in the music gives you that image or understanding? Is it an overall impression or do the details match as well? Is the connection based on the general mood or on specific parts/aspects of the music?

As the students become more adept at explaining their connections the teacher can become more demanding on detail as well as on the use of musical vocabulary. In the beginning students often struggle with using the appropriate terminology because they will have learnt it in a different, narrower, context of conventional musical analysis. But judicious help from the teacher with the musical terms results in successful scaffolding of the students' learning. The process tends to lead to the students absorbing the musical vocabulary more thoroughly than in conventional music lessons because of having worked on the concepts that the musical terms denote. Just like in any other part of the school curriculum, conceptual investigation through P4C deepens the learning experience.

Approach (c) seeks to clarify social issues surrounding music through comparisons, including unusual juxtapositions.

Philosophical enquiry in the music lesson leads to clear gains:

- it gives students opportunities to develop and reflect on concepts that relate to the multifaceted phenomenon of music in contemporary culture and society, and music as a cultural entity with a long and rich history
- it provides a forum for reflecting on and articulating musical experience in an enquiring community by (initially) linking music, which is difficult to talk about, to things out there in the world that are easy to talk about. This process enables the development of a language through which profound musical experience can be genuinely shared. Its ultimate aim is to equip students with the cognitive and linguistic abilities to discuss music much like the best music critics do: through a combination of technical analysis and reporting

on aesthetic experience, in a virtuous cycle of listening, discussing, reflecting and acquiring new understandings

- it prepares students for receiving new musical experiences with an open mind
- the more reflective students become as listeners and enquirers the more likely they are to transfer this attitude to composing and performing activities
- it fosters the development not only of concepts but also of metaphorical language – both features of higher order thinking
- repeated listening to – and hard thinking about – music helps lodge the musical material firmly in the students' minds where it continues to exert its influence well beyond what can be articulated about it in words.

# Activities using music and P4C

Type A: the philosophy of music – what is and is not music?
Type B: deciphering musical meaning – the aesthetics of music
Type C: the place of music in society – to whom do different kinds of music belong?

In the following section the suggested musical starting points are presented under the three headings listed above. This is designed to help both teachers and students to consider some of the many aspects that music plays in both individual and communal lives. The questions and concepts listed after each starting point may arise in the course of the discussion or the teacher can feed them in as appropriate. The musical material suggested below is heavily weighted towards European/ Western classical music, reflecting the area of experience and expertise of the present author but, naturally, music from all idioms and traditions can be used.

## Activity 1: Type A – What is music?

### Stimulus
Musical excerpts as outlined below.

### Resources
Music: Excerpt of different genres of twentieth-/twenty-first-century Western classical music and world music, using diverse tools of

expression, for example, Rap; Steve Reich – *Clapping Music* (consisting of two people clapping in a complex rhythmic structure; Steve Reich – *Music for Pieces of Wood* (using just a few piano keys in a percussive manner, repetitively); Karlheinz Stockhausen – *Stimmung* (for vocal solo ensemble, slowly changing chords with no perceivable rhythm structure); African drumming; Ernst Toch – *The Geographical Fugue.*

### Guidance
Play two excerpts and invite questions that, ideally, respond to the two excerpts together.

The central question of the discussion is whether either of the excerpts can be categorized as music. For this question to be answered criteria have to be established for 'music' and 'not music'. These criteria need to be proposed, grouped, ordered and tested. Further examples of music excerpts, offered by either the students or the teacher, need to be examined, compared and contrasted with previous ones. The discussion is unlikely to lead to a consensus and is likely to inspire students to research the subject further by finding more examples of controversial pieces and/or by establishing several subcategories of music genre, style or period.

### Philosophical questions and concepts
*Questions*

- Which excerpt is music/not music? By what criteria?
- Is there an agreed list of minimum criteria for a piece to be considered music?
- Does it make a difference if there is a named composer?
- Does it matter if it doesn't sound pleasant?
- Who decides what is and is not music?

*Concepts (likely to arise)*
Music/not music, rhythm, pitch, structure, composer, composition.

## Activity 2: Type A – Who is the composer? What is a composer?
### Stimulus
Nature sounds *contrasted with John Cage.*

*Resource*

Copies of recordings of nature sounds, for example, whales calling, the sea lapping at a pebbly shore, the sound of a stream, wind blowing, and so on; and John Cage: 4'33" Tacet.

*Guidance*

The teacher plays the nature sounds and explains or performs the Cage piece (or a shortened adaptation of it). The students are invited to formulate questions, ideally encompassing both pieces.

 *Philosophical questions and concepts*

*Questions*

- Can either of these pieces be considered music? Under what circumstances?
- Can either of them be said to have a composer? If not, who is the composer of them?
- What is/isn't a musical composition?
- Can a listener be a composer?
- Can there be a composition if there is no-one there to hear it?
- Is this the same question as: 'Does a tree falling in the middle of a forest make a sound if no-one hears it?'

*Concepts*

Music/not music, noise/sound/music, listening as creative act; listening as composing; intention; accidental/deliberate sounds.

## Activity 3: Type A – Birdsong

*Stimulus*

Birdsong *contrasted with Messiaen.*

*Resources*

The sound of birdsong, for example, by the Royal Society for the Protection of Birds (RSPB) and an excerpt from a birdsong-inspired piece by Olivier Messiaen, for example, *Le réveil des oiseaux* or *Epode from Chronochromie* or *Catalogue d'oiseaux.*

### Guidance

The teacher plays an excerpt from the birdsong recording that matches as closely as possible the bird(s) listed in the Messiaen piece and invites questions.

### Philosophical questions and concepts

*Questions*

- Is birdsong music? By what criteria is/isn't it?
- How do the two recordings compare?
- Do birds know they sing? Does it matter whether they do or not?
- What is the difference between talking and music-making?
- What compositional tools does Messiaen employ?
- Can his piece be considered non-music? By what criteria?

*Concepts*

Singing, talking, communication, interpretation, intention, sublimation, abstraction.

## Activity 4: Types B and C – The range of the female voice

### Stimulus

*Soundtracks of female voices.*

### Resource

Music from a range of female singers, for example, solo plainchant by Anonymous 4, an unaccompanied folk song from the British Isles, an African folk singer, jazz by Sarah Vaughan and Luciano Berio's composition: For Cathy (written for the voice of his singer wife Cathy Berberian), consisting of a great range of vocal noises, including laughter and cat noises, but excluding 'proper' singing.

### Guidance

The teacher plays excerpts from the recordings, asking students to list and compare the features of each voice. Next each singer is placed in her historical and cultural/ethnic context. The different contexts are compared and the voices considered as representations of the contextualized musical idioms.

*Philosophical questions and concepts*

*Questions*

Type B

- Which songs have an identifiable composer and which ones don't? How does this affect our thinking?
- Which singers sing contemporary music and which ones sing older music? How does this difference affect their performance?
- Which singers have freedom to improvise? How is this freedom related to the musical idiom?

Type C

- What is/might be the cultural background to each of the singers?
- What might be the social status of each singer?
- How does each musical performance fit into its host culture?
- Are there gender issues?

*Concepts*

Folk song, art song, jazz, contemporary music, improvisation, vocal technique, period performance; status, value, recognition, anonymity, singing as shared (or private) social activity in contrast with singing as performance.

## Activity 5: Type B – Different trees

*Stimulus*

Music for 12 Trees.

*Resource*

*Music for 12 Trees* by Daniel Peret.

*Guidance*

Play two contrasting pieces, revealing that the composer thought of these pieces as depicting different kinds of trees.

After each piece the students are asked to draw the type of tree they think is reflected in the music. The students compare their drawings and explain what aspects/elements of the music gave them the ideas for their trees.

Experience shows that there will be a variety of tree shapes in respect of both musical excerpts. Drawing as a first response to music can be liberating for students. As they articulate their interpretation they are encouraged to use adjectives that link their experience of the music with the tree images the music conjures up, for example, strong, static, rigid, flowing, light, swaying, wintery, and so on. These adjectives constitute a bridge between their description of the trees and their metaphorical description of the music. Through it students begin to acquire the means of describing music in a way that not only analyses the music but also gives an account of the students' musical experience. The same words they have used to describe the concrete and familiar trees become applicable, in an abstract and metaphorical manner, to the description of the music. They also begin to articulate their understanding of the different compositional tools employed to achieve different effects.

### Philosophical questions and concepts

*Questions*

- What character is expressed in the music?
- What musical tools are employed to convey that character?
- What is the difference between the two kinds of tree as depicted in the music?
- Which elements or aspects of the music pinpoint the difference?
- What could the two excerpts represent other than trees?

*Concepts*
Musical expression, depiction (in music and in drawing), translation, character (of tree and of music), comparison.

### Notes
Daniel Peret is a Swiss music therapist and composer whose recording *Music for 12 Trees* is only available privately at the moment. However, the activity derived from it was included here because it is a productive exemplification of the use of drawing to mediate musical experience. Teachers will easily find pairs of contrasted pieces that hint at, for example, strong, old and rigid trees like oak and slender, tall, mobile ones like birch or willow.

## Activity 6: Type B – A musical portrait

### Stimulus
Gustav Mahler's 6<sup>th</sup> symphony.

### Resource
A recording of Gustav Mahler's 6<sup>th</sup> symphony (First movement).

### Guidance
The teacher plays the opening movement of *Mahler's 6<sup>th</sup> symphony*, revealing that Mahler thought of this movement as a portrait of a person he knew well, perhaps later revealing that the person was his wife Alma.

The students are asked to articulate their perceptions about the personality depicted in the music and justify their ideas with specific references to the music.

Here the students are connecting the two complex areas of personality and musical depiction – both fundamentally beyond the reach of verbal expression, therefore needing metaphorical or analogous reasoning. By seeking to articulate their understanding of someone's personality as gleaned from the music they are developing their complex metaphorical thinking as well as considering the tools of musical expression in late Romantic European music.

### Philosophical questions and concepts
*Questions*

- Is the person depicted old or young, male or female?
- What are his/her character traits?
- Does he/she have a close relationship with the composer?
- How does the composer feel about this person?

*Concepts*
Musical depiction, personality, character, relationships, identity, gender.

### Notes
All ideas have to be justified with specific references to the music.

A similar piece is Elgar's *Enigma Variations* – said to be portraits of Elgar's friends plus a self-portrait.

## Activity 7: Type B – Film music

*Stimulus*
Film Soundtracks.

*Resource*
Music from soundtracks to films.

*Guidance*
The teacher plays two excerpts that are contrasted in mood; informs students that these are soundtracks to cartoons that were lost in a big warehouse. Can they work out the nature of the film from the music? If the students work in groups they can compare their speculations with those of other groups.

*Philosophical questions and concepts*
*Questions*

- What might be going on in the story?
- What could the title of the cartoon be?
- What are the clues in the music?
- Could there be a different interpretation?
- Are there specific (stock) cartoon characters identifiable from the music? What is their role in the film?

*Concepts*
Mood, character, contrast, narrative, depiction in music/film.

## Activity 8: Type B – How do advertisements work?

*Stimulus*
TV/Film recordings.

*Resource*
Recordings of television/film advertisements.

*Guidance*
Play an advertisement without music to half the class and with music to the other half. Students should report on their perception of the attractiveness/desirability of the thing advertised. The two groups compare their responses.

*Philosophical questions and concepts*
*Questions*

- How has the music affected the viewers' response?
- What compositional tools were employed?
- Was the effect intense or subtle?
- Did the music reinforce the images or go against them?
- Can a different kind of music be devised for the same advertisement?

*Concepts*
Relationship between visual and aural perception, manipulation, emotional response.

## Activity 9: Type B – Assess the cover

*Stimulus*
Contemporary songs.

*Resource*
A popular contemporary song and at least two cover versions of it.

*Guidance*
Play the original song a number of times to familiarize every student with it. The context of the song may be discussed. Next the cover versions of the song are presented one by one. Students should be invited to compare the different versions by listing their similar and different features.

*Philosophical questions and concepts*
*Questions*

- What are the messages in the original? Are they credible/appropriate/inspiring?
- Are the covers exact copies of the original songs or variations/adaptations of it?
- Are there differences in mood, style, message?
- Which version is the best and why?

*Concepts*
Cover, authorship, adaptation, homage, message, style, instrumentation, character.

# Activity 10: Type C – Who is the singer?

## Stimulus
'Love and Death in Venice'.

## Resource
Music from Derek Lee Ragin counter-tenor, for example, from the recording 'Love and Death in Venice', paper and drawing materials.

## Guidance
Play the music and ask the students to draw the person whom they imagine to be the singer. The drawings are shared and discussed, assumptions about the voice type, gender and cultural background of the singer identified. The teacher shows students a photograph of the singer and the issues raised by the singer being male and black are further discussed.

## Philosophical questions and concepts

*Questions (before revealing the photo of the singer)*

- What clues are there in the music as to the period and style of the composition?
- Who is a typical performer of/ listener to this kind of music?
- What about the voice type and technique?

(after showing the artist's photo)

- Who assumed the singer was male/female? Why?
- What previous experience did they draw on?
- Who assumed the singer to be black/white/other race? Why?
- What conclusions can be drawn?

*Concepts*
Tradition, style, convention, period performance, counter-tenor, castrato, assumptions, generalizations, jumping to conclusions.

## Notes
As a follow-up students can research other musicians who 'go against type'.

# Further reading

Liptai, S. (2005) 'What Is the Meaning of This Cup and That Dead Shark? Philosophical Inquiry with Objects and Works of Art and Craft', *Childhood & Philosophy*, 1 (2) (July/December), online at www.filoeduc.org/childphilo/n2/SaraLiptai.htm

Tan, C. (2008) 'Teaching Philosophy Using Music Videos', *Thinking*, 19 (1), 44–8.

# Further resources

## Music

Recordings, MP3s or downloads of different types of music: classical and world music, jazz, pop, devotional music, dance music, experimental music, and so on.

Many record companies publish compilations or tasters of their recordings. These are often modestly priced and have relatively short excerpts. The *Gramophone Magazine* includes a compilation compact disc with every issue. Recordings compiled around a theme (e.g. 'seasons' or 'exciting music' or 'music for relaxation') are also useful, as are recordings of nature sounds.

## Websites

The Department for Education's latest document on the teaching of music, published in November 2011: *The Importance of Music – A National Plan for Music Education*.
www.education.gov.uk/publications/standard/publicationDetail/Page1/DFE-00086-2011

The website of the International Society for Music Education. The organization's mission statement implies an approach to music education that is similar to the P4C approach.
www.isme.org

# References

Kramer, L. (2007) *Why Classical Music Still Matters*. Berkeley and Los Angeles: University of California Press.

Love and Death in Venice – CD EMI: 0964812.

# 13

# P4C in Drama

Neil Phillipson and Gordon Poad

## Chapter Outline

| | |
|---|---|
| Introduction | 235 |
| Connections between drama and P4C | 236 |
| Activities using drama and P4C | 242 |

# Introduction

In the GCSE Subject Criteria for drama it is stated that learners should be 'inspired, moved and changed' by their experiences in the subject (QCA, 2007, p. 3). Three years ago my first real experience of drama affected me in just such a way. While working as a Head of Science in Stoke-on-Trent, I became involved with a drama project which, together with the inspirational man who led it (now my co-author), moved me to tears and caused me to completely rethink my view of teaching and learning. Since then I have been privileged to witness the work of numerous drama practitioners who have created the most fantastic educational experiences for children in Stoke, developing them as learners and as people. Through them I have come to understand drama as a tool for exploring the human condition, for 'dramatising and reflecting on the experiences and circumstances which people face throughout a lifetime . . . playing out alternative solutions to human problems and dilemmas' (Manna, 2011, p. 1). When drama is described in this way, the connections to P4C become apparent, and indeed this group of inspirational educators are connected by their exploration of what happens when drama and P4C are brought together in the same space.

This chapter sets out to explore some of the connections between P4C and drama, showing how they can work side by side to enhance each other and the experience of learners. In Part 2, the connections I have identified are illustrated with examples from work with young people. This chapter draws heavily on the writing and practice of Gordon Poad, who developed the teaching strategy of dramatic enquiry. The chapter is enriched with comments and practical examples from experienced drama practitioners Peter Kennedy and Susanna Harding.

# Connections between drama and P4C

These 'connections' are presented in distinct sections, but it will soon become apparent to the reader that they are interconnected; each 'section', for example, could be said to involve the development of critical thinking. This format draws attention to what seem to be key areas of synergy between the two approaches as used in schools.

## Critical thinking and creative problem solving

It has long been understood that children use play to help them make sense of the world around them. Drama in education, and more latterly 'process drama', have their roots in this same idea – the use of drama to explore issues, themes and dilemmas and to solve problems through improvisation, not to create a theatrical performance. This requires use of the 'higher order' thinking skills of application, analysis, evaluation and creativity in making judgements and solving problems – in other words it requires critical thinking.

Settings, like communities of enquiry and drama groups, that create the conditions for the construction of new understanding through social interaction, can develop critical thinking skills, as explained by Marie-France Daniel: 'because of cognitive conflicts arising from divergent peer viewpoints, the pupil is led to: question, doubt, recognize problems, suggest alternative solutions, criticize suggested alternatives, identify criteria for determining the most coherent alternative, and finally apply the chosen solution to daily experience' (Daniel, 2007).

Experienced drama practitioner Susanna Harding explains how P4C impacts on her practice:

I have always used reflection and critical thinking as an integral part of my drama practice but I am currently introducing the particular processes of P4C in order to enhance and formalise deeper critical and creative thinking – as a way of feeding into and inspiring drama and writing . . . P4C formalises that thinking and offers to take participants out of a particular narrative or character mindset in order to explore the wider philosophical issues. These issues in turn might feed into or enhance, impact upon or inform the thinking you take back into a Drama.

An example of Susanna's work illustrating how philosophical dialogue and 'process drama' can work together to encourage critical thinking and understanding is provided in Activity 5 (Part 2).

## They offer complementary methodologies

The P4C method of moving from open questioning in response to a stimulus to focused dialogue is explained in the introduction to this book. Drama can work in much the same way. In GCSE drama specifications (see, for example, Edexcel, 2008, p. 9) learners are required to employ a range of drama strategies and media to deepen their understanding of a theme, topic or issue raised in response to a stimulus. The stimulus might take the form of a poem, artefact, piece of music, playscript, and so on. Successful learners aim to demonstrate an outstanding understanding of the dramatic potential of the theme, topic or issue.

A first step towards this might surely involve identifying and deepening a learner's understanding of the concepts involved – which presents a perfect opportunity for P4C to add value to the process. Concepts that seem to learners deceptively simple can be 'problematized', taking them into what has been described as the 'Learning Pit' (Nottingham, 2010, p. 185). Thoughtful facilitation will help them to extricate themselves from this pit by a social co-construction of new understanding through dialogue. This new understanding can then be explored further as it enriches the development of new drama. In Part 2, Drama in Education practitioner Peter Kennedy provides an example of how P4C structures can deepen the dramatic exploration of a stimulus (Activity 3).

## They both rely upon and develop a spirit of collaboration

Some of the benefits of P4C in the classroom develop gradually, over a period of sustained practice. However, other benefits are quicker to emerge; one of these is the development of a more collaborative atmosphere among a group of learners. Learners are often accustomed to the idea of teachers being the givers of information, seeing themselves as passive recipients of new 'knowledge'. Within a community of enquiry, this model is quickly challenged. Learners realize that their own knowledge and wisdom are valued, and that by supporting and challenging each other they can become co-constructors of new understanding. They realize too that they share responsibility for the success of their enquiry – the success of one learner helps another to make progress. Improvements in motivation and concentration quickly follow. Crucially – and wonderfully – learners who may not normally regard themselves as successful in the classroom often flourish in this new environment; they are delighted to see that the wisdom they have accumulated through experience is valuable and the regard in which they are held by their peers is often elevated. With proper attention to the continued development of collaborative and caring thinking (Sharp, 2007) these effects grow and flow from the community of enquiry into the wider curriculum.

Just as this kind of interdependence is central to P4C, so is it vital to the success of a drama class. Members of a company must learn to communicate effectively, to listen to and respect each other and, at times, to depend upon each other. They need to be sensitive to the ways in which groups work effectively, to be willing to take shared responsibility and accept the outcomes of a democratic approach to decision making. Experience of working in a community of enquiry can help to develop the conditions necessary for this level of collaboration. Equally, the use of drama within P4C can help to increase the engagement of the group. A dramatized philosophical problem affords the possibility of expressing ideas with more freedom and more communication resources to play with, thereby providing access for a wider range of learners, including those who find a traditional dialogue-based enquiry challenging and may prefer more active forms of learning. See, for example, the range of strategies employed by Peter Kennedy in Activity 3 (Part 2).

Some young learners face a huge barrier to active engagement in dialogue or drama – fear. For them, giving expression to personal thoughts and feelings in front of their peers is an enormous risk; the unsympathetic rejection of their ideas could have a lasting impact on their confidence. For some, the potential for humiliation within drama is even greater. The explicit development of a caring and collaborative community of enquiry makes it an ideal forum for creating a sense of security and trust that helps to overcome anxiety. This gives learners the confidence to take a risk and hence to grow. A well-facilitated community of enquiry can also help to foster what Carol Dweck calls a 'growth mindset' – an understanding that our abilities are not fixed and that challenge can help us to grow (Dweck, 2007). At the root of 'caring thinking' is the ability to empathize, the importance of which is further discussed in last section of Part 1 ('Both help to develop empathy', pp. 240–2). The author of Emotional Intelligence, Daniel Goleman, states that: 'Empathy requires enough calm and receptivity so that the subtle signals of feeling from another person can be received and mimicked by one's own emotional brain' (Goleman, 1996, p. 104). A calm and receptive environment is descriptive of a good community of enquiry – see, for example, Joanna Haynes' work on relaxation (Haynes, 2002, pp. 68–80).

## Both provide a safe environment for testing the application of values

As part of the Socratic questioning used to develop critical dialogue in P4C, young people are often asked to consider the consequences of their ideas. For example, a learner asserting that 'friends should support you, not tell you that you are wrong', might be asked to consider the implications of the application of this principle to various situations.

Such a statement could also form the starting point for some 'process drama' in which scenarios are created to explore situations in which the decision to support a friend or not is problematical. This could be achieved through asking the participants to develop a sequence of tableaux to collectively construct a diary entry, or develop a collective role through which the entire group may speak. Here again, the techniques of drama and P4C are complementary. Creating a context in which learners can explore the application of principles can make the process more concrete and help them to engage, providing an excellent stimulus for subsequent philosophical dialogue. In Part 2, Peter Kennedy uses a combination of drama and P4C to explore possible courses of action for King Lear as he considers how to divide his possessions among his daughters (Example 4).

## Both help to develop empathy and the ability to express reasoned and balanced arguments

One of the criteria of GCSE drama (QCA, 2007, p. 4) is that learners should be enabled to develop a basis for their future role as active citizens. This suggests that students of drama should develop confidence in public speaking and in their ability to express an informed and balanced opinion on a particular issue. Being balanced requires several skills and dispositions, not least of which is the capacity to be open to opposing arguments, to be willing to admit the possibility that one's existing view may have been formed in ignorance and to be open to changing one's view as new information is received. Developing this disposition within a community is central to the success of P4C.

Balance also requires the ability to take proper account of the views of people with different perspectives on a dilemma. Here drama is invaluable as it can require learners to take the roles of people caught in such a situation. Spending a period of time behaving as if you were somebody else – mimicking their movement, mood and manner, for example – can provide real insight into their way of thinking and help to develop the disposition to empathize. As Daniel Goleman points out, the ability to empathize is central to the life chances of us all:

. . . failure to register another's feelings is a major deficit in emotional intelligence, and a tragic failing in what it means to be human. For all rapport, the root of caring, stems from emotional attunement, from the capacity for empathy. (Goleman, 1996, p. 96)

In a world in which we are surrounded by intolerance and mistrust, having active, global citizens with the ability to empathize and to develop an understanding of different cultures and value systems will be essential if the struggle for harmony is to be won.

Several of the examples in Part 2 show P4C and drama working together to develop empathy. Developing the skills needed to construct a balanced and informed argument is central to Activity 2 (Part 2).

The complementarity between Drama and P4C has been explored by Gordon Poad for a number of years, and has led to the development of dramatic enquiry. He describes this teaching strategy as follows:

The dramatic enquiry is a distinct fusion of P4C and drama / Theatre in Education. It provides learners with a compelling, imagined, motivation for engaging with philosophical enquiry. They are placed in the middle of a dilemma which requires them to apply reasoning, critical thinking and imagination in order to work out the best courses of action to take. Dramatic enquiry uniquely provides theatre based frameworks and strategies that allow learners to engage with concepts and philosophical dilemmas from multiple perspectives in contexts which challenge their thinking beyond their everyday lives and current levels of experience. The practice demands emotional and social intelligence in a way that reflects reality. In certain forms it can provide learners with all of the tools of the theatre to engage with dilemmas, including metaphor, distance, time and space. (Phillipson and Poad, 2010a)

Earlier I refer to the impact that the experience of working with the drama project had on me. This project is described below (Activity 2). It was a transformational experience as it made apparent the value of drama in education and showed the power of working with learners as co-constructors of understanding – stimulating and responding to their questions and ideas, engaging their emotions as well as their intellects, creating a real 'need to know' – an intrinsic motivation to learn. It showed what could be achieved when teachers and learners were prepared (and supported) to take risks, and how the creation of a 'real' product (in this case a piece of theatre), with all the pressures and responsibilities it entails, can bring so much out of a group of people – perhaps more than they knew they had to give – and lead to such a rich, multidimensional learning experience. In short, it gave me a glimpse of what education could be like, and it is a vision that has inspired me ever since.

# Activities using drama and P4C

Below are activities created by colleagues while exploring the synergy between drama and P4C. Each helps to exemplify the points made in Part 1. I hope that they might inspire readers to explore for themselves the transformational potential of mixing these two complementary approaches. (Please see 'Further resources' on p. 250 for a resource on the drama techniques referred to in this section.)

## Activity 1: The Happiness Machine – a thought experiment

*Stimulus*

The Happiness Machine, based on a thought experiment by Robert Nozick, is a day-long, immersive dramatic enquiry (created by Gordon Poad and Grace Robinson with the help of the Reveal Theatre Company and Haywood High School in Stoke-on-Trent).

*Resources*

Paper (A3 or larger) and marker pens; props to support the following setting:

The setting is the laboratory of Dr Nozick, a scientist.

[H]is life work is almost complete. He invites the country's leading scientific minds to his maximum security laboratory, in absolute secrecy, to reveal his creation. They don't know it yet, but they are about to make a decision that could change their lives forever. (Partners in Creative Learning, 2008)

## Guidance

The learners are inducted into the role of leading scientists and posed with the dilemma of whether or not they would enter a machine that would offer eternal happiness, but which they would never be able to leave to re-enter the real world as the shock could prove fatal. Ultimately, they are led to consider the philosophical questions at the heart of the dilemma.

## Notes

From experience of this activity the students maintained their role throughout the day and the atmosphere among the participants was one of mutual respect, with performers deferring to the students' role as leading scientists. This resulted in the pupils adopting this register, communicating with each other in role and engaging with the dilemma in sophisticated and thoughtful ways.

## Philosophical questions and concepts

- What is happiness?
- Can we be happy if we never experience sadness?
- Does happiness give life meaning?
- If our life is without happiness, should we try to change our lifestyle? Why?
- In Figure 13.1 the children have written 'Is happiness what it seems?'

**Figure 13.1** Children raising philosophical questions

## Activity 2: Girl A

*Stimulus*
A trial scenario – Girl A.

*Resources*
Pens and paper; props to support the following setting:

 Sometime in the near future, financial systems have collapsed and the world faces an unprecedented crisis. A 'World Council' is formed in response, which passes some uncompromising legislation. A law is passed requiring all 16-year-olds to report for genetic screening. If they are found to have genes related to one of a number of genetic diseases targeted for eradication, they are sterilized; in this way, the diseases can be eradicated along with the tremendous cost to the public finances that they generate through expensive healthcare. A girl, known only as Girl A, has evaded the screening programme and has been brought to trial. The trial is seen as a test case – if a conviction is not secured, the law will be considered unworkable. (Phillipson and Poad, 2010a)

*Guidance*
The learners take on the role of jurors and barristers for the defence and prosecution. They formulate questions for witnesses including an expert in genetics (their science teacher) and people with a range of different perspectives (and philosophical positions) on the genetic screening laws (other members of staff). They evaluate the evidence given, assessing bias, the strength of ethical arguments and the relative merits of factual and opinion-based evidence. They co-construct the personal story of Girl A using a range of drama techniques. P4C sessions allow them to discuss some of the key concepts at the heart of the trial before they pass their verdict on the accused.

*Notes*
This project was used to provide a stimulating introduction to GCSE science for students aged 14 at Thistley Hough High School in Stoke-on-Trent. Teachers and dramatic enquiry practitioners collaborated to create the scenario. After each tutor group had engaged in a day of enquiry, a small group went on to co-construct a production of Girl A,

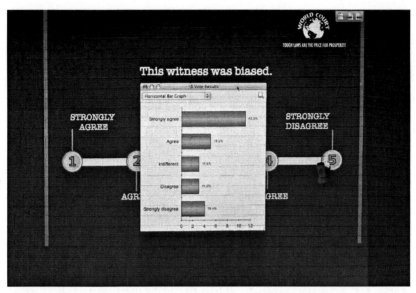

**Figure 13.2** Children's response to the statement 'This witness is biased'. Photograph taken by Andrew Billington in the New Vic Theatre, Newcastle-under-Lyme on 8 July 2009

which was staged at two local theatres. Audiences were participants in the enquiry, just as the students had been. The full story of this work has been published elsewhere (Phillipson and Poad, 2010a, 2010b).

### Philosophical questions and concepts

- To what extent should individuals make sacrifices for the many?
- Is freedom to reproduce a fundamental human right?
- Is outlawing the transmission of certain genes an absolute moral wrong?
- If we seek to control our characteristics by manipulating our genes, how will we know when to stop?

## Activity 3: *Two Scavengers on a Truck*

### Stimulus

A poem – *Two Scavengers on a Truck, Two Beautiful People in a Mercedes* by Lawrence Ferlinghetti.

### Resources

Projection of the poem so that all the class can see.

*Guidance*

Project the poem and read it to the class.

- Create a soundscape of the city as a setting for the event to take place.
- Create tableaux in groups of four (two scavengers and two beautiful people) to represent the moment described in the poem.
- Thought-track all four characters from the image to find out what they are thinking but not saying.
- Rewind the tableau to improvise the dialogue between the scavengers and the dialogue between the couple in the Mercedes before the two vehicles meet at the stop light.
- Fast-forward the tableau to improvise the dialogue between the scavengers and the dialogue between the couple in the Mercedes after the two vehicles have left the light.
- Discuss what they think the poem and the drama are about and encourage learners to reduce their answers to key themes or ideas (suggesting they can only answer in single words can help this), for example, unfairness, contrast, social mobility, jealousy, materialism.
- List these ideas and themes and then allocate each to a small group or pair who have to create a philosophical question incorporating their allocated theme/idea.
- Children vote (using a specified voting system) on which question they would like to debate.
- Move into philosophical enquiry.

*Philosophical questions and concepts*

*Questions*

- What do we mean by equality?
- Are all people equal?
- Can we ever evaluate a person's life choice?
- How should we determine the value of someone's career?

*Concepts*

Fairness and unfairness.

## Activity 4: *King Lear*

*Stimulus*

*King Lear* (in two parts) – an improvisation and a role-play.

### Resources
Projection of the phrase below, 2 large sheets of paper, pens.

### Guidance
**Part A**: Project/write the phrase 'He's only got himself to blame' on the board and ask pupils to contribute to two large sheets of paper entitled 'Who?' and 'Why?' When some ideas have been generated, divide the class into pairs and ask them to select an idea and create a 30 second improvisation that includes the phrase 'He's only got himself to blame'. Pupils should know who they are in relation to the character ('He') that they are talking about (e.g. sibling, parent, teacher, friend). These are then shared through drama techniques such as 'eavesdropping' or 'spotlighting'.

The purpose of this activity is to generate thoughts and ideas around the theme of responsibility for your own actions ('you reap what you sow'), understanding that all actions have consequences, and so on.

**Part B**: Adopt the role of King Lear and give the whole class a collective role as his advisors. (NB the students undertook a separate activity to familiarize themselves with the main characters, particularly the names and ages of the three daughters of King Lear).

Thank you for coming to my help once again. You know how much I value your advice and how you have helped me on many previous occasions. As you know I am becoming increasingly old and frail and I have decided that it is time for me to pass my kingdom on to my three daughters: Cordelia, Goneril and Regan. I have brought with me the map of my kingdom so that we can study it together and decide how best to divide it between the three of them. (Personal correspondence with Peter Kennedy – the practitioner involved)

Negotiate with the class (in role as advisers) what you (King Lear) should do; the teacher's role is to make this difficult for the class and to reveal extra bits of information (e.g. *To be honest with you – but please don't tell them this – I do have a favourite, Cordelia, and I was planning on giving her a little bit more than the others*).

As the negotiations progress, capture the emerging concepts. These can be pursued in role (allowing the learners to use the protection of the advisers' roles) or in a more conventional enquiry format.

*Philosophical questions and concepts*
*Questions*

- Are there any circumstances when you might not treat your children equally?
- Is it right for children to inherit positions of leadership from their parents?
- Is it good for children to inherit their parents' wealth?

*Concepts*
Fairness, love, favouritism, responsibility.

## Activity 5: Odin

*Stimulus*
The story of Odin.

*Resources*
Props to support the following re-enactment of the story of Odin.

*Guidance*
Learners use drama to re-enact nodal points from the story of Odin on his quest to find the runes and therefore gain knowledge of all things. These significant moments may include Odin deciding to begin his quest, his clinging onto the Tree of Life and his dreaming of being able to understand everyone's thoughts. The learners decide upon and deliver one line each to show what they think Odin might be thinking or feeling during such a moment (e.g. 'I'm so cold', 'I wish I knew everything', 'I can't hang on any longer!', 'where are those runes?'). Once they have connected with the idea of what they imagine Odin might be feeling or thinking in such circumstances – therefore investing in the situation and character – they turn these feelings and thoughts into stimuli for a P4C session.

*Philosophical questions and concepts*

- Does knowledge give life greater meaning?
- If we know more, does this make us happier?
- What's the point of knowing everything?
- What is knowledge for?
- How can one possibly know when one knows everything?

## Notes

From experience of this piece of work, learners have been particularly interested in the fact that they wouldn't have to go to school any more if they knew everything, and how much power this would give them at home.

Following the P4C sessions, learners have returned to the scenes of Odin to improvise a monologue each in which Odin is justifying to himself why he is prepared to go through anything to get these runes. The learners demonstrated not only an increased ability to think around the subject and enter Odin's consciousness at a more complex level, but also an increased general sense of confidence about exploring their own thoughts through comment and improvisation.

## Activity 6: The Staffordshire Hoard

### Stimulus

The Staffordshire Hoard.

### Resources

Images of the Staffordshire Hoard, video clips about its discovery and theories about its history (see Resources section at the end of the chapter).

### Guidance

Support learners to identify concepts arising from a consideration of the Hoard and to formulate questions about it. Use P4C and Drama to explore the learners' ideas.

### Notes

When this activity was tried with one group of 12-year-old learners, questions around issues of heaven and hell led to further questions about whether the owner of the Hoard was more likely to be a Christian or a pagan. At this point drama techniques such as role on the wall, hot seating as a whole group (where everyone offers an answer each) and improvisation of imagined scenarios were used to flesh out two possible characters – one Christian and one pagan – and then to explore how each might relate to the Folded Cross, an early symbol of Christianity. This approach achieved a more sensory and more affective outcome than P4C alone had done, therefore creating another layer of understanding. This is sometimes referred to as 'body thinking'.

*Philosophical questions and concepts*

- Do we need religion to tell us what is right and wrong?
- Does a person's belief determine their character?
- If we have no belief system can we still have laws?
- If we have no belief system is everything permitted?
- What is a 'just' war?

# Further reading

Almond, D. (2008) *The Savage*. London: Walker Books.

Innocenti, R. (1985) *Rose Blanche*. Mankato, MN: Creative Education.

Pullman, P. (1995) *The Firework-Makers Daughter*. London: Random House.

# Further resources

## Websites

Several commonly used Drama strategies are mentioned in the text. They can add an extra dimension to a philosophical enquiry by, for example, engaging learners physically as well as mentally (as in the creation of tableaux) and making thinking 'visible' (as in thought tracking). A compilation of useful drama strategies are available at

http://dramaresource.com/strategies

The Staffordshire Hoard is the name given to the largest collection of Anglo-Saxon gold ever found. The Hoard was discovered in 2009 near Lichfield in Staffordshire. Educators in Stoke-on-Trent have explored its potential as a stimulus for enquiry-based learning and have found it very effective.

www.staffordshirehoard.org.uk for more information on The Hoard.

The 'teach it' site contains a good list of stimuli suitable for exploration through Drama, together with lesson ideas.

www.teachit.co.uk/index.asp?CurrMenu=1167&T=2187#2187

More resources to support teachers wanting to try dramatic enquiry can be found at

www.cap-a-pie.co.uk

## Stimulus for enquiry: Images

*A Fishermans Goodbye* by Philippe Lodowyck Jacob Sadee

*Two Men Contemplating the Moon* by Caspar David Friedrich

*Moonrise at Sea* by Casper David Friedrich

*Wanderer Above the Sea of Fog* by Casper David Friedrich

## Stimulus for enquiry: Poetry

*Two Scavengers on a Truck, Two Beautiful People in a Mercedes* by Lawrence Ferlinghetti (see Activity 3 on p. 245)
*The Hero* by Siegfried Sassoon

## Stimulus for enquiry: Film

Gibbons, A. *The Piano*. This short animation has proved a powerful stimulus for dramatic enquiry in primary schools in Stoke.
www.youtube.com/watch?v=-ZJDNSp1QJA

# References

Daniel, M-F. (2007) 'Epistemological and Educational Presuppositions of P4C: From Critical Dialogue to Dialogical Critical Thinking', *Gifted Education International*, 22 (2 & 3), 135–47.

Dweck, C. (2007) *Mindset: The New Psychology of Success*. New York: Random House.

Edexcel (2008) 'Unit 1 – Drama Exploration', Edexcel GCSE in Drama (2DR01), p. 9.

Goleman, D. (1996) *Emotional Intelligence*. London: Bloomsbury.

Haynes, J. (2002) *Children as Philosophers*. Abingdon, NY: RoutledgeFalmer.

Manna, A. (2011) in J. K. Dowdy and S. Kaplan (eds), 'Introduction' in *Teaching Drama in the Classroom*. Rotterdam: Sense Publishers, p. 1.

Nottingham, J. (2010) *Challenging Learning*. Berwick upon Tweed: JN Publishing.

Partners in Creative Learning (2008) 'Dramatic Enquiry in Stoke-on-Trent' (unpublished report).

Phillipson, N. and Poad, G. (2010a) 'Use of Dramatic Enquiry to Explore Controversies in Science', *School Science Review*, 92 (339), 65.

— (2010b) 'Using Dramatic Enquiry to Explore Controversies in Science', *Creative Teaching and Learning*, 1 (2), 32.

Qualifications and Curriculum Authority (2007) 'GCSE Subject Criteria for Drama'.

Sharp, A. M. (2007) 'Education of the Emotions in the Classroom Community of Inquiry', *Gifted Education International*, 22 (2 & 3), 248–57.

# Acknowledgements

Special thanks to Anne Bromley, Susanna Harding, Peter Kennedy and Grace Robinson for allowing their work to be used during the writing of this chapter.

Thanks to Partners in Creative Learning for their support of Dramatic Enquiry in Stoke-on-Trent and to Andrew Billington for photography.

# 14

# P4C in Physical Education and School Sport (PESS)

Paul Dearlove

---

## Chapter Outline

| | |
|---|---|
| Connections between PE and P4C | 252 |
| Activities using PE and P4C | 255 |

# Connections between PE and P4C

I wonder what might run through your mind when you arrive at your rare physical education experience in Year 9 and find yourself sitting in a circle being encouraged to articulate your thoughts about such topics as, 'competition', 'rules' and 'performance-enhancing drugs'?

I wonder what you might think as you get together with colleagues at your first departmental meeting of the year to be encouraged by your departmental head to take a focussed walk with colleagues around the schools grounds, pausing every now and again to air your thoughts? Thoughts such as 'What are the benefits to our learners in the quality physical education experiences we provide in our school?' and 'What makes them quality experiences?'

I wonder what you might think as you journey through Year 13, facilitating regular philosophical enquiries with younger students on 'What makes a great team?', 'Why do people climb mountains?', 'Is sport the same as war?', 'Where does the confidence to try something new come from?' and other questions the younger pupils have created by themselves?

[C]hildren learn responsibility best and gain a sense of moral values by **discussing with good guidance** from the earliest age real and controversial issues. (QCA, 1998, p. 64)

Some of the most powerful learning experiences are found in the stories that young people share around a campfire or conversations they have after a 7-a-side competition. I wonder if there is a common theme emerging? Was there 'something' about those shared experiences that encouraged the young people involved to articulate their thoughts and reasons about the changes they notice in themselves through this shared experience? Were the bonds created through these high quality physical experiences engendering openness among those with whom they have shared the experience? Did the nature of this deeper 'trust' that seemed to be developed during the challenge encourage and promote the dialogue? Did there have to be perceived risk for this deeper shift in self and the dialogue about it to take place? Could the changes in perspective that the young people were reporting be somehow enhanced by the dialogue about them?

If talking about the challenging physical experiences they have is productive in young people making 'meaning' of that experience, and informs and forms their 'self' in some way then surely, as a quality mediator, we should be creating the opportunity for these intense learning moments to occur. We should also be facilitating deeper dialogues about those moments to enable the changes to be articulated, not only for their own learning journey but also for the benefit of others engaged in journeys of their own. Will engagement in those dialogues build the necessary bridge between 'this' piece of learning and 'that' future challenge I face? If so, then physical education is uniquely placed to not only enable the challenging experience to take place but also the dialogue to support the learning about that experience.

I hear and I forget, I see and I remember, I do and I understand (Confucius)

Although our current knowledge about the importance of dialogue to the learning process is still growing, current dialogue researchers such as Chris Argyris, Peter Senge, William Isaacs, Neil Mercer and Robin Alexander see dialogue as a form of talk that tries to face the difficulties of conversation, of human interaction and thought. Robin Alexander proposes, among other things

[O]f all the tools for cultural and pedagogical intervention in human development and learning, talk is the most pervasive in its use and powerful in its possibilities. Talk vitally mediates the cognitive and cultural spaces between adult and child, between teacher and learner, between society and the individual, between what the child knows and understands and what he or she has yet to know and understand. Language not only manifests thinking but also structures it, and speech shapes the higher mental processes necessary for so much of the learning which takes place, or ought to take place, in school. (Alexander, 2005, p. 2)

Through dialogue we become aware of our own values, assumptions and beliefs that influence the way we perceive and solve problems. By knowing the influence group dynamics have on conversations, it is possible to question them critically and to achieve a more fundamental understanding. Dialogue is therefore understood as a reflective learning process – critical, caring, creative and collaborative in nature. As David Bohm commented, 'a new kind of mind thus begins to come into being which is based on the development of a common meaning that is constantly transforming in the process of the dialogue' (Bohm, 2004, p. xix).

Physical education should encourage learners to be inspired, moved and changed by following a broad, coherent, satisfying and worthwhile course of study and to develop awareness and appreciation of their own and others' cultures in relation to physical education. A PESS curriculum should encourage creativity and decision-making skills to enable learners to plan effectively for performances and to respond to changing situations. The marriage of dialogue with an engaging physical experience therefore gives us the opportunity to maximize moments for students and the philosophical approach developed by Matthew Lipman offers such an opportunity.

It makes good sense for colleagues with more classroom time to introduce the principles and practice of philosophical enquiry. Then, in PE, we could consider approaching a key concept like 'teams' with our GCSE, AS or BTEC candidates in the following way, through which the students begin to take control of the dialogue themselves rather than being spoon fed.

Spoon feeding in the long run teaches us nothing but the shape of the spoon (Forster, 1951)

# Activities using PE and P4C

## Activity 1a: Thinking about the concept of 'team'

### Stimulus
'Story from pictures' thinking game (see below).

### Resources
A series of pictures of what might (or might not) be considered teams, for example, a family picture, a group of elephants, pod of orcas, horse and rider, the Red Arrows in flight, ice hockey players in a 'tête-à-tête' and so on.

### Guidance
As an introductory task, make available to the students a 'story from pictures' thinking game such as the selection of pictures featured above. The students then, in small groups, study and select a picture(s) that says something about 'team' for them as an individual.

Ask the students to share their thoughts about what the picture brings to mind about the concept of a team and why they think this is important. Their thoughts are noted and become the outcomes for a practical team game outside. For instance, consider the picture of a horse and rider – what does it say about the concept of 'team'? Is this a team? If so, then what is the evidence? If it is not a team, then what evidence is there to the contrary?

Ask the students to then focus on the criteria of a successful team. They may make suggestions such as trust, cooperation, working together, caring, shared goals and purpose and effective communication. You will then have the opportunity to challenge them through asking for evidence, reasons, analogies and similarities and differences and to begin to encourage them to challenge each other. For example, what might the arguments be to support this not being a team?

## Activity 1b: Ranking exercise

### Guidance

As you draw out from the group some of the characteristics of 'team' as they understand it, ask the students to rank these characteristics in order of most important to least. In order to achieve this, encourage them to talk further about the meaning of the words and why 'this' is more important than 'that' for them. You may wish this to take place in small groups, or even pairs, to allow for further fruitful dialogue as groups challenge each other over their ranking.

Outside, engage the group in a small team activity. Each team has a camera operator and an observer who are 'capturing' the team behaving in the manner in which they described, which might be, for example, *communicating a goal for the activity and ensuring all share this purpose*, with pictures/video footage saved for use as a stimulus for further enquiry. You may also suggest they revisit their ranking exercise to see if there has been any change of mind in the light of experience. Students could record aspects of this activity on a 'thinking wall' or corridor if space is available for them to display their learning. For example:

- Pictures with possible concept words attached
- A list of examples of teamwork
- Examples of the reasons used by participants
- Examples of questions used to stimulate dialogue (and interest in viewers of the display)

As the students view their own pictures of 'team' in operation, ask them to turn their thoughts, after a period of personal reflection, into philosophical questions they would like to answer. These become the focus for the enquiry the 'community' will engage in.

The example above uses thinking tools, a practical activity, reflective strategies and a picture of the learners in action as a stimulus for an enquiry into the concept of 'team'. What interests *them*? What puzzles *them*? What are *they* wondering about?

*Philosophical questions*

- When does a group become a team?
- What are the characteristics of **great** teams?
- Is risk necessary for teams to perform their best?
- Do we all need to be team players?
- Is failure necessary in order to be successful?
- Is it possible to understand something without having knowledge about it?
- Is praise beneficial in developing self-esteem?

Engaging in these enquiries enables the facilitator and participants to challenge thinking and understand where individual students are in their own thinking. It also gives the opportunity, in a safe place, for them to articulate their thoughts and to change their minds in light of what they hear. As one Year10 participant said, *'I'd just like to disagree with myself here'*. At a later stage the opportunity is created to put into practice the 'new' learning and to reflect on whether or not their enquiry has made any difference to how they act.

## Activity 2: Fairness

Fair exchanges seem to be intrinsically rewarding, but what does it mean to be 'fair'? Unfairness seems to drive people to right perceived injustices, complain vehemently to referees and refrain from feeling empathy with those who we feel have been unfair to us. Unfairness can also generate a strong 'threat' response within our minds (Tabibnia and Lieberman, 2007). Enquiring into this rich concept with young athletes, coaches, referees and volunteers can give young people a deeper understanding of why they behave in the way they do.

*Stimulus*
Pictures, articles or film clips.

*Resources*
An article about Oscar Pistorius (the blade runner) about whether he should compete with able-bodied athletes. (Athletics officials ruled in 2008 that athletes like Pistorius had an advantage over able-bodied runners and could not compete with them. Pistorius then appealed and the

ban was removed. In 2011 he won a medal at the World Championship, the first double amputee to do so.)

### Guidance

To elicit questions around the concept of fairness, show a picture, a newspaper article or film clip that raises issues about 'fairness', for example, an article about Oscar Pistorius. Do Pistorius' lightweight prosthetic legs allow him to move his legs faster?

 *Philosophical questions*

- Is it fair to wear a high technology swimsuit that obviously enhances performance?
- Is it fair, when we have goal-line technology that will settle disputes over whether balls have crossed the line, to rely on fallible humans?
- How does a referee or umpire administer the rules in a fair way?
- Where do our fairness values come from?
- How can two human beings who are uniquely different be judged fairly on their performance?
- Is it possible to hold a fair race?

## Activity 3: Collaboration and leadership

The acquisition of leadership attributes is often seen as an aim of a quality PESS activity. In physical education, learning should be an active, constructive process. If students are to learn new information, ideas or skills, they must work actively with them in purposeful ways. They need to integrate this new learning with what they already know, or use it to change what they think they knew. 'In collaborative learning situations, I am not simply taking in new data or ideas. I am creating something new with the data and ideas. I am constructing meaning or creating something new and this is crucial to my learning process' (Tough, 2009).

One of the tasks of a twenty-first-century PESS curriculum is to encourage development in a number of key concepts, such as competence, performance, creativity, healthy lifestyles and all the processes involved with these concepts, such as outwitting opponents, accurate replication of actions, phrases and sequences, exploring and communicating ideas, concepts and emotions, performing at maximum levels, identifying and solving problems to overcome challenges of an adventurous nature (as in outdoor activities), exercising safely and effectively to improve health and well-being and to be able to take on different roles such as officiating, coaching/leading as well as participating.

There is often some advantage in collaborating with other professional colleagues, such as the English and history departments, around a common theme with the aim of creating something 'new' for both teachers and students. Within the concept of 'leadership', for example, students could explore the leadership characteristics being displayed in a particular historical period or by characters in a play or novel. If learning depends on the rich context in which it occurs, then these kind of collaborative learning activities that immerse students in challenging tasks or questions are essential. By beginning with 'problems' or questions for which students must organize relevant facts, ideas and resources, they are more likely to develop practitioner skills very quickly. Rich contexts also challenge students to practise and develop higher-order reasoning and problem-solving skills.

### Stimulus
Odd one out.

### Resources
Photographs of recognized leaders.

### Guidance
Present a picture of the key character whose leadership is being explored and have two other pictures either from the same play/book/film or from the same moment in time. For example, Martin L. King Jr, El-Hajj Malik El-Shabazz and John F. Kennedy.

Other examples may include:

- Stalin, Roosevelt, Churchill
- John Terry, Steven Gerrard, Rio Ferdinand
- Stalin, Trotsky, Czar Nicholas II

Ask the students who is the odd one out and why? Through this activity, students begin to understand that often there can be many 'appropriate' answers and that actually, each of the three could be the odd one out for different reasons. This exercise also gives an insight into where their thinking is at that moment. Repeating it as a midpoint review or a post-activity reflection can also reveal if and how their thinking has changed.

### Notes

Engaging the learners in a practical application of any theoretical finding can serve to build a bridge for them in their minds. Round-robin team-building activities are often successful ways for students to experience first-hand the concept of leadership in physical education lessons. These activities may be embedded in a journey or story in which the team must address issues, problems and questions in order to progress or may use stand-alone tasks that can be repeated. Learners can volunteer to lead a task or a leg of the journey, though sometimes it is useful to discuss who has the necessary attributes to lead the next phase, and make a decision on who might lead in the light of these discussions.

Having generated from the group some leadership characteristics, give each small team the challenge of moving from task to task with leaders taking the opportunity to 'lead' in the way the group are prepared to follow. Alternatively, simply watch who emerges as the leader and ask each team to figure out what they were doing.

### Philosophical questions

- What attributes and attitudes were demonstrated that helped individuals and the team?
- What did you do well? Not so well?
- Were you successful?
- What have you learned?
- What questions have risen for us about the nature of leadership?

## Activity 4: A case study

A Year 11/12 group worked together as part of their VI form induction and took part in an afternoon of events very similar to those described above. Their interest was in developing a leadership programme in Years 12 and 13. They spent time together on that day enquiring into some of the philosophical questions. Other questions became the focus for other philosophical enquiries as the leadership programme developed.

## *Stimulus*

The stimulus for the sessions was *Our Iceberg Is Melting*, a book by Kotter and Rathgeber (2006). A summary and some sections of the book were read by the students prior to the event.

## *Guidance*

The young people were divided into groups using a team questionnaire completed before the day and used to create 'balanced' teams for the sessions (Belbin, 1993).

## *Philosophical questions*

- Are leaders people with all the answers?
- Where do effective leaders position themselves?
- How do leaders make wise decisions?
- Was Hitler a good leader?
- Where should we place priority, the leader or the team?
- If I know where to go, why don't you follow?
- When young people speak, why don't adults listen?
- Where should leaders place their energy for success?
- Is praise essential to promote high performance?

This induction developed over time into a week-long residential experience at an outdoor centre. A range of adventurous, collaborative and enquiry-based learning opportunities were created, including philosophical enquiries. One enquiry involved students selecting a picture of one of the activities they had experienced for themselves. They were asked:

Which picture would you chose and what question(s) would you ask? This led one group to explore assumptions in the following claims:

- If young people have compulsory PESS lessons at school they will come to enjoy/love physical activity.
- School is an appropriate context in which to introduce young people to physical activity.
- If young people are taught about the importance of physical activity for health at school they will wish to remain physically active for life.
- If young people are exposed to a range of different activities they will find something they like or are good at and will choose to continue being active after school hours and beyond school life.

- If young people take examinations in PESS (theory and practical) they will be better informed and more likely to continue with physical activity.

Opportunities exist to extend the activity through revisiting the questions raised, looking for connections between the questions and identifying other associated concepts that could be drawn out of the experience. Reality, truth, change, identity and emotions are some of the concepts the group aired, all of which provided a rich source of dialogue.

## Activity 5: Case study – the residential

For many PESS departments the residential is a small but important part of the learning opportunities they arrange. Residential experiences that use P4C will increase the impact that these powerful learning opportunities have on students. The following is an example of a residential summer school for students who had been identified as Able, Gifted and Talented. The whole summer school was a collaborative learning experience for the young people, who were late primary and early secondary age and all on the G and T register. Students from the programme wowed their knowledgeable audience at BAALPE (AfPE) and Ofsted conferences with their presence, wisdom, confidence and creativity and described their experiences as life changing.

The programme was based around a creative response to a series of adventures. Participants were given video cameras, still cameras, recording equipment and journals to encourage them to capture learning in a variety of situations. A series of short inputs on dance, drama, art and ICT were made available to participants, leaving them to decide which would be most beneficial for them. Philosophical enquiries featured prominently throughout the programme. There were also a number of physical adventures called 'Challenges by Choice', based in the outdoors. The programme climaxed with a 24-hour problem-solving journey, involving the young people negotiating a series of 'challenges' which led them back to 'home' base. They navigated, abseiled, gorge-walked, built shelters and solved puzzles and problems. They then turned all this into a range of creative events to show parents on the final afternoon.

*Excerpt from a student's residential journal*

*Sitting in a circle under the large Rowan tree in the grounds provided us with some welcome shade and a chance to reflect on our first hour at the centre. We the 'new crop' had already overcome our first challenge in persuading our incredibly unhelpful large bag down the drive and over the 'sleeping policemen' (Why on earth did they call them that?)*

*We had already opened an envelope containing a piece of a jigsaw that, when assembled correctly, enabled us to find the rest of our team. Chaos! The jigsaw turned into a map which led us to discover the parts of the centre we needed to know about immediately, our base, and the facilitator with whom we would be working for the week. His name would be Pa-l all week 'cos we lost a 'u', Sorry Paul!*

*And so we met for the first time in the shade of the big Rowan. We shared names, and aspirations, created our team name and logo and flag and broke bread together.*

*Sitting in the light drizzle outside the cave it suddenly seemed to dawn on many of us just what we had let ourselves in for. We focussed on team, and creating a safe way of working for ourselves in this alien environment, shared some fears and discussed a goal for ourselves, and descended into the cool inky darkness, a silent breathless moment.*

*An hour later, buzzing, soaking wet, muddy faces and a small piece of contraband lead in pocket we tumbled into daylight, reborn, renewed, laughing, relieved, proud, a team.*

*First the stories of derring do, deep and freezing water, how tight the squeeze, how dark without lights, how far under the mountain, how beautiful, how scary. Then the deeper thoughts, I never thought . . ., I know I can now . . . . Thank you for helping me when . . . . Wait 'til me mam hears about . . . . Were we taller now? Closer? Was anything possible now we . . . . Or is it my imagination? Oh yes I get the sleeping policemen as well . . . now.*

## Last thoughts

Perhaps physical education, sport and philosophy have a unique gift to offer twenty-first-century learners. In times of rising obesity, a fast approaching Olympics, shifting sands in terms of funding and seriously disaffected young people, this is not a proposal to sacrifice physical activity for dialogue.

However, if we can engage with physical education students at a deeper level, then they can explore courage, curiosity and the ability to find things out for themselves. They learn that they can 'mess about' with new ways of doing things, make mistakes and learn how to 'imagine' their way through challenges as well as persist and follow hunches. They are comfortable with collaboration, sharing ideas and giving rich feedback as well as receiving it with open-minded humour and can give good reasons and agree and disagree with others – without falling out.

They can experience the 'flow' of immersing in something and can also take a step back and reflect on how things are going. Then they can construct meaning about the need for healthy, positive and active lifestyles, and make that adventurous choice *for themselves.*

## Further resources

Cain, J. (1998) *Team Work and Team Play.* Dubuque, IA: Kendall Hunt.

Cain, J. and Smith, T. (2002) *Book on Raccoon Circles.* Tulsa, OK: Learning Unlimited Publishing.

Dweck, C. Mindset (2006) *The New Psychology of Success.* New York: Random House Publishing.

Greenaway, R. (1991) *More than Activities.* Glasgow: Bell and Bain Ltd, Save the Children.

Hannaford, C. (1995) *Smart Moves.* Alexander, NC: Great Ocean Publishing.

### Websites

www.forestschools.com

www.mindinternational.co.uk

www.outdoor-learning.org

www.reviewing.co.uk

www.teachmeteamwork.com

www.teamworkandteamplay.com

## References

Alexander, R. (2005) 'Culture, Dialogue and Learning: Notes on an Emerging Pedagogy', *Education, Culture and Cognition: Intervening for Growth.* International Association for Cognitive Education and Psychology (IACEP) 10th International Conference, University of Durham, UK, 10–14 July.

Belbin, R. M. (1993) *Team Roles at Work.* Oxford: Butterwoth-Heinemann.

Bohm, D. (2004) *On Dialogue*. London: Routledge.

Kotter, J. and Rathgeber, H. (2006) *Our Iceberg Is Melting*. London: Macmillan.

QCA (1998) *Education for Citizenship and the Teaching of Democracy in Schools*. London: QCA.

Tabibnia, G. and Lieberman M. D. (2007) 'Fairness and Cooperation Are Rewarding: Evidence from Social Cognitive Neuroscience', *Annals of the New York Academy of Sciences*, 1118, 90–101.

Tough, P. (2009) 'Can the Right Kinds of Play Teach Self-Control?', *New York Times Magazine*. Available at www.nytimes.com/2009/09/27/magazine/27tools-t.html?pagewanted=all [accessed 11 November 2011].

# 15

# P4C in Information and Communication Technology (ICT)

Nick Chandley

## Chapter Outline

Connections between ICT and P4C                                    266

Activities using ICT and P4C                                       269

# Connections between ICT and P4C

Steve Jobs, co-founder of Apple Inc., said, in the 29 October 2001 issue of *Newsweek*, 'I would trade all of my technology for an afternoon with Socrates.' This seems a surprising quote from a man seen by many as one of the most influential people in the field of computer technology, yet without vision, creative and critical thinking, a reflective attitude and the ability to listen to others and to ask the right questions, the story of Steve Jobs' life may have been a very different one. Socrates was, of course, the master of all these and it's easy to see how such an innovator as Jobs could hold him in such high esteem. Philosophy and ICT, however, seem initially to be polar opposites – one born almost 3,000 years ago and one that has grown in the space of one lifetime; the fundamentals of one dealing with the nature of reality, knowledge and right and wrong and the other with hardware and software; the lifeblood of one being communication through the spoken and written word and the other through simple binary code. The methodology of P4C helps to bring these two opposites together and this chapter will demonstrate how. The first question we need to explore, however, is 'why bother?'

It could be argued that a great weight of responsibility rests on the shoulders of ICT teachers across the land. In no subject has there been such exponential growth over the last decade as that of computer technology and its influence pervades every walk of life. Computer literacy is an ever-increasing aspect of job specifications and there are few areas of the workplace that don't involve some aspect of technology, either directly or indirectly. New occupations have arisen as a result of this – web design, software development, and so on – and there is a vast manufacturing and support industry as a result. As if to compound matters, this is an exceedingly fluid area of the market, with new hardware and applications joining the race to become the fastest, the biggest, the most efficient, the most popular, the most advanced and, quite simply, the best. Computer technology has the power to make life easier, safer, longer and more comfortable at the same time as having the potential for devastating chaos and destruction. If there had ever been any doubt before, we must surely now be in the age of computing. It is vital therefore that we allow time for our students to consider the wider implications of the technology they have at their fingertips, and P4C is the ideal strategy to support this.

The increasing use of technology in all aspects of society makes confident, creative and productive use of ICT an essential skill for life. ICT capability encompasses not only the mastery of technical skills and techniques, but also the understanding to apply these skills purposefully, safely and responsibly in learning, everyday life and employment. (QCA, 2007, p. 121)

In addition to the huge increase of computer technology in the workplace, there has been significant growth in the domestic market. In 2011, 77 per cent of British households had internet access, a 25 per cent increase over the previous four years and more than double the figure in 2001 (Office for National Statistics, 2011). The implication here is that the majority of pupils will have the use of a computer at home and indeed a survey of over 1,000 parents indicated that more children between the ages 5 and 7 were able to operate a computer (86 per cent) than tie their shoelaces, swim, tell the time or ride a bike (Kelkoo, 2011). This, coupled with Ofsted's (2009) findings that, in primary schools, 'sometimes pupils' ICT capability was so good that it outstripped their teachers' subject knowledge' (p. 9), suggests that students may be better equipped to succeed in ICT than in many other subjects. Why, then, does there seem to be a surprising trend appearing in GCSE ICT?

Findings by the Royal Society (2010) have shown that the numbers of students taking GCSE ICT fell by 33 per cent between 2006 and 2009, with a similar reduction in A Level between 2003 and 2009. This has led to many leading organizations, including Microsoft and Google, participating in a study to find possible reasons and solutions. Professor Matthew Harrison, Director of Education at the Royal Academy of Engineering, states that

Young people have huge appetites for the computing devices they use outside of school. Yet ICT and Computer Science in school seem to turn these young people off. We need school curricula to engage them better if the next generation are to engineer technology and not just consume it. (Royal Society, 2010)

Ofsted adds to the debate, stating that 'teachers gave too much emphasis to teaching students to use particular software applications rather than helping them to acquire genuinely transferable skills' (Ofsted, 2009, p. 4). The subject of ICT is perfectly placed, however, to develop the kind of skills students will need to succeed, not just in ICT but in life. The potential for talk – the right kind of talk – is immense, as students are encouraged to reflect on their findings, discuss any similarities and differences between theirs and those of their peers, explore the moral and ethical aspects of a whole host of issues and, simply, think about what they're doing. P4C encourages students to do this together, working collaboratively and creating, literally, a community that enquires – a community of enquiry – and the opportunities are certainly there within the ICT curriculum. Students should, for example, develop a range of open and closed questions, reflect and evaluate critically, use ICT safely and responsibly and take part in informed discussions about the social, economic, ethical and moral issues raised by ICT (QCA, 2007).

P4C can both benefit the subject of ICT and the student. Within the introductory pages of this publication you can see how P4C develops a community within the classroom – a community of good thinking – but within this chapter we begin to explore how P4C can be used specifically within the subject of ICT. There follows a description of a typical P4C session – a 'community of enquiry' – that both uses electronic sources as stimuli and focuses on moral, ethical and, in this instance, possibly political issues in ICT. This first activity will be described in some detail, following which we will identify how and where this might fit within not just the curriculum for ICT but also the wider contexts of Personal Learning and Thinking Skills and the place of digital technology in society.

# Activities using ICT and P4C

## Activity 1: Plagiarism

### *Stimulus*

BBC News article (2011) – see pp. 272–3.

This article is centred around plagiarism – the unauthorized and unattributed passing of another's work as one's own, whether deliberate or not. The ease with which information can be found on the internet has resulted in cases of plagiarism growing, although new technologies mean that detection rates are also rising.

### *Resources*

A3 paper and broad felt pens.

### *Guidance*

*Opening activity*

Ask students, in pairs, to discuss the question 'Is anything *entirely* new?' List any suggestions and invite challenges from the whole group.

*Main activity*

1. Ask students to access the following news article, found at www.bbc.co.uk/news/world-europe-12608083
2. Read out the article and access the two media clips about the article – one video, one audio.

3. Allow students personal thinking time of around a minute.
4. In pairs, ask students to share their first thoughts about this article then regroup after a few minutes and ask pairs to summarize their discussion to the whole class. The teacher simply acts as moderator of this discussion and gives no personal opinion.
5. Each pair to link up with another pair and share thoughts about the stimulus and the issues it raises. Note down on one side of A3 paper any questions that arise from this discussion.
6. After 6–10 minutes, stop the class, check progress and ask each group to select their favourite question from those generated and write it in large type on the reverse of the sheet. Post these on the wall around the room or ask each group to hold their question up for others to see.
7. Read out the questions and ask the class if any are unclear or need explanation. This ensures that there are no misunderstandings as students move into the vote.
8. Ask each student to decide on their favourite two questions. Read the questions out again and students stand when each of their chosen two is called out. Record the votes and announce the question with most. There are many other voting methods that could be employed but students can often come up with their own creative way to decide the most popular question.
9. Ask the group whose question gained the most votes to give their thoughts on the question. Invite others to join in, with each contribution encouraged to begin with 'I agree/disagree' with (name of a student). Also encourage students to talk to each other rather than through you, the facilitator.

### Notes

From this point in, you should, in the role of facilitator, encourage the students to discuss, in increasing depth, the question chosen. This may mean leaving the original question for a while in order to explore a concept that has arisen. For example, if a student states that plagiarism is unfair, the facilitator may further this dialogue by asking 'What makes it unfair?', 'Does being fair mean everything being equal?' This exploration of the concept of fairness then allows the students to be in a better position to respond to the original question. At no point should you 'enter' the dialogue, as teachers are often viewed as having all the answers. You should simply 'manage' the dialogue, by asking for clarification, examples/analogies, explanation, and so on, as well as occasionally asking questions that deepen the enquiry. Example questions follow each activity, but are neither prescriptive nor necessarily the best ones.

### Philosophical questions and concepts

*Concepts*

Plagiarism, copying, stealing, fairness, deception, honest/dishonest, cheating, fake, trust.

*Questions*

Stealing

- If plagiarism is stealing, what has been stolen?
- Is stealing an idea the same as stealing a car?
- Is some stealing worse than others? More acceptable than others?

Cheating

- Is cheating ok if no-one finds out?
- What is the same about cheating and stealing and what is different?
- Can you cheat a computer?

Honesty/dishonesty

- If someone describes themselves falsely on a Facebook profile, does that make them dishonest?
- Can we *always* be completely honest?
- If someone does one dishonest thing, does that make them a dishonest person?

Fairness

- What does it mean to be fair?
- Is playing chess with a computer a fair game?
- Does everyone have to be treated *exactly* the same to be fair?

## German Defence Minister Guttenberg resigns over thesis

German Defence Minister Karl-Theodor zu Guttenberg has stepped down after he was found to have copied large parts of his 2006 university doctorate thesis.

Mr Guttenberg, considered until recently a possible candidate for chancellor, has already been stripped of his PhD. He told a news conference that it was 'the most painful step of my life'.

Tens of thousands of German academics have written to Chancellor Angela Merkel complaining about his conduct. The plagiarism scandal led to him being nicknamed Baron Cut-and-Paste, Zu Copyberg and Zu Googleberg by the German media. But Ms Merkel had continued to stand by him, with her party facing three state elections later this month.

Mr Guttenberg told reporters in Berlin that he was relinquishing all his political offices and he thanked the chancellor for her support, trust and understanding.

'I must agree with my enemies who say that I was not appointed minister for self-defence, but defence minister', he said. 'I was always ready to fight, but have to admit I have reached the limit of my strength.'

The chancellor told reporters she was confident he would be able to clear up the problems surrounding his thesis and held out the prospect of his return to government.

'I am convinced that we will have the opportunity to work together again in the future, in whatever form that may take', she said, adding that the former minister had 'a unique and extraordinary ability' to relate to people.

A 39-year-old aristocrat popular with the electorate, Karl-Theodor zu Guttenberg is a member of the Christian Social Union (CSU), the Bavarian sister party of the chancellor's Christian Democrats. He came under pressure after a Bremen University law professor began reviewing his 2006 thesis with the aid of the internet.

Reports emerged of a passage from a newspaper article that featured word for word, and then of a paragraph from the US embassy website being used without attribution. Analysts then estimated that more than half the 475-page thesis had long sections lifted from other people's work.

As his popularity began to wane Mr Guttenberg's political allies began to desert him. Parliamentary Speaker Norbert Lammert spoke of his actions as 'a nail in the coffin for confidence in democracy'.

**Cont'd.**

For the opposition Social Democrats, Wolfgang Thierse, vice-president of the lower house of parliament, the Bundestag, said Chancellor Merkel had been wrong to assume that what her defence minister had done as a private individual had no bearing on his position as minister.

By Tuesday the newspaper Die Welt reported that the number of academics who had signed the letter objecting to his continued role in the government had climbed to 51,500.

One of the most blistering comments came from law professor Oliver Lepsius, who succeeded his doctoral supervisor at Bayreuth. 'We have been taken by a fraud. His brazenness in deceiving honourable university personnel was unique', he wrote.

*Article text reproduced with kind permission of the BBC. Full article may be found at www.bbc.co.uk/news/world-europe-12608083*

## Reflection on this activity

Students are expected to independently research and to justify their arguments using evidence drawn from a variety of sources, including the internet. This enquiry therefore allows them to enter into rational dialogue about a very real issue within ICT, that of plagiarism. What this activity has not done, though, is to simply set out what plagiarism is and how to avoid it. Instead, it has supported the students through their own investigations and encouraged them to link wider concepts, of which they may have experience and/or knowledge in other areas of life, to that of plagiarism.

## Is this ICT?

Many students, and teachers, might argue that it is not as it doesn't follow the conventions of their 'usual' ICT lesson. It does allow interaction at some point with the computers but in this lesson the focus is not the computer or the software applications but the implications of such things on society. In this sense then, it is not a lesson on computers but a lesson on their *impact* and as such is as much an ICT lesson as is manipulating text within a word processing package or entering formulae into spreadsheets. After all, as Edsger W. Dijkstra, the eminent computer scientist said, 'computing science is no more about computers than astronomy is about telescopes' (Marder, 2011, p. 14).

There is potential too for follow-up lessons of the more traditional style. Students may create their own 'news' page, perhaps based on plagiarism or maybe something entirely different. They could take, edit and insert their own video and/or audio clips and manipulate images and text, maybe creating a class web page for the news items to be inserted. They might look for other articles on plagiarism on the internet and compare the sources, identifying similarities and possible discrepancies in the reporting. All these activities will be based on a real-life context stemming from the initial lesson, in which the students explored an issue in depth. This is surely learning of the highest quality, firmly rooted in the subject of ICT, but there is more.

There can be little doubt that such a lesson also contributes significantly to Personal Learning and Thinking Skills. Students work together, develop and ask questions, make connections, use reasoned arguments, listen to others, acknowledge different opinions and beliefs and attempt to present a clear and well-supported argument, all core essentials of a curriculum that promotes thinking. It has also, apart from the initial stimulus, been firmly in the domain of the students. They generated the questions, voted for the one to take forward and explored it in a way that mattered to them, drawing upon their own knowledge and experience to do so. Once more, high-quality learning that means something to the students and which helps them develop the kind of skills they need for life as well as for learning.

The following activities may be carried out in a similar fashion to Activity 1.

## Activity 2: Internet usage in the United Kingdom

*Stimulus: Office for National Statistics data on internet usage in the United Kingdom.*

The internet is now a part of many people's lives around the world. Recent data from the Office for National Statistics shows how the internet is being used by age and by gender. This is an indicator therefore of how much an impact it is having on society in general and enables the student to identify trends, similarities and differences across age

**Table 15.1** UK internet usage by age and gender, 2011 (in percentage)

| | 16–24 | 25–34 | 35–44 | 45–54 | 55–64 | 65+ | Men | Women | All |
|---|---|---|---|---|---|---|---|---|---|
| Social networking, e.g. on Facebook or Twitter | 91 | 76 | 58 | 42 | 30 | 18 | 54 | 60 | 57 |
| Finding information about goods and services | 63 | 77 | 80 | 83 | 85 | 78 | 78 | 77 | 77 |
| Using services related to travel and accommodation | 45 | 58 | 58 | 63 | 63 | 55 | 58 | 56 | 57 |
| Internet banking | 49 | 72 | 63 | 51 | 50 | 31 | 58 | 52 | 55 |
| Reading or downloading online news, newspapers or magazines | 48 | 65 | 57 | 50 | 46 | 41 | 57 | 47 | 53 |
| Seeking health-related information | 30 | 51 | 50 | 38 | 42 | 39 | 38 | 46 | 42 |
| Looking for information about education, training or courses | 58 | 46 | 36 | 32 | 19 | 11 | 34 | 39 | 36 |
| Downloading software (other than games software) | 38 | 38 | 32 | 23 | 21 | 16 | 39 | 20 | 30 |
| Looking for a job or sending a job application | 49 | 42 | 31 | 24 | 14 | 2 | 31 | 29 | 30 |
| Telephoning or making video calls (via webcam) over the internet | 22 | 28 | 21 | 16 | 18 | 17 | 23 | 19 | 21 |
| Selling goods or services over the internet | 28 | 45 | 35 | 31 | 21 | 16 | 35 | 27 | 31 |
| Doing an online course | 9 | 9 | 6 | 9 | 3 | 3 | 6 | 7 | 7 |
| Reading or posting opinions on civic or political issues | 16 | 19 | 16 | 9 | 15 | 8 | 18 | 11 | 14 |
| Taking part in online consultations or voting on civic or political issues | 5 | 8 | 9 | 7 | 9 | 6 | 7 | 7 | 7 |
| Consulting Wikis to obtain knowledge in any subject | 59 | 52 | 51 | 43 | 39 | 26 | 51 | 43 | 47 |
| Professional networking using websites such as LinkedIn | 8 | 18 | 17 | 14 | 9 | 3 | 16 | 9 | 12 |

Base: GB adults who accessed the internet in the last three months

*Source*: Internet Access – Households and Individuals, 2011. Office for National Statistics. www.ons.gov.uk/ons/publications/re-reference-tables.html?edition=tcm%3A77–226727

groups and gender and to think creatively in identifying possible reasons for these. For example, why might men download more software and women use the internet more than men for information on education and courses?

### Resources

Excel spreadsheet (see p. 275) on internet usage in the United Kingdom, available at www.ons.gov.uk/ons/publications/re-reference-tables.html ?edition=tcm%3A77–226727

This spreadsheet may either be viewed online or downloaded.

### Guidance

*Opening activity*

'If I could only use my computer for one thing, it would be . . .'. Students share their responses.

*Main activity*

1. Ask students to access the ONS website and locate the above spreadsheet. Either download it or view it on the whiteboard.
2. In pairs, students browse the table and jot down any first thoughts. You may wish to ask them, for example, to look at statistics with significant differences or gender bias.
3. Display the spreadsheet on the whiteboard and ask for responses. Scribe any connections/distinctions noted by the students.
4. In the same pairs, students develop two questions, maybe, but not essentially, using the 'first thoughts' discussion as inspiration.
5. Join up with another pair, share each other's questions and decide on one to put forward. This may be one they already have or a new one as a result of their discussion. Encourage students to look for links between their questions.
6. The session now follows the same route as Activity 1.

 ### Philosophical questions and concepts

*Concepts*

Dependence, needs/wants, progress, generation gap.

*Questions*

Dependence

- Could we do without computers?

- Would our lives be better, worse or no different without computers? The internet?
- In what way(s) have computers made life better? Worse?

Needs/wants

- What's the difference between needing and wanting?
- What things do we need?
- Does society now *need* the internet?

Progress

- Will computers always get better?
- Does everything progress? Get better?
- Does progress mean getting better?

Generation gap

- Do older people think any differently to younger people?
- Do you think any differently to younger people?
- What is the best age to be?

### Extension activities

The minimum age sampled in this survey is 16. Would the results be different for 11- to 15-year-olds? Students could predict which of the aspects of internet usage might change most, if at all. Would there need to be any other uses added? Would any need to be taken away altogether? Students could then design their own survey, creating a questionnaire and building a database, then collating the results in the form of a spreadsheet, with simple formulae being added to cells. Do the results differ significantly in any way? Students should then be given time to reflect on their results together.

## Activity 3: The impact of technology on the environment

### Stimuli: Video and photographs of the impact of technology on the environment.

The stimuli for this activity can be found at www.worldchanging.com/campaign and www.edwardburtynsky.com (navigate to China, recycling and select the photograph titled 'China Recycling #9).

The march of technology leaves behind it a trail of waste. A range of examples can be found on this video, all taken by celebrated photographer Ed Burtynsky and set to a soundtrack by Michael Montes.

## Guidance

*Opening activity*

Prepare the video on the whiteboard, paused on the photograph 'Concrete Forest, China'. This photograph is titled Urban Renewal #6, Apartment Complex, JiangjunAo, Hong Kong, China, 2004. How many people might live there?

*Main activity*

1. Ask the students to access the above web page and video or display the video on the class whiteboard. Allow students to view the entire video.
2. Focus the students on the issue of e-waste by asking the students to access 'China Recycling #9' on Edward Burtynsky's website above and/or display it on the class whiteboard.
3. After thinking time, ask for responses in the form of one key word or concept. List on the board and ask students to identify any connections between words/concepts and any other concepts that arise from such connections. For example, if someone suggests 'waste', then this might link with 'recycling' and may then lead onto the concept of 'responsibility'.
4. In groups of four or five, ask the students to then formulate a range of questions based upon the words listed on the board.
7. The session now follows the same route as Activity 1.

 ## Philosophical questions and concepts

*Concepts*

Environment, nature, exploitation, waste/e-waste, recycling, care.

*Questions*

Environment

- Is damage to the environment inevitable to maintain progress?
- Can one person make a real difference?
- Should we be prepared to make sacrifices to benefit the environment?

Nature

- What makes something 'natural'?
- Are humans a part of nature?
- If humans are a part of nature, does that make anything they do a part of nature too?

Exploitation

- Should human beings be allowed to take natural resources for their own good?
- If we take something from the environment, are we able to put the same back in return?
- Is the environment there for human beings to exploit?

Waste/e-waste

- If all computers can't be recycled, what should we do with those that aren't?
- Should governments restrict purchases of electronic equipment to reduce e-waste?
- Whose responsibility is e-waste?

Care

- What does it mean, to 'care'?
- Is the care you show for a person different to the care you show for other things?
- Can we care for something we can't touch or see?

### Extension activities

Students could make their own version of the World Changing video, taking a series of pictures around school or the local environment on the theme of waste and recycling and creating an emotive short film with soundtrack. They might also investigate and prepare presentations on a range of waste issues, using Edward Burtynsky's work as inspiration. This might be done, for example, using PowerPoint, inserting their own video clips and pictures and possibly sound too, with students presenting their finished project to the whole class.

## Activity 4: 24-hour surveillance

*Stimulus: Video on using technology for surveillance.*
The stimulus for this activity can be found at www.bbc.co.uk/learning-zone/clips/24-hour-surveillance/6398.html Technology has advanced to the point where our movements can be tracked in a variety of ways and for a range of purposes. This 8-minute video follows a day in the life of a young woman, showing how her movements are recorded, often without her knowledge.

### Resources
A3 paper and broad felt pens.

### Guidance
*Opening activity*
Ask the students, in pairs, to observe as much as they can of their partner and then turn their backs on each other. Each one changes a small detail of their appearance, turns around to face their partner again and each tries to guess the change. How much of what we see do we remember?

*Main activity*

1. Watch the video on the whiteboard, asking the students to make notes on anything they find interesting
2. After thinking time, ask the students to feedback on their notes.
3. Ask the students to discuss, in pairs, what might be impacted on by such surveillance. If nothing has arisen from their initial feedback, you may need to give an example, such as 'privacy'.
4. Ask pairs to join up with another pair, share ideas and write down as many questions as they can think of related to the video and their subsequent discussion. You might also ask them to group questions according to area of impact. For example, all the questions related to privacy. Allow 5/7 minutes for this and then bring them all back together.
5. Ask each group to briefly give an idea of the range of questions they've generated, then to decide which is the one they'd like to put forward to the rest of the class.
6. The session now follows the same route as Activity 1.

## *Philosophical questions and concepts*

*Concepts*

Privacy, spying, civil liberties, freedom.

*Questions*

Privacy

- Is everyone entitled to privacy?
- Is there a difference between something that's private and something that's secret?
- If such surveillance cuts crime, is it justified?

Spying

- What's the difference between spying and simply watching?
- Are some kinds of spying justified but others not?
- Can computers spy?

Civil liberties

- What kind of things should *everyone* be entitled to?
- Can I choose what I'm entitled to?
- Who decides my civil liberties?

Freedom

- Are we free to do what we want?
- What governs how we act?
- Has computer technology increased or decreased our freedom? Or made any difference at all?

## *Extension activities*

Students could set up their own surveillance (web) camera on their lessons and then reflect on how they felt to be observed. They might also look, using the internet, at different countries and their approaches to civil liberties and rights. They could look at the different ways organizations, such as supermarkets, websites and online stores such as Amazon, use technology to gather information. Is this in our interest or theirs? There are natural links here with data protection too, so students might look at the kind of data that is stored about them and the rights of people to access information about themselves through the Freedom of Information Act.

## Conclusion

This chapter has hopefully served to demonstrate that philosophical enquiry can be a very effective strategy for the ICT curriculum. Not only does it give students something different, it also encourages them, through supported, facilitated activities and dialogue, to ask questions about a range of issues that are relevant to the lives they lead. In addition to this, such lessons can be a springboard to activities in every aspect of ICT and help give a genuine context for learning. In a population that is expanding beyond control, it is vital that we support our students in developing the skills they'll need in order to prosper – the skills that are so inherent in the P4C approach. Not everyone can be the next Steve Jobs and maybe our students wouldn't trade their technology for an afternoon with Socrates, but they can at least be inspired by them as they try to make sense of this ever-changing world.

# Further resources

Other aspects of moral, ethical and social issues in the subject of ICT may include:
Copyright, including downloads from the internet:

www.bbc.co.uk/schools/gcsebitesize/ict/legal/2copyrightrev1.shtml

The National DNA Database:

http://news.bbc.co.uk/1/hi/uk/7532856.stm

www.tes.co.uk/teaching-resource/Video-debating-the-National-DNA-Database-6071017

E-safety:

www.learninglive.co.uk/teachers/e_safety/index.asp

www.staysafeonline.org/tools-resources/resource-documents

For a range of resources across many aspects of such issues in ICT, see

www.teach-ict.com/gcse_new/social_ethical/politics_ethics/home_politics_ethics.htm

www.james-greenwood.com/2009/08/10/moral-issues-in-ict-handout-resource

# References

BBC (2011) 'German Defence Minister Guttenberg Resigns over Thesis'. *BBC News* 1 March [online] Available at www.bbc.co.uk/news/world-europe-12608083 [accessed 12 September 2011].

BCS (2010) 'BCS Welcomes the Curriculum Review'. http://academy.bcs.org/content/conWebDoc/38133 [accessed 5 September 2011].

Kelkoo (2011) 'Techno Tots More Likely to Be Able to Work a Computer Than Tell the Time'. http://press.kelkoo.co.uk/techno-tots-more-likely-to-be-able-to-work-a-computer-than-tell-the-time1.html [accessed 12 September 2011].

Marder, M. (2011) *Research Methods for Science.* Cambridge: Cambridge University Press.

*Newsweek* (2001) 'The Classroom of the Future'. *Newsweek* 29 October. Available at: www.highbeam.com/doc/1G1-79408808.html [accessed 7 November 2011].

Office for National Statistics (2011) 'Internet Access – Households and Individuals, 2011'. www.ons.gov.uk/ons/publications/re-reference-tables.html?edition=tcm%3A77-226727 [accessed 2 September 2011].

Office for Standards in Education (2009) *The Importance of ICT – Information and Communication Technology in Primary and Secondary Schools, 2005/2008.* London: Ofsted.

Qualifications and Curriculum Authority (2007) *The National Curriculum for England at Key Stages 3 & 4.* London: QCA Publications.

The Royal Society (2010) 'Current ICT and Computer Science in Schools – Damaging to UK's Future Economic Prospects?' http://royalsociety.org/Current-ICT-and-Computer-Science-in-schools [accessed 5 September 2011].

# Appendix
## A Brief History of P4C and SAPERE
Steve Williams

---

## Chapter Outline

The origins of P4C                                    284
P4C starts in the United Kingdom                      287
Other approaches in the United Kingdom                291

## The origins of P4C

P4C first emerged in the United States in 1972 from the work of Professor Matthew Lipman and his colleagues at the IAPC (Institute for the Advancement of Philosophy for Children) in Montclair University, New Jersey. The IAPC was part of the Department of Philosophy and Religion (Lipman, 2008, p. 121), and there were contributions from the department of education where Lipman's main collaborator, Ann Sharp, was a professor. Initial funding came from the National Endowment for the Humanities and continued from other sources. At that time, as now, there was widespread dissatisfaction with the 'state of education'. There was also a growing interest among educators in 'critical thinking' and 'informal logic' as means of enabling students to 'think for themselves' in preparation for life and further learning.

Following the pragmatist philosopher John Dewey, Lipman believed that education should not only be a preparation for future living but also a process of living:

[P]resent education fails because it neglects this fundamental principle of the school as a form of community life. It conceives the school as a place where certain information is to be given, where certain lessons are to be learned, or where certain habits are to be formed. The value of these is conceived as lying largely in the remote future; the child must do these things for the sake of something else he is to do; they are mere preparation. As a result they do not become a part of the life experience of the child and so are not truly educative. (Dewey, 1987)

It was inevitable, then, that Lipman envisaged more than limited programmes for the teaching of critical thinking or informal logic. He believed that the practice of philosophizing about life and learning should be stimulating and worthwhile. It would cultivate fallibilism and reasonable judgement, both *in* the present and *for* the future (see Lipman, 1988, 2003, 2008). To these ends, he made two impressive innovations in the creation of his P4C programme.

## Philosophical novels

Lipman wrote 'novels' to bring philosophical topics alive for students. The young characters in these works talked about the same kinds of perplexing questions he hoped student readers might raise if they were sensitive to philosophical dimensions of their experience. Characters exemplify the practice of inquiring together into questions that matter to them; they demonstrate ways to make that inquiry more rewarding by sharing opinions, giving reasons, considering the reasons of others, asking for examples, questioning assumptions and testing hypotheses. Their teachers are depicted as an important source of intellectual encouragement and stimulation. Lipman hoped all of education could be like this: intellectually encouraging, respectful of the concerns of young people and effective in strengthening their powers of judgement.

The novels, like Plato's dialogues, are open-ended and packed with twists and turns of philosophical argument so as to interest readers and prompt them to reconsider their own presuppositions. Children are invited to engage with the voices in the text as well as with those of their own peers and teachers. Lipman wanted the novels to be:

a challenge to teachers as well as pupils. If both groups were to find them interesting, there would be *discussions* of the texts, in which both teachers and pupils would participate. Such discussions could revolve around different interpretations. (Lipman, 2008, p. 118)

So, from the start, P4C was seen as a practice undertaken jointly by teachers and pupils. The novels mediated two things to both groups: aspects of the discipline of philosophy and the practice of P4C.

## The community of inquiry

What sort of practice did Lipman envisage? He took a phrase from another American Pragmatist philosopher, Charles Peirce, that suggested a direction – 'the community of inquiry'. Lipman wrote: 'what impressed itself upon me ... was the practice implied by the phrase', that of participants (the model from Peirce being scientists) who 'operated under two sets of requirements, one being the requirements of inquiry itself and the other being the requirements of communal life' (2008, p. 118). There is respect for others as people but also a concern to offer one's ideas up for scrutiny.

### Routines, manuals and training

These two central features of the IAPC program – the novels and the community of inquiry – were supported by classroom routines for questioning and dialogue, extensive manuals for teachers with focused tasks and advice, and training networks bringing together teachers and philosophy graduates.

Lipman and his colleagues took the training of teachers very seriously. They wanted to preserve a respect for the two overlapping and constituent practices of P4C: philosophizing and teaching. Lipman was clear on the one hand that he 'knew enough to reject the idea of using children's classrooms as a dumping ground for unemployed and untrained philosophers' who had 'never been exposed to an hour of preparation for teaching' (2008, p. 130).

On the other hand, he saw that most teachers were untrained in philosophizing. They needed to become familiar with some of the philosophical ideas behind the novels, see the materials and routines used in schools and get some support when they tried out the program with their own students. Lipman wanted to work with teachers who were 'disposed to examine ideas, to engage in dialogical inquiry and to respect the humanity of children being taught' (2008, p. 131).

To this end he engaged people with a strong philosophy background as 'teacher educators' who also acted as school 'philosophers in residence'. Teacher educators took a course at the IAPC to prepare them to work with children and teachers and to know the course materials.

Teachers observed the philosophers in residence and took a substantial course in preparation for teaching the programme and working for a community of inquiry. Teachers used the materials with their pupils and received feedback from the teacher educators. Networks of teachers were established in order to facilitate ongoing contact, information and support.

These innovations, in combination, provided the launch pad for P4C world-wide. In some countries, including the United Kingdom, the practice was amended to varying degrees.

Of the original Lipman initiative, we can agree with Alex Kozulin that it 'can be considered content-based because it is grounded in specific content material (a philosophical novel). Its originality is in constructing this material rather than taking ready-made material from classical sources such as Plato's dialogues or Descartes' *Method*' (Kozulin, 1998, pp. 82–3). As we can see, however, it is much more than *only* a content-based program.

# P4C starts in the United Kingdom

P4C came to the attention of teachers in the United Kingdom with the screening of the BBC documentary 'Socrates for Six-Year-Olds' in 1990 (BBC, 1990). It presented Lipman and his colleagues – most notably, Catherine McCall – putting their program into practice in local New Jersey schools. Many viewers were impressed not only with the theory but also with the practice and the outcomes of P4C. Pupils from 6 to 13 seemed to become more willing and able to reason together. Some appeared to enjoy and value their philosophy sessions and many performed better in a range of assessments.

In response to the documentary, at least 2,000 people requested more information. An initial meeting took place for those who could attend and in 1991 an organization was set up to develop P4C in the United Kingdom. SAPERE (Society for the Advancement of Philosophical Enquiry and Reflection in Education) was, in contrast to the IAPC, a network of individuals rather than a special unit attached to a university. A majority of members were teachers keen to incorporate the practice of P4C into their work with children and teenagers. Some people in the United Kingdom had been doing P4C before SAPERE was formed and they took a leading role in the organization.

It was set up without funding from outside organizations and has continued to survive for 20 years as a self-reliant charitable organization. In the early 1990s, SAPERE focused on making links with the IAPC and inviting guest speakers and trainers to Britain. As local expertise in the practice of P4C grew, SAPERE organized courses led by UK trainers, developed its own course materials and supported – with conferences and publications – the relatively small network of teachers trying out P4C.

After appropriate training, some secondary teachers in the United Kingdom successfully trialled materials from the IAPC programme (see, for example, Village Community School, 1993). However, some drawbacks to using the novels became apparent:

- They were not as engaging for either children or teachers as Lipman had hoped. And if the materials did not inspire interest, then there was no alternative to turn to.
- The programme of novels, exercises and discussion plans demanded a great deal of time to get through.
- They were not very amendable to a range of curriculum designs or topics, nor were they very adaptable to the interests of pupils because most of the available time is taken up working through the given materials.

In the early 1990s P4C had made a tentative beginning, though the environment was not particularly supportive. Teachers were still coming to terms with the introduction of the National Curriculum after the Education Reform Act of 1988. Timetable space for P4C was understandably hard to achieve. It would be true to say that, for teachers in those early days, commitment to P4C was not a route to professional advancement. Many reluctantly gave up in order to pursue more traditional channels of career progression. Nonetheless, a core of P4C enthusiasts continued to experiment, educate themselves pedagogically and philosophically, maintain networks and introduce the practice to others via training courses and conferences. They were supported by a handful of academics in philosophy or education departments of universities.

## UK developments

### Philosophy with picture books

Philosopher and educator Karin Murris had been working on using picture books rather than specially written novels as the starting point for philosophizing. In 1992 she wrote *Teaching Philosophy with Picture Books* (Murris, 1992). Following the IAPC, she produced a 'manual' of exercises and teacher guidance together with recommendations about which books to use. She argued that picture books were appealing to children, familiar to teachers, had potential to stimulate philosophical dialogue and could fit easily into the primary school curriculum. Teachers and children often talked together about picture books; now they could add a valuable philosophical dimension to their dialogues. All the rest of Lipman's innovations were maintained: the community of enquiry, the manuals, the regular routines, the training and networks.

The teachers who tried out *Teaching Philosophy with Picture Books* in primary schools were impressed with the results. They reported that children seemed to become more able to reason, more curious, more confident in expressing their views and more willing to listen to others. In 1994 a research project sponsored by Dyfed County Council in South Wales found that children involved in the approach gained in thinking, listening and language skills and also self-confidence, particularly when discussing ideas (Dyfed, 1994).

Karin Murris and Joanna Haynes have continued developing P4C with picture books both in practice (see Murris and Haynes, 2002) and in theory (Haynes and Murris, 2011).

A wider circle of primary schools took up this initiative and, again, achieved good results. Other materials such as folk tales, poems, short stories, news items and philosophical dialogues became available. Once the link with the novels was broken, teachers began to experiment with their own choices of story, with short films, images, objects, role-play and drama. Educationalist Robert Fisher produced a popular series of books for primary schools using folk tales and poems (see Fisher, 1996, 1997). He also wrote a popular introduction to the field (Fisher, 2003).

P4C in the United Kingdom became not so much a content-based programme presenting philosophy to children via a set text but rather a practice involving teachers and pupils exploring the philosophical dimensions in their shared experiences – not only of shared stories and films but also going beyond those to questions arising from other subject areas and their lives, and to beliefs and interests beyond school, unmediated by any set text.

In secondary schools, teachers used the community of enquiry ideal and the routines for dialogue. They built on ideas they had encountered on P4C training courses to find philosophical dimensions in their own subject areas and also to improve the reasoning of their students. They, too, were impressed with the results. They often found P4C to be complementary to their own disciplines.

### New curriculum initiatives

As time went by, the reputation of P4C in the United Kingdom grew by word of mouth between schools and through local education authority advisors and events. Its progress was assisted by a variety of national initiatives such as the introduction of Citizenship and SEAL (Social and Emotional Aspects of Learning), a rediscovery of 'Thinking Skills', the proliferation of 'Gifted and Talented' programmes, and the idea of 'A Creative Curriculum' (P4C has always stressed the connection between critical and creative thinking). As teachers attended training courses on these new initiatives they often heard about P4C in positive terms. In fact, given some uncertainty about the best ways to achieve the aims of these diverse curriculum interventions, P4C seemed to offer a tried-and-tested direction to take. In addition, those teachers who wanted to try out P4C but hitherto had failed to justify its adoption in their schools now found new arguments opening up via the initiatives.

However, the opportunities for schools to train staff in any new curriculum approach or teaching practice were constrained. Schools have a limited number of 'training days' available per year (normally five) and they are able to send selected members of staff out of school to attend courses upon payment of the course fee and of replacement teachers. As P4C courses in the United Kingdom receive no outside funding, schools have to bear the full cost. Given these factors, most schools opt for a short course of two days to get them started in the practice of P4C, though they may follow-up the introduction with further training. Enthusiastic teachers may also educate themselves by further reading, philosophical study or involvement in teacher networks. And, of course, some teachers may already have experience of philosophical study.

So here, in the training, is another difference between work in the United Kingdom and the original IAPC design for P4C. In the United Kingdom, with no outside investment, SAPERE had to operate in the niches that arose out of the changing UK education system with its succession of training days and government initiatives. Training and support is therefore seen as a scale of involvement. Teachers taking the introductory courses find it benefits their teaching, but further training and support is recommended, both in the philosophical and educational aspects of the practice of P4C.

The practice of P4C is now undertaken in many schools in the United Kingdom to varying degrees. In some, the most basic elements are used simply to enhance speaking and listening and encourage reasoning. In others where teachers are disposed to examine ideas with young people in a philosophical way and work towards a community of enquiry, it has a much greater impact.

# Other approaches in the United Kingdom

## Community of Philosophical Inquiry

Dr Catherine McCall is a Scottish philosopher who worked with Matthew Lipman on the P4C program at Montclair University in the 1980s and appeared in Socrates for Six-Year-Olds showcasing CoPI (Community of Philosophical Inquiry), her own methodology (see McCall, 2009). As with the IAPC program, CoPI uses specially written novels to stimulate philosophical dialogue, particularly in the early stages of work with participants. Later, other stimuli are introduced including works of literature and the visual arts.

Dr McCall works not only with children but also with businesses and community groups. In 1990 she set up EPIC (European Philosophical Inquiry Centre) to implement CoPI in schools and in the community, and the Postgraduate Centre for Philosophical Inquiry at Glasgow University to teach and to supervise Ph.D. research in CoPI. Postgraduate education in CoPI is now continuing at Strathclyde University under the leadership of Dr Claire Cassidy. Dr McCall now travels throughout the world introducing CoPI to new constituencies.

## The Philosophy Foundation

The Philosophy Foundation (formerly The Philosophy Shop) is a charity that trains philosophy graduates to do philosophy in schools and facilitates their visits. The Philosophy Foundation develops its own materials, often in the form of stories, to stimulate dialogue with young people. Many of the themes covered in the stories are taken from well-known philosophical puzzles and paradoxes. The aim is to develop children's 'autonomous learning skills and higher-order thinking skills' with a view to them applying those skills elsewhere.

# Further resources

*Research summaries.* A summary of research into P4C can be found at http://p4c.com/benefits-p4c There are links to research articles. The SAPERE website has a similar page: http://tinyurl.com/p4cresearch2

A comparison of approaches to P4C in the United Kingdom: 'Get 'em while they're young', in the *Philosophers' Magazine*

www.philosophypress.co.uk/?p=1186

SAPERE website:

www.sapere.org.uk

Epic website:

www.epic-original.com

Philosophy Shop website:

www.thephilosophyshop.co.uk

IAPC website:

http://cehs.montclair.edu/academic/iap

# References

Dewey, J. (1897) *School Journal*, 54 (January), 77–80. Available on the internet at http://dewey. pragmatism.org/creed.htm

Dyfed County Council (1994) *Improving Reading Standards in Primary Schools Project*. Dyfed County Council, Wales.

Fisher, R. (1996) *Stories for Thinking*. Oxford: Nash Pollock.

— (1997) *Poems for Thinking*. Oxford: Nash Pollock.

— (2003) *Teaching Thinking: Philosophical Enquiry in the Classroom* (2nd edn). London: Continuum.

Kozulin, A. (2001) *Psychological Tools: A Sociocultural Approach to Education*. Cambridge, MA and London: Harvard University Press.

McCall, C. (2009) *Transforming Thinking: Philosophical Inquiry in the Primary and Secondary Classroom*. London and New York: David Fulton.

Lipman, M. (1988) *Philosophy Goes to School*. Philadelphia: Temple University Press.

— (2003) *Thinking in Education* (2nd edn). Cambridge: Cambridge University Press.

— (2008) *A Life Teaching Thinking*. Montclair, NJ: IAPC.

Haynes, J. and Murris, M. (2011) *Picturebooks, Pedagogy and Philosophy*. London: Routledge Research in Education.

Murris, K. (1992) *Teaching Philosophy with Picture Books*. Reading: Infonet (this is now out of print).

Murris, K. and Haynes, J. (2002) *Storywise: Thinking through Stories, DialogueWorks* (this is currently out of print but a new version will be available in January as an e-book on the website www.p4c.com).

Worley, P. (2010) *The If Machine*. London: Continuum.

# Index

Abbott, Edwin A. 84
abstract self-portraits 203, 204
ad hominem 36
advertising 210, 231
aesthetic criteria, identification/
    negotiation of 200
Alexander, Robin 2, 254
Ammonia and Haber process 110–11
a posteriori 69–71
Appiah, Kwame Anthony 56
a priori 69–71
archiving and questioning 44–5
Arendt, Hannah 130
argumentation 30–1
argumentative writing 40
arguments and justifications 60–1
argumentum ad hominem 36
Argyris, Chris 254
art and architecture 83
art and P4C, activities using
    abstract images 202–3
    ambiguous images 205–6
    female beauty 208–9
    flipchart paper 204–5
    form and function 211–12
    portrait 209–10
    visual art 207–8
astronomical images 98
attainment targets and exam results 38–9

Baker, Jeannie 200
banana trade 192–3
beliefs and arguments 9
benzene, ring structure of 110
birdsong 226
Bohm, David 254
Boyne, John 53
Brooks, Duwayne 161
Browne, Anthony 200

causes and choices 45–6
certainty and science 107–9

chaos and complexity theory 86–8
chemicals, understanding 120–1
chemistry, ethical issues in 116–17
Cherbury Iron Age camp 194–5
classroom dialogue. see Dialogue in P4C
cognitive conflict 31–2
Cohen, Jack 87
Collingwood, R. G. 21
community of enquiry 4–5
    discussion in 70
community of philosophical
    enquiry 142–3
Community of Philosophical
    Inquiry 291–2
composer
    guidance 226
    music 225
computer literacy 267
computer technology 267
concepts 153, 154
contestable 21, 183
    definition 133
    enquiry into
        God 137–41
        methodology for 135–6
    hierarchy of 134–5
    within religious traditions 134
concepts of scale 187
conceptual understanding 135
conflict of opinions 31–2
connection-making 5
contextualize (element) 139–40, 142
Craste, Mark 200
credibility 35
critical thinking
    deficiencies 26–7
    definition 26
    steps for developing 27–32
cultural understanding and diversity 191

deductive reasoning 69
dehumanization 61–2

deliberate philosophizing 6–8, 11, 14, 20, 53
Dewey, John 129, 284–5
dialogue in P4C 156–9, 254
 connection-making 5
 and mathematics 69–70
 sequence of enquiry 3–4
 skill-building activities 5
dialogue
 structure for 3–4
 and thinking 40
Dijkstra, Edsger W. 273
discourse 15
dispositions and reasonableness 172–4
DNA, discovery of double helical
  structure of 111
Doonan, Jane 200
drama
 creative problem solving 236
 GCSE Subject Criteria 235
 methodologies 237
 and P4C, activities using
  Girl A 244–5
  improvisation and role-play
   246–8
  poem 245–6
  Staffordshire Hoard 249–50
  thought experiment 242–3
 techniques 242, 249
dramatic enquiry 241
Dweck, Carol 239

Egan, Kieran 80
electromagnetic spectrum 99
emotion maps 186–7
English and P4C, activities using
 causes and choices 45–6
 'It just happened!' 46–8
English and P4C, connections between
 attainment targets and exam
  results 38–9
 humanistic education 38–9
English literature 53
English literature and P4C, activities using
 *The Boy in the Striped Pyjamas*
  being reasonable 64–6
  dehumanization 61–2
  father 62–4
 *The Merchant of Venice* 60–1
English literature, philosophical
  dialogue in

*The Boy in the Striped Pyjamas* 53–4
 comic tradition 57–8
 fake-letter strategy 57–8
 *Harrison Bergeron* (story) 66
 humanistic activity 56
 imaginative response 54–5
 inviting students for 58–9
 objections to 55–7
 Stanley Milgram's experiments 66
 *Tuck Everlasting* 66
English teaching.
   *see also* English literature,
    philosophical dialogue in
 humanistic education 38–9
 and philosophical dialogue 39–40
  sequence of activities
   integrating 40–5
environmental impact of ICT 277–9
environment, physical and human
  dimensions of 190–1
epistemology 181
ethical awareness 93
European/Western classical music 224
'Evaluate' (element) 140–2
experimentation and
  hypotheses 102–3

fairness 21, 56, 134, 246, 248, 257–8, 271
fair trade and food miles 192, 195–6
female singers 227
 guidance 227
 philosophical questions 228
 resource 227
female voice. *see* female singers
fiction writers 53
field excursions 193
film music 231
Fisher, Robert 205, 290
fishing rights 189–90
*Flatland: A Romance of Many
  Dimensions* 84
floating demonstration 100–2
free-standing images 200
freewriting
 challenges for students 49
 definition 49
 and dialogue 50
 purpose of 50
functional mathematics 78–80
future foods 114–16

Galileo's paradox 73
GCSE drama 237, 240
GCSE ICT, numbers of students taking 268
geography
  concepts in 184
  definition 181
  enquiry in 179–81
  humanistic and radical 181–2
  images in 185
  and P4C, activity using
    banana trade 192–3
    change 190
    emotion maps 186–7
    fair trade 195–6
    fishing rights 189–90
    *Home* (film) 187–8
    landscape 184–6
    preconceptions 191–2
    values in environment 190–1
  Tsunami in Japan 182
  values and interpretation 183
Girl A 244
God concept, enquiry into 137–41
Goldsworthy, Andy 206
Goleman, Daniel 240
graphicacy 180
growth 80–3
Guttenberg, Karl-Theodor zu 272–3

Haber process 110–11
habits, PSHE session 151–2
Hampshire enquiry model 133, 140–1
Happiness Machine 242
Harding, Susanna 237
Haring, Keith 205
*Harrison Bergeron* (story) 66
Harrison, Matthew 268
Haynes, Joanna 199, 239, 289
HeLa cells, immortality of 112
Hilbert, David 74
Hilbert's Hotel paradox 74
history
  dispositions reasonableness and 172–4
  language and questioning in 170–2
  and P4C, activities using
    being a soldier 175–6
    holocaust 176
    slavery and identity 176–7
    war 174–5
  philosophical skills and concepts
    in 168–70

Hoard, Staffordshire 249
Hodgkin, Howard 202
holocaust 176
*Home* (film) as stimulus for
    questioning 187–8
24-hour surveillance 280–1
Hume, David 39
humour and humility 34
hypotheses
  connection between P4C and
    science 100
  and experimentation 102–3
  exploration of 102
  floating demonstration 100–2
  laws and theories 103–4

IAPC 284, 286–9, 291
ICT
  capability of 267
  curriculum 268
  implications on society 273–4
  and P4C, activities using
    environmental impact 277–9
    Internet usage 274–7
    plagiarism 269–74
    surveillance 280–1
  and P4C, connections between 266–7
ICT teachers, responsibility of 267
IERG. *see* Innovative Education
    Research Group
images and music 212
implying and inferring 152–5
Innovative Education Research
    Group 80
interdependence 188
Internet usage in United
    Kingdom 274–7
  by age and gender 275
  impact on society 274–5
  Office for National Statistics data
    on 274, 277
Isaacs, William 254

Jobs, Steve 266, 282
justice, concepts of 5, 20–1, 52, 57, 60, 61,
    134, 142, 186
justifications and arguments 60–1

Kekulé's structure of benzene 110
Kennedy, Peter 239
King Lear 246

Klee, Paul 202
Kozulin, Alex 287

lab chops 115
landscape and P4C 184–6
language in history 170–1
language of reasoning
  enlightened use of 15
  expressions in 14–15
  routines to develop 16–17
Law, Stephen 160
laws and theories 103–4
leadership 258–60
Learning Pit 237
Lipman, Matthew 4, 26–7, 29, 147, 199,
      254, 284–91
Living Difference Revised 2011 131, 133,
      134–5, 144
Long, Richard 207
Louden, Robert B. 56
lysergic acid diethylamide (LSD) 109

Macke, August 202
Malvolio 57–8
mathematical ideas and concepts 70–1
  concept of infinity 70
  concept of irrational numbers 71
  concepts of certainty and
      uncertainty 70–1
mathematics and P4C, activity using
  art and architecture 83
  chaos and complexity theory 86–8
  functional 78–80
  growth 80–3
  Mexican wave observation 88–9
  musical chords 83–4
  number theory 73–6
  probability 76–8
  sorting and categorizing
      statements 71–3
  space, shape and dimensions 84–6
mathematics and P4C, connections
      between
  dialogue 69–70
  reasoning 68–9
McCall, Catherine 287, 291–2
Mercer, Neil 254
Mexican wave observation 88–9
Milky Way galaxy 98
Murris, Karin 199, 289

music 215
  advertisement 231
  composer 225
  conventional teaching 217
  education 215, 216
  European Renaissance and Baroque 219
  female singers 227
  film 231
    and pop 219
  outside school 216
  philosophical enquiry 216, 217, 220
  philosophy of 221
  ragas 219
  resources 225
musical chords 83–4
musical excerpts 224
musical vocabulary 223
music and P4C, activities using
  advertisement 231–2
  birdsong 226–7
  composer 225–6
  female voice 227–8
  film music 231
  musical excerpts 224–5
  musical portrait 230
  singer 233
  trees 228–9
music lessons 223
musicness 221
mysteries as stimulus 195

National Curriculum 38, 148, 170, 173,
      179, 182–4, 216–17, 288
Newswise 152, 155, 157, 159, 160, 165
Nozick, Robert 242
N-ray research 99
number theory 73–6

Odin
  guidance, resources 248
Ofsted 128, 130, 262, 268
opinion line 63–4
opinions 18–19, 28

paintings 202, 203, 209
P4C. see Philosophy for Children
p4c.com 12, 51, 165
Peirce, Charles 4, 286
perception 97
Peret, Daniel 228

performance-enhancing drugs 252
permanence, concept of 206–7
Personal and Social Education 148–9
Personal Social Health
    Education. *see* PSHE
PESS. *see* Physical Education and School
    Sport
philosophical concepts
    conceptual contestability 20–1
    definitions 21
    and empirical sciences 21
philosophical dialogue
    and English teaching 39–40
    sequence of activities
        archiving and questioning 44–5
        questioning and discussion 41–4
        reading and viewing texts 40–1
philosophical enquiry 94, 200, 216
    exemplification 202
    progress in 24–5
    in RE at 'Evaluate' 141–4
    reconfiguration of PSHE 150
philosophical novels 285
philosophical questions and
        concepts 46, 61
    arguments and justifications 61, 62
    dehumanization 61–2
    dialogue 158–9
    reasoning 156
    stereotyping 162–3
philosophical teaching and learning 48
philosophical writing 39–40
*Philosophy: A School of Freedom* 164–5
Philosophy for Children. *see also* Specific
        cases
    benefits of introducing 1–2
    origins of 284–7
    as a practice 2
    process 147–8
    in schools 1
    starts in United Kingdom 287–91
        new curriculum initiatives 290–1
        philosophy with picture
            books 289–90
    structure of
        community of enquiry 4–5
        sequence of enquiry 3–4
        skill-building activities 5
Philosophy Foundation 292
photography 202, 208

physical education
    activities 255
    connections 252
    encourage learners 254
Physical Education and School
        Sport 252
    case study 260–3
    collaboration 258–60
    community 256
    curriculum 258
    fairness 257
    last thoughts 263–4
    leadership 258–60
    open-minded humour 264
    ranking exercise 256
    residential experiences 262
    team activity 256
physics, ethical issues in 119
Picasso's line drawing 205
pictures/video footage 256
Pistorius, Oscar 257, 258
plagiarism and ICT 269–74
Poad, Gordon 236, 241, 242
portraits 203, 204, 209–10, 230
'positivist' geography 181, 182
probability 76–8
PSE. *see* Personal and Social
        Education
PSHE 146
    citizenship and ethics 159–60
    curriculum review 163
    definition 147
    and P4C, activities using
        dialogue 156–9
        inferring and implying 152–5
        openness 163–4
        reasoning 155–6
        stereotyping 160–3
    skills and habits 150–2
PSHE education and schools 148
pulsars, discovery of 111–12

QI books. *see* Questions and Ideas books
questioning and archiving 44–5
Questions and Ideas books
    definition 49
    freewriting in 49–50
    possible uses 49
    prompts for 50–1
Quinn, Marc 208

RE. *see* Religious Education
reading and viewing texts 40–1
reasons 29–30
reasonableness and dispositions 172–4
reasoning 68, 155–6
  deductive 69
  and reflection 8
recordings, TV/Film 231
relationships and P4C 10–11
religious belief systems 130
religious concepts 135
Religious Education
  background of 128
  enquiry pedagogy for 129–30
  models of enquiry in 130–1
  and philosophical enquiry 132
  philosophical enquiry in 127
  purpose of 128–9
resources on P4C 12
respect concept, enquiry into 34, 39,
    136–7, 149
Romantic European music 230
round-robin team-building activities 260
Royal Society for the Protection of
    Birds 226
RSPB. *see* Royal Society for the
    Protection of Birds

scale of involvement
  practice of P4C 11
  variables in 11
science
  definition 93
  *vs* non-science, activities
    differentiating 95–7
  P4C and nature of 94–5
  perspectives on 94
science and P4C, activities using
  certainty and science 107–9
  concept development
    defining species 121–3
    stimuli for 119
    understanding chemicals 120–1
  hypothesis 100–4
  observing invisible 98–100
  origin of life 104–7
  science *vs* non-science 95–7
science ethics and P4C 112
  in biology 114

  in chemistry 116–17
  in physics 119
  stimulus for philosophical
    enquiry 113–14
science lessons
  ethical awareness 93
  objectives of 92
  and P4C, connection between
    enquiry process 92
    hypothesis 100–4
    observing invisible 98–100
    origin of life 104–7
    question creation 93
    science *vs* non-science 95–7
  in secondary science curricula 92
scientific discovery and P4C 109–12
  double helical structure of DNA 111
  Haber process 110–11
  immortality of HeLa cells 112
  pulsars 111–12
  ring structure of benzene 110
  stimulus 109
sculptures 206, 208
  female beauty 208
self-management 164
Senge, Peter 254
'sense of place' 184
sense perception 97
Sharp, Ann 12, 21, 238, 284
skill-building activities 5
slavery and identity 176–7
Socrates 148, 266, 282
*Socrates for Six-Year-Olds* 12, 287, 291
sorting and categorizing
    statements 71–3
space 186
  shape and dimensions 84–6
species, defining 121–3
Splitter, Lawrence 21
spontaneous enquiry 95
spontaneous philosophizing 6–7
stealing 271
stereotyping 160–3
Stewart, Ian 87
straw man arguments 26, 36
surveillance and ICT 280–2
sustainable development 149, 184,
    190
Swan, Malcolm 69

Tan, Shaun  200
team concept  256
*The Boy in the Striped Pyjamas*
    (novel)  53–4
Thompson, Colin  200
toleration, concept of  23–4
trickery  35
*Tuck Everlasting* (novel)  66
*Twelfth Night*  57

Uffington White Horse  193–4
The UK riots and media  41–2

unfairness  246, 257
Urey-Miller experiment  104–6

visual art  207, 208

Ward, Helen  200
Williams, Raymond  39
wobblers  32–4
writing for dialogue in English lessons
    freewriting  49–50
    purpose of  48
    QI books  49